Leave No DNA

LEAVE NO DNA
It Will Convict You

Other books by the author:

The FBI and I

Setup Framed and Railroaded

LEAVE NO DNA

It Will Convict You

by
Albert -Sayers

Library of Congress Control Number:

ISBN: 0-8187-0401-2

Printed in the U.S.A.
Harlo Printing Company, 50 Victor, Detroit, Michigan 48203

This book narrates a true unsolved murder case in the so-called. "Cold Case" Category! Therefore, names of people and places have been changed to protect the innocent and for other obvious reasons.

I borrow from Winston Churchill who said, whimsically, "A lie gets halfway around the world before the truth has a chance to get its pants on."

DEDICATION

This book is dedicated to VERNE BATES and JOHNNY DOBROCZYNSKI whose unselfish and untiring help have made this book possible. From Manhattan Beach to Harlo Printing Company in Detroit and back, their contributions and communications in design and construction have largely made this book what it has turned out to be. Thanks, fellas!

INTRODUCTION

It was the fall of 1991.

I had just finished packing my old Chevy pickup when the phone rang. I was going to ignore it but something told me. . . .

"Bello here," I said.

"Steve Bello, right?" It was Lola Lucia, one of the top criminal defense attorneys in the State Bar Association. "Stan Levine gave me your name - said you work cheap and seem to know what you're doing - said you seem to catch on pretty well, especially in homicide cases if things are not too difficult."

"Fuck you, Wise-ass," I said.

I had the old pickup loaded, tuned up and primed with gas topped off in the tank and a six pack of the right weight of oil tucked in behind the driver's seat, prepared to go to Colorado and Wyoming, where I had spent the first two of my twenty-five years as an FBI agent. They tell me the fishing is better there now than it was then. Now retired from the Bureau and possessing a California PI license and a concealed weapons permit, I can pick and choose my own cases and don't have to take any shit from any two-bit, ladder climbing, kiss-ass-so-called "Supervisor" any more. It's funny how the really top-notch agents made it to the top administratively while the mediocre assholes seemed to linger in the mid-levels and ex-

isted for the sole purpose of trying to make the street agents' lives a living hell.

"No, wait," she said, Don't hang up, I was just yanking your chain; Stan said you are the best but that you have a pretty short fuse and I was just testing a little."

"Only when I'm alone or with somebody, " I said, "What's on your mind?"

"Well I've got a court-appointed homicide case, and...

"I knew it. No money, right?"

"Well, not much money but this is a real ball-buster - been going on now for over three years - almost four, and my - that is, our - client has been languishing in the slammer, without being permitted bond and without a lawyer - capital case, you know, I just got the case a month ago. I'm gonna have to start throwing writs and motions and whatever or a trial date is going to come up more quickly than I would like and there's a ton of work to do."

"I like the way you said "our" client. I think I'm goin' to like you, but I smell some rotten fish," I told her. "Three years in the jailhouse and just now gettin' an attorney. They do like to soften 'em up, don't they? What did they do, bury him and forget about him? Isn't there something about "a speedy trial" and all that good bullshit?"

"No, some just-out-of-law-school neophyte waived that right and took him to preliminary. He was bound over and that's where he sits."

"Well, okay, let's have a sitdown. Shit! Trapped again!"

I unloaded the pickup and put my gear back in storage, kicking myself every step of the way.

One of the best things about our criminal jus-

tice, system is that an indigent defendant can sometimes get top-notch legal defense at taxpayer, i.e.,
court, expense. This is because almost all top law
firms and partnerships have a certain percentage of
their legal talent devoted to pro bono work on an
as-needed, rotating basis. Their lawyers for any particular indigent-client case are appointed by the court.
Of course in these cases, the lawyer works at a dras-
tically reduced rate or no fee at all. They do get expenses though or, theoretically, they could starve to
death and go broke while necessarily devoting all
their working life defending a complicated and de-
manding months-or-years-long case. As it turned out,
this is the type of potential disaster Lola had caught;
a big, ugly, 250 pound black gangbanger from South
Central, accused of murdering a young woman while
in the process of burglarizing her brand new condominium during her first night there.

   In her office, Lola introduced me to her partner
Marjie Fay, a tall, pretty blonde, who looked like anything but a lawyer to me but who I later found out,
not only by word of mouth but by observation, could
hold her own, and more often than not win, against
any adversary in a knock-down-drag-out battle in a
court of law.

   "I've visited Jody in jail on several occasions and
interviewed him at length each time," Lola said. "I've
read the discovery material we've been able to get
(waving her hand at two large cardboard boxes lying
on the floor) and practically memorized the police
"Murder Book" (several thick, black loose leaf bind-
ers, containing the Detective Bureau's investigation,
in one of the boxes). They have him charged with
attempted rape also. Marjie and I are convinced that
Jody is totally innocent of these charges. In spite of

his rap sheet and gangbanging lifestyle, Jody gives out good vibes, but we have a problem."

"What's that?," I asked.

"The problem, and in this type of case it's a big one, is, Jody has two priors, both felonies, a crime against property and a crime against a person - Burglary on the one hand and Assault With Deadly Weapon on the other. The ADW was done on the owner of the residence while in the process of doing the burglary. He has done four years in Folsom for those crimes. The present charges sound almost like a carbon copy - Right? No jury will ignore those raps; consequently, knowing this, the prosecutor will play on them like Horowitz on a grand piano."

"So what have you got that makes you so sure and what do you want me to do?"

"At this point, I'm not going to tell you what I have. That may or may not come later. I want to test our theory and see if you come up with the same conclusion we have. But first I want you to take your camera, go down to the crime scene, at least the part you can get into, and photograph everything in sight - everything - from every angle possible. Then I want you to spend all the hours you need, as soon as possible, to study the Murder Book and the other discovery material. Then I want you to go back and photograph anything you think is important, again, based upon what you have read in the Murder Book and the other discovery material. Any questions?"

"Yes. Have you had any other investigator working this case? If so, I want no part of it. I'll just fold my tent and steal silently into the night and away from here. If your answer is "No," I'll jump right in and do the best job my education, training and experience will permit and I'll give you a written report on every-

thing I do. But I must have absolute investigative control. I will do almost anything you want or ask me to do but I will not break the law in any respect and I will not give up my sources to you or anyone else. If you fire me at any time during the course of my investigation, you cannot rehire me for this or any other investigation. If you can deal with those cautions, I'm your man. My fee schedule is what the court will allow plus what expenses the court will allow. How about it?"

"Grab those boxes, get the hell out of here and go to work," she replied. Handing me a check for two hundred bucks already made out in my name, she said, "Here, this'll get you started."

Marjie blew me an eyes-closed, wet smooch as I went out the door. That'll bear developing, I thought.

After my Mary's death at the wrong end of a deranged bank robber's Uzi two years ago, I hadn't thought about romance much, but lately there have been almost forgotten stirrings in my gut when I see someone who reminds me of her. After Mary, there has been no peace for me. The animal who slew her does not even know of the man he destroyed that day nor of the devastation he brought to my life. Well, maybe I can do something about that or at least bring some kind of closure to the agony of the innocent.

INVESTIGATOR'S PRELIMINARY REPORT

Investigation is predicated upon receipt of a request, received from Loretta (Lola) Lucia, Attorney at Law, Los Angeles, California.

She requested investigation which would be supportive of the defense of one Jody B. Williams, who is in the Los Angeles County Jail charged with a "Special Circumstances" Murder, Burglary and Attempted Rape. Ms. Lucia furnished six volumes of material pertaining to what has taken place in the case since the night of May 30-31, 1989, when one Terri J. Horgan was reportedly murdered in her condominium at 3200 Alder, Unit #66, Urban, California.

The following are results of investigation:

Initially, efforts have been made to read and correlate the six volumes of material furnished by Ms. Lucia. This particular activity has continued during the investigation up to and including the date of this report. It will probably be a continuing activity and a source of investigative leads as long as this investigation takes place.

The Urban Police Department has primary investigative jurisdiction in this case for the People of the State of California, with the prosecutive jurisdiction being with the Office of the Los Angeles County District Attorney.

The defense of Jody B. Williams was originally the

primary responsibility of the Los Angeles County Public Defender's Office, however, it has since evolved into the hands Of Ms. Lucia.

Inasmuch as this investigator was not privy to the facts, the development of suspects and other aspects of this case, including the crime scene search and the resulting laboratory work which developed evidence and suspects at the beginning and as the case progressed up to now, this investigator must draw upon education, training and experience in order to develop facts and evidence which might be of value to the defense of Mr. Williams.

Besides Mr. Williams, other suspects thus far developed by the Urban Police Department have been Dan, Black, Donald (Don) Arnold and Sammy Battle. They will be further identified later in this report. They were all employees of the builder or the security firm hired by the builder at the time of the crime.

The Urban Police Department (UPD) investigators theorize that the point of entry of the unknown subject who murdered Terri J. Horgan in her town house on the night of May 30-31, 1989, was a window over the garage about 13 feet above the ground and that he gained access to the window by use of a stepladder. This is contested by those who believe the point of entry was the sliding glass door leading into the premises from a patio on the west side of the townhouse, after the screen door protecting that sliding glass door was slit.

The strongest evidence placing defendant Jody B. Williams at the scene of the murder, i.e., in the townhouse, is not the alleged pubic hairs found in the room where the body of the victim was found, but the fingerprints found on the bent screen, allegedly from the above-mentioned window and the smudged palmprint found on the sill of that window.

The best evidence of the sliding glass door being the point of entry, in addition to the slit screen, is the footprint found in the mud at the base of the low wall leading to the patio where the sliding glass door is located, along with the mud smudges found on the door of the bedroom where the body was found. Also, mud smudges were found on top of the wall immediately above where the footprint was found.

With regard to the bent screen found just inside the front door of the townhouse, the reports do not show how the screen was bent; whether it was bent vertically, horizontally or diagonally, one way, or the other; consequently no one theorizes on how the screen got bent.

Defendant Williams has stated that if his palmprint is on the above-mentioned windowsill, it was put there when he removed the screen so that he could see when his supervisor was coming. This was so that he could safely grab a nap during his tour of duty. This would also, according to him, explain his fingerprints on the bent screen.

Since this investigator is inclined to agree with those who believe the point of entry by the killer was through the patio sliding glass door and not through a window 13 feet off the ground, the following seems to be a reasonable scenario as to how Williams's fingerprints were found on the bent screen and his palm print was found on the windowsill (if, in fact it was his palm print):

Williams has admitted being in the victim's townhouse on one or more occasions before the date of the murder and after the carpet was laid. This was, it is believed, after the screens were installed on or about May 5, 1989. This was also before the townhouse was under lock and key at night.

Williams entered the townhouse through one of the three entrances, i.e., the garage, the front door or the sliding glass door. In removing the screen, he pulled up on

the two tabs at the bottom of the screen and then, shifting his hands so that he could grasp the screen for removal, it slipped out of his hands and fell the 13 feet to the driveway or alley in front of the garage. Since he had closed the garage door, if he had entered that way so as to avoid discovery as being in the townhouse, he went out the front door, retrieved the screen which was bent when it hit the ground, and returned inside the townhouse, leaving the bent screen just inside the front door. Since work was still being done by several different people inside and outside the townhouse, anyone noticing the screen there would simply think it was a screen that had been bent (in any number of ways) and needed replacing. The placing of Williams's fingerprints on the screen could have occurred when he was carrying the screen into the townhouse rather than at the time he removed the screen.

PROLOGUE

He looked at his watch. "One thirty," Jody said sotto voce, in his lazy, mumbling way acquired and conditioned by his years in Folsom and his contacts with the police in South Central Los Angeles. "Shit, only two and a half hours into this shift. Guess I'll catch a few Zs," Jody thought, which had become his habit since he'd gotten this job - sort of inherited it when his brother Lumus had quit. "Hell, this is a construction site - nothin' happens around here this time of night; besides, what's there to steal - or who's there to bother?"

Jody had been paroled out of Folsom for less than a month after doing three and a half out of a four year stretch for First Degree Burglary (459 PC) and Assault with a Deadly Weapon (245 PC); the ADW for swatting the occupant of the house with a putter he found standing in a corner when the guy surprised him.

He felt grudgingly fortunate to get this job, seeing as how it is not that easy for a parolee, especially a Black parolee from South Central, just out of the joint, to find steady work. Jody still viewed this as a chickenshit job, and he was going to leave it as soon as his fingerprints came back from CII. Lumus had told him this sometimes took weeks, counting the time the employer took two or three weeks, if ever, to

submit the fingerprint cards to CII and then the extra
two or three weeks the CII Bureaucracy took to clas-
sify, search, and get the information back to the employer. Thus he would have earned a little nest egg
during that limbo time before his criminal record was
discovered by his employer and he would have to
leave. He figured he could dance his Parole Office
(PO) around, telling her he was getting day labor jobs
on a catch-as-catch-can basis but was looking for a
steady job every waking hour. He knew that she, like
every PO in Los Angeles County was so overloaded
with cases that she could not supervise him as closely
as she would like and he, like almost every other
parolee in the county system, regularly took the ad-
vantage.

Besides, although he was living with his dad and
step-mother, he was also drawing "GR" (General
Relief) from the county and it would not do for them
to know he was working full time - not just yet, anyway.

Before going to Folsom, Jody had been a very
active member of the Rolling Sixties Crips. His brother
Lumus had suffered two gunshot wounds from being mistaken for Jody, but Lumus was not
"ganged-up;" in fact was not even known to law enforcement, except possibly as an entry in the descrip-
tive and background information in Jody's Criminal
History File. Jody's father, Fred Williams, and his
step-mother, Estellene, were respected members of
the neighborhood, Fred being a soon-to-be-retired
twenty-five year security guard for a large industrial
firm and Estellene being an active member of her
church as well as being involved in civic and chari-
table activities. She was a gentle person but, getting
to know her, one would realize that she had back-

bone like a Drill Sergeant. She apparently acquired Jody as a step-son a little too late to have much influence. Jody's mother Vonnie, was what could almost be described as non-entity, if that describes anything. She was virtually putty in his hands. She lived deeper in South Central and was "On the County." His sister, Danielle, was married and had four children. She and her husband were both employed full time and had sufficient income to raise their children more or less comfortably.

Pursuing his desire for sleep after being up since Noon and partying with his homies most of the afternoon and evening, although he did arrive at work at 11:00 p.m., on time, Jody entered the almost finished Condo #66. He ascended to the second level of this split-level building and proceeded to the east window of the room overlooking the alley. He moved the only piece of furniture which had been delivered to that level, a pure white settee placed directly beneath the window, to one side. He then opened the right-hand, movable side of the casement-type window, reached out and removed the window screen and brought it inside. In maneuvering the screen through the window, he bent it almost double. He half-heartedly tried to straighten the screen but seeing that it was a lost cause, he laid it aside. Then, putting his hand on the windowsill to brace himself, thrust his head and upper part of his five foot eight inch , 250 pound body outside so that he could look up and down the alley to see if his boss, Bill, was in sight making his nightly rounds of inspecting the guard force. Seeing no one, Jody replaced the settee beneath the window, then descended to the entry level, taking the bent screen with him and placing it next to the front door. He intended to later take it to

the alley and place it directly beneath the window to make it appear that it had been insecurely fastened by the building screener and had fallen the thirteen feet to the hard surface of the alley, thus bending it. He was so punchy from lack of sleep, that he forgot. He went to the living room, which was devoid of furniture, lay down on the carpet and immediately fell into a deep sleep, using his gym bag for a pillow.

Sometime during the night, Jody felt a nudge at his rib cage and, groggily thinking it was Bill, he grunted a couple of times, indicating acknowledgment but turned his gargantuan body over and continued sleeping.

At about 5:00 a.m., Jody was awakened by Bill, his supervisor, who discovered him while making his rounds. Bill admonished him severely about sleeping on the job and told him he would have to write him up. Jody whined and pleaded but to no avail. He then finished his shift on patrol and, at 6:00 a.m., went home, lighting up and finishing a marijuana "roach" while walking to the bus line. Jody had no idea that while he slept, a young woman was murdered in an upstairs bedroom.

Chapter I

CRIME REPORT

Urban Police Department

REC. REPORT: Det. E. P. HALL

Section & Code: 287(A) P.C.
Location: 3200 Alder, #66
Date and Time Reported: 5-31-89, 12:05 p.m.
Occurred, Day of Week: Unknown, Wednesday;
    Dates and Times: 5-31-89, between (unknown)
    & 11:45 a.m.
Victim: Terri Horgan, DOB 11-19-62; White Female.
Suspect: Unknown
Person Reporting: MARY GANDY, victim's mother.
        Q & A Results:
Yes   No
( )   (X)   1. Suspect arrested
( )   (X)   2. Suspect named
( )   (X)   3. Suspect can be identified/located
( )   (X)   4. Suspect vehicle
(X) ( )   5. Injury or rape
( )   (X)   6. Witness
( )   (X)   7. Stolen property traceable
(X) ( )   8. Physical evidence

(X)   (   )   9.   Distinctive MO
(   )   (X)   10. Loss over $5000
(X)   (   )   11. Additional investigation recom-
                     mended
(X)   (   )   12. Victim will prosecute
(   )   (X)   13. Victim/suspect related - How
(X)   (   )   14. Victim contacted
(X)   (   )   15. Witness contacted
(X)   (   )   16. Neighbor contacted
(X)   (   )   17. Area checked
(X)   (   )   18. CSI Report
(   )   (X)   19. Suspect/MO Page included

The victim was not a Neighborhood Watch member and was under age 60.

The case was assigned to Det. Rick Lander.

CRIME REPORT - CONTINUATION REPORT

DETAILS:

On Wednesday, 31 May 89, 12:06 hours, I was detailed to 3200 Alder, #66, in regards to a Deceased Person Report.

Upon arrival, I was met by Compton Fire Department Paramedic Trainee Todd Genaro, who was in training with Urban Fire Paramedics, and Carson Paramedics Randy Anderson and David Powers. Fire Fighter Genaro advised me they had been detailed to Unit #66 in regards to a rescue call. They received their call at 1155 hours and were on the scene at 1204 hours.

Upon their arrival, they were met by Mary Gandy and escorted to a small upstairs bedroom. In the bedroom, they found the deceased lying on the floor. The subject was obviously dead.

Pursuant to my request, the following were sent to my location: One Lieutenant, two Sergeants, seven Detectives (including Det. Lander) and three Sworn Officers.

At the location upon my arrival were the victim's mother and four others who were affiliated with the building construction company or its subcontractors. These subjects were all later interviewed by detectives and statements were recorded by them.

Also, in addition to the aforementioned paramedics, an Urban Fire Department Engine Company consisting of a Captain and three Fire Fighters were at the location.

Fire Fighter Genaro stated they hooked a vital sign monitor up to the subject's back, using a gel type substance. During this process, they partially pulled up the back of the subject's shirt. No vital signs were detected. Lividity was observed. In addition, the subject had numerous abrasions to her arms and face. The paramedics' opinion that foul play had occurred.

I then went to the location of the deceased. I found the subject in the upstairs northwest bedroom. Her head was pointed to the west and her feet to the east. She was laying on her stomach. The subject was wearing a lounging type suit, consisting of a maroon and aqua colored blouse and light blue pants with pink cuffs. Adjacent the victim, were blankets and a pillow. There was no bed or other furniture in this bedroom.

On the pink carpet, I observed what appeared to be blood stains south of the victim. An adjacent mirrored closet door was partially pushed off its track. Scattered on the floor, were a pen, a lipstick, keys, and one white tennis shoe. There were marks on the

wall indicating the possibility of a struggle. Due to these circumstances, I requested a Supervisor, Crime Scene Investigation and Detectives, resulting as stated above.

Subsequently, the deceased's father, Mr. Gandy, also came to the location. Much later Security Guard Phinney was interviewed by detectives at the front door.

My investigation revealed the following:

The location of occurrence is in a townhouse subdivision known as Paradise West. The complex is still under construction with only some of the units occupied. The townhouse in question is located near the rear of the development in the middle area. The townhouse consists of three levels. The first level being an enclosed attached garage; the second level being the main entry way, living room, dining room, kitchen, and bathroom; the third and upper most level consists of two bathrooms, a large master bedroom, and a smaller bedroom. The deceased's townhouse is on the north side.

I observed a window screen bent in half located just inside the front door. This screen possibly came from an east facing window in the dining area.

I noted that the glass sliding door in the west facing living room was closed but not locked. The screen door was also closed but not locked. There was a small cut in the screen door above the latching device. This door leads out onto a semi-enclosed patio on the west side of the townhouse. I observed a brownish discoloration on the exterior wall on the west and north side.

On the banister area atop the staircase on the upper most level, I observed what appeared to be a torn brassiere, attached to the brassiere, were nu-

merous strands of dark hair and what appeared to be blood stains.

The window screen in the larger master bedroom on the east side of the townhouse was off and laying prompt against the wall. This window was opened.

I observed a 1982 Ford Mustang two door, white, License -------- inside the attached garage. The garage door was opened. Subsequent investigation revealed that this vehicle belonged to the deceased.

On the front right seat of the locked Ford, I observed a handwritten note. On the note was listed the name Dorian Kane, the word "Psychologist," the address "1136 Marion," the name "Diane," and phone number "(818) 271-1816.11

I interviewed Mary Gandy, who identified herself as being the mother of the deceased. Mrs. Gandy advised me of the following information:

Her daughter, Terri Horgan, had purchased the townhouse in October 1988 before it had been constructed. She stated her daughter normally lived with her and her husband at their residence in Hollywood Riviera. As construction was being completed on the townhouses, Terri was slowly moving items into same. Mrs. Gandy stated that she and her daughter were the only people who had keys to the townhouse. She further advised that the townhouse had been on a master key for construction purposes, but it was unknown if it had been removed from same.

Mrs. Gandy stated that her daughter, Terri, was a golfer and was due to take a lesson at the Los Angeles Country Club in West Los Angeles on 31 May 89, in the morning hours. Due to this fact, her daughter had decided to stay overnight at her townhouse so that she would be closer to her destination in the morning.

Mrs. Gandy said that her daughter had requested that she come to the townhouse around noon on 31 May 89, to let in some construction and delivery people. Terri did not expect to be home until at least 1300 hours.

Mrs. Gandy stated she spoke with Terri on the telephone at approximately 1715 hours. Mrs. Gandy said she phoned her at Terri's sister's house. The sister is Bridy Gandy. Bridy lives on Brownwood Street in Los Angeles - unknown exact numbers in the address.

During this conversation, Terri advised her mother that she was going to a group therapy meeting in West Los Angeles. Mrs. Gandy told me she did not know why Terri was going to the group therapy, and that she did not know the location of the group other than it was in West Los Angeles.

Mrs. Gandy said she drove to the townhouse on 31 May 89, approximately 1145 hours, to wait for the expected people. Upon her arrival, she observed her daughter's Mustang in the opened garage. She thought this was unusual as she did not expect her daughter to be home for at least an hour.

She then entered the house and observed construction personnel working inside. The air conditioning person was working in the attic area of the master bedroom. He had been let in by Dan Black, who is one of the people responsible for the building construction.

Mrs. Gandy also saw that the door to the small bedroom was closed. Looking for her daughter, she opened same. She then saw her daughter lying face down on the floor. She called to her daughter several times and upon not receiving any answer, she partially removed the blanket over her daughter's body.

She then touched her daughter's wrist and found to be cold. She then ran downstairs and called for paramedics.

Upon the paramedics' arrival, they noted that Terri Horgan was obviously dead.

Mrs. Gandy informed me that her daughter had no boyfriend and that she did not work or go to school. She was active with an athletic gym group, located at an unknown location in West Los Angeles. Her daughter was also known as Terri Gandy. The mother stated her daughter had changed her name approximately one year ago, but the reason she did so, was not clear to the mother. Terri never married.

Mrs. Gandy stated that Terri had recently had a problem with one of the security guards in the "Paradise West" complex. Mrs. Gandy told me that her daughter had advised her she felt very uncomfortable with this subject and called him "Crazy Security Guard." Mrs. Gandy further related that her daughter had had a problem with this security guard on the past Saturday. Apparently, the guard was trying to be overly helpful and while doing so, was annoying Terri. Although what happened is not quite clear, Mrs. GANDY stated that it had something to do with the security guard wanting to throw out Terri's trash. Apparently, during this process, Terri's wrist watch had gotten deposited into the trash bag. Terri subsequently had to request the assistance of another security guard, a male black, no further description, in order to locate her trash bag in a communal trash area.

Mrs. Gandy described this annoying security guard as being a male white in his 20's, approximately 5'8" to 5'10", 160 lbs., with brownish hair. She was not sure of the guard's name, but probably might be something like "Jody." Further, she stated the guard

works for Interstate Security. Mrs. Gandy stated that in past conversation with this guard, he "sounds dumb." Further, Mrs. GANDY stated she had heard from her daughter that the guard was going to be fired, as it had been reported he had been annoying other residents.

I notified the Coroner's Office and they assigned a case number. Coroner's Investigator Jackson and Coroner personnel McHenry and Lopez came to the location for the gathering of evidence and removal of the remains.

Investigator Jackson told me that the deceased was in full rigor mortis with lividity. A sexual assault test kit had been administered at the scene. Further, the Coroner's investigator told me that the death was consistent with strangulation by ligature.

The deceased was removed by Coroner personnel to the County Medical Examiner's Office.
E.P.Hall, 31 May 89.

MODUS OPERENDI (MO) INFORMATION

SURROUNDING AREA: Residence
STRUCTURE: Town House
COMMERCIAL: No
TARGET: No
POINT OF ENTRY: Unknown
METHOD OF ENTRY: Unknown
TOOLS USED: None
SECURITY SYSTEM: None
SUSPECT ACTIONS: Victim's clothes cut/rip
PRETENDED TO BE: Unknown
VICTIM WAS: Injured/Hit - Strangled
EVIDENCE: Blood - Clothes - Fingerprints - Foot Prints - Hair - Photographs

WHILE IN THE PROCESS OF MOVING INTO A NEW TOWNHOUSE, THE VICTIM STRANGLED TO DEATH BY MEANS OF A LIGATURE. VICTIM IS LEFT ON FLOOR OF BEDROOM.

SUPPLEMENTARY REPORT

187 P.C. MURDER INVESTIGATION
Victim: TERRI GWEN HORGAN nee Gandy

Investigative Summary
By
Detective RICK LANDER

On 05 31 89 at approximately 1215 Hours, I, Detective RICK LANDER, arrived at 3200 Alder Street, Unit #66, in regard to a possible 187 P.C. Upon arrival I was briefed by Sgt. McKENNA who was at the scene prior to my arrival. I entered Unit #66 and walked through the crime scene including the upstairs portion where the victim was lying face down in the northwest bedroom. I observed the condition of the victim and further noted items strewn on the floor of the northwest bedroom, along with a female purse in a bathroom adjacent to the same bedroom with its contents strewn across the top of the bathroom counter. I assisted in directing CSI officers DIAMOND and IRELAND in the photographing and collection of physical evidence. I was also present when the Coroner Officers arrived and viewed their actions while at the location.

While at the location I became aware that victim TERRI HORGAN's mother, MARY GANDY, and father, Dr. JOHN GANDY, resided at 315 Via Del Valle, Holly-

wood Riviera, California. Dr. GANDY's business was nearby.

I further became aware that victim TERRI HORGAN had been seeing therapists including a group therapy, and in connection with this was able to obtain the names of Dr. DORIAN KANE, telephone 549-1339 and a DIANE, telephone 821-9611. These items were received from a piece of paper found in the victim's vehicle.

While still at the location on 31 May 89 I was advised by fellow investigators Detective HUNTER and Detective CONLEY that a security officer by the name of SAMMY BATTLE had had some kind of minor confrontation with victim TERRI HORGAN a few days prior to the discovery of her body.

On 31 May 89 I was contacted by a resident of the condominium complex who identified herself as MARIA RIVAS, female with a DOB: 25 March 59, Residence 3200 Alder Street, #28. Miss RIVAS stated that a couple or three days prior to 31 May 89, she was in her unit, #28, during the evening hours. She recalled at approximately 2200 to 2230 Hours a male security guard knocked on her front door and asked her if she had smelled a skunk. She recalled telling him that she did not smell anything at this time, however, that odor was common due to the nearby wasteland where there were plenty of animals, including skunks. Miss Rivas then recalled that this security guard then engaged her in small talk which she thought was extremely unusual due to the late hour and the fact that he was hired and to work there and to guard, not engage homeowners in conversations. I had previously been provided photographs of all the security guards who were currently working at that complex and upon showing Ms. RIVAS the various photo-

graphs, she identified one, SAMMY BATTLE, as being the same person who had knocked on her door that night. Ms. RIVAS recalled that the conversation between the two lasted approximately three or four minutes, at which time her mother, who also lives in Apartment #28 showed herself at the front door. She stated that shortly thereafter the conversation ended and BATTLE walked away.

On 31 May 89 I was able to make telephonic contact with DIANE BRADY, telephone 937-7513. DIANE BRADY advised me that she had been recommended by victim TERRI HORGAN'S sister, BRIDY GANDY, because the victim had been having back and neck problems. DIANE BRADY stated that she had an appointment on 30 May 89 with the victim TERRI HORGAN for a one hour therapy. She stated that on 30 May 89, the victim arrived at her home address at 1530 Hours. She stated that the therapy lasted one hour and at approximately 1630 Hours the victim left her home. She stated this was the first time and the last time she had any contact with the victim and stated it was a straight professional relationship and that the victim had stated nothing unusual at that time.

On 31 May 89 I spoke with the wife of Dr. DORIAN KANE. I was advised by Mrs. KANE that TERRI had been seeing Dr. KANE for approximately one year on a weekly basis for private counsel and therapy. In reviewing the doctor's schedule book she noted that the last contact Dr. KANE had with the victim was a telephonic therapy on 29 May 89 between the hours of 1330 and 1500 Hours. Mrs. KANE stated she would advise her husband of TERRI's death and further forward my business number to him.

On 01 JUN 89 at 0820 Hours, Detective CONLEY

and I went to the GANDY residence in Hollywood Riviera. We had a conversation with the victim's family, which included Mr. and Mrs. GANDY and her sister, KATE GANDY. During the conversation we were advised by KATE GANDY that the victim, TERRI HORGAN, had been at KATE's house on 30 May 89 from the hours of 1700 to 1730. KATE stated that she left her house at approximately 1730 Hours for group therapy, however, did not know the exact location where it was to be held. She recalled that one of the group leaders was JANE and that the group therapy was on a weekly basis, the hours from 1800 to 1900 Hours. KATE further stated that following the therapy the group would go to a local cafe, which she believed was on Santa Monica Boulevard near Sawtelle Boulevard in West Los Angeles, for coffee. Normally after the group had coffee, KATE was aware that TERRI would then return home.

The family stated that the victim's normal habits were very structured. They stated that she usually went to bed early and rose early and normally was very prompt for all of her appointments or scheduled meetings. The family felt that TERRI was very mature for her age and was security minded. The family was aware that TERRI had at least $50.00 in U.S. currency and probably more in the area of $100.00 or so in U.S. currency in her purse on 30 May 89. Mrs. GANDY stated that she knew she had to pay her golf pro $50.00 on the morning of 31 May 89 and she stated she normally paid him in cash. She was also aware that her daughter always carried some currency with her. The family stated that TERRI was wearing a medallion on a choker chain which they believed had the initials of "WCGC" and a picture of a golfer with a pearl in place of the golf ball around her neck. She

also normally wore a watch, gold in color, with an expansion band. Again, in talking of personal habits, the family stated that TERRI was very into golf and outside of taking weekly golf instructions from her golf pro, GRADY NEWMAN, she also played several times a week in practice at a couple of other clubs in the area. TERRI was also a member of the Hockaby Hills Country Club where she frequently played golf.

The family explained to us that TERRI had changed her name to HORGAN and dropped her middle name approximately one year prior to her death. We were further informed that she did this of her own accord and felt that it gave her more identity as an individual and independence. KATE explained to us that the name HORGAN was picked out by TERRI due to the fact that the name stems from a history meaning "Healthy and Hearty Woman."

The victim's mother stated that TERRI would have had several credit cards in her purse, some of which were Mastercard California First Bank, a Visa from the Wells Fargo Bank, a Union gas card in the name of JOHN GANDY, abbreviated first name "GABE," a May Company card and her check book from Home Federal Savings and Loan. On this same date, 01 JUN 89, the GANDYs explained to Detective CONLEY and myself the actions of themselves and the victim, TERRI HORGAN prior to her death. This information will be outlined in detail further in this same report.

On 01 JUN 89 at approximately 1430 Hours, Detective CONLEY and I made contact with GINA DiBELLO, 1380 Western Avenue, Apartment 8, Lomita, California. It should be noted that prior to contacting GINA DiBELLO, Detective CONLEY and I had been advised by Detectives HUNTER and

MIZELL that they interviewed security guard BATTLE at 1380 Western Avenue, Apartment 8, on 31 May 89, in connection with their follow-up investigation of the homicide. We were advised that BATTLE was currently living at this location and we were informed that BATTLE was living there with his sister.

Upon contacting GINA DiBELLO she advised us that she was not a relative of Mr. BATTLE, only a friend. She stated that she is a wife of PETER DiBELLO and that she, along with her husband and three children, live in Unit 8. She stated that she was helping out SAMMY BATTLE by allowing him to stay and sleep at their unit until he got on his feet. We asked GINA DiBELLO if she could go over the events that took place on 30 May 89 and she gave the following statement. She stated that she was home that date and in the early evening or around 8:00 p.m., SAMMY BATTLES had arrived home from work. She stated at approximately 9:00 p.m. she walked to Darby's Coffee Shop about three blocks away to visit her husband who is employed there. She stated when she left SAMMY BATTLE was still at the location watching her three children as he frequently did. She stated she took the last bus from that location and returned home at approximately 11:15 p.m. on 30 May 89 and noted that SAMMY BATTLE was still at the location with her children watching television. She stated shortly after that she left Unit 8 and walked to the Wait-A-Minute Bar where she remained until approximately 2:00 a.m. GINA DiBELLO stated that she walked back to her apartment after 2:00 a.m. and remembered that SAMMY BATTLE was asleep on the front room floor with the television running. GINA DiBELLO stated that she remained up until approximately 0330 Hours, having a couple of additional

drinks, at which time she fell asleep. GINA stated the following morning when she awoke SAMMY BATTLE was still asleep on the front room floor and it appeared to her he had never left the location.

On 01 JUN 89 I telephoned 434-9773 and spoke with JANE REIMER. She advised me that she is a group leader for a group therapy in which victim TERRI HORGAN had been attending for several months on a weekly basis. JANE stated that TERRI attended the therapy group on 30 May 89 and was there between the hours of 1800 and 1915 to 1930 Hours. She stated that following the group therapy the members had gone to have coffee, however, she did not attend. She stated that TERRI had made no unusual statements during the time that she was there and appeared to be very excited about both her golfing success and the fact that she would be moving into her new home in the near future. JANE REIMER stated that victim TERRI did not give out her home number or new address, and JANE and the other members of the group can recall that no one in the group knew exactly where the condominium project was located.

On 01 JUN 89 at approximately 1300 Hours Detective CONLEY and I attended a coroner's autopsy on the victim TERRI HORGAN. The autopsy was performed by Dr. ROONEY. Upon viewing the victim, I, Detective LANDER, took several photographs of her physical condition, with these photographs being retained as evidence. At the conclusion of the autopsy Detective CONLEY and I were advised by Dr. ROONEY that the victim had died of ligature strangulation. We were informed that the victim had a bruised area on her right eye and cheek and a second bruised area on the top portion of her head. We noticed that

the victim had numerous abrasions on her elbows and forearms which Dr. ROONEY felt was caused just prior to the time of death. (See autopsy report.)

On 02 JUN 89 at 0740 Hours Detective CONLEY and I conducted a taped interview with subject SAMMY BATTLE. During this interview subject BATTLE explained his actions prior to and following the discovery of the victim, TERRI HORGAN. (See transcript of taped interview).

On 02 JUN 89 at 1000 Hours I received a telephone call from BOBBIE HILLER. BOBBIE HILLER stated she was a psychologist in a cull group leader with JANE REIMER. She said she had sat in numerous group meetings in which the victim had taken part on a weekly basis. She stated that TERRI was a private individual and did not have many friends when she was growing up. She stated that she felt her father was responsible for some of this due to the fact that he was very stern and had a weak relationship between himself and her mother. BOBBIE HILLER stated that TERRI felt up during the last meeting on 30 May 89 and again was excited about her success in recent golf. She recalled that TERRI was wearing the medallion she had won in a golf tournament and was further excited about moving into her new home. Miss HILLER felt that besides members of the group in which TERRI was extremely popular with, the victim also felt secure and confident in speaking with her other therapist (name unknown) and met with him on a weekly basis, and her golf pro who had been assisting her in her golf game. BOBBIE HILLER had no knowledge of any relationship that TERRI was involved in with any male or female and felt if there had been one she would have mentioned it during the therapy meetings.

On 02 JUN 89 at approximately 1050 Hours Detective CONLEY and I had a taped interview with subject DON ARNOLD, 37508 19th Street, Saugus, California, telephone (805) 732-2343. The entire interview was tape recorded with the tape later being transcribed. The following is a small synopsis of the interview. ARNOLD stated he had previously been living with a female by the name of CONNIE ARNOLD and they had married approximately one year previous to this date. He stated that CONNIE had two children from a previous marriage, both boys, one being seventeen and the other being eight. ARNOLD stated that he was currently driving a 1989 Chevy Blazer, burgundy in color. ARNOLD stated he had been a resident for approximately five years and previous to this had resided in Texas. He recalled that on 30 May 89 (Tuesday) he, ARNOLD, had let in a heating man in Unit #66. He stated that in the afternoon prior to the hours 1530 and 1545 Hours a delivery service delivered a sofa to the victim and further recalled that these delivery people spoke with the victim at her apartment. ARNOLD further stated that he recalled a newer white smaller sedan was parked in the garage and felt that this newer vehicle was possibly a BMW. He stated that following work on 30 May 89 he secured Unit #66 at approximately 1530 or 1545 Hours and at that time was unaware if any other person was in the location. He stated he then left the complex and drove to Saugus. He stated that he, along with one of his step-children, went to Shakey's where they bought pizza and returned back to his house where he washed his truck. He stated that he stayed up until approximately 1130 (Hours) at night, at which time he went to bed. He stated he awoke as usual at ap-

proximately 0330 Hours, dressed and left to return to work in Urban, arriving at approximately 7:00 a.m. (Refer to transcribed interview for further information and details of conversation).

On 02 JUN 89 at approximately 1500 Hours I received a telephone call from BOB MARTIN, telephone 549-8029. Mr. MARTIN stated he is a member of the therapy group and was present on 30 May 89 with the victim TERRI. He stated he has known the victim since February and that following this session he, along with the victim and other members of the group, went to Timmie's Cafe for coffee. He stated that the conversation was casual and that her statements were more directed towards her golf and moving. He stated that the victim left Timmie's Cafe at approximately 2015 Hours, however, he did not see what car she was driving. MARTIN stated that the victim was popular with the group and he had no idea as to who or why anyone would want to hurt her. MARTIN stated that he was aware she was purchasing a new home somewhere in Urban, however, he had no personal idea as to where.

On 04 JUN 89 the GANDY family was re-contacted at their residence. Present during this interview was Mr. and Mrs. GANDY and one of the victim's sisters, BRIDY GANDY. During this interview thoughts were exchanged concerning the murder of TERRI HORGAN and, again, conversation concerning all parties' actions prior to and following the death of TERRI. This interview was tape recorded with the tape being retained by me. (See transcript of taped interview for further information and detail). On 05 JUN 89 at 0800 Hours I was telephoned by Mrs. GANDY who stated that she recalled some facts which she could not previously remember during our

taped interview. Mrs. GANDY stated that on Sunday night, 28 May 89, TERRI had left her car at her condo overnight and had gone home with Mrs. GANDY to their house in Hollywood Riviera. She stated that Monday, 29 May 89, TERRI was scheduled to play golf with her father. She stated that on the morning of 29 May 89 her father had apparently forgotten the car arrangement and had left to play golf, leaving TERRI still at the house. Mrs. GANDY drove TERRI down to her house at approximately 8 a.m. in the morning so that she could pick up her car and meet her father to play golf. She stated that TERRI had, in fact, played golf that day and had returned to her house in Urban at approximately 1300 Hours. TERRI telephoned her mother at that time and advised her that she was home. Mrs. GANDY recalled driving to TERRI's house at approximately 1600 Hours on 29 May 89, at which time she picked up her daughter and they went shopping until 1800 Hours. Mrs. GANDY, driving her car and the victim driving her car, both drove back to the Hollywood Riviera address to spend the night.

On 05 JUN 89 Detective CONLEY and I picked up various items collected as evidence by the coroner's investigation from the Coroner's Office and delivered these items along with the victim's brassiere found at the crime scene to the Sheriffs Crime Lab for examination and comparison.

On 07 JUN 89 at 0750 Hours I contacted the victim's golf pro, GRADY NEWMAN, by land line. NEWMAN recalled that TERRI had been taking weekly lessons from him for approximately one year. He stated he last spoke with the victim on Tuesday, 30 May 89 at approximately 1400 to 1430 Hours where they discussed the lesson which was scheduled for

the morning of Wednesday, 31 May 89. He recalled
that they talked about the fact that if he (NEWMAN's)
wife had the baby which was due any day, that the
lesson would be cancelled. However if his wife did
not start labor, he would try to make it on the morning of 31 May 89. He stated that TERRI would normally arrive between 7:30 a.m. and 8:00 a.m. for her
scheduled lesson every Wednesday morning which
was conducted between 8:30 a.m. and 9:30 a.m. He
stated that the victim did not socialize with other pa-
trons and normally just practiced her golf game and
upon completing this, would leave alone. Mr.
NEWMAN could not think of any reason or person
who disliked her nor could he think of anyone who
would commit such an act upon her.

I At this time in our investigation I and fellow investigators CONLEY, McKENNA, HUNTER,
CAMPBELL and MIZELL compared notes and statements given by numerous individuals connected with
either the condominium complex or the victim's family. We noted that subject ARNOLD's statements were
inconsistent with statements given by other people.
ARNOLD stated there was a sofa delivered on Tuesday, 30 May 89. However, it was determined and verified by Detective CONLEY that the sofa was delivered on Saturday, 27 May 89. This fact was also
pointed out by the victim's mother who was present
when the delivery was made. ARNOLD stated that
there was a white car parked in the garage at 1530
Hours when he secured the unit on 30 May 89. Again,
the victim was at the location verified by her mother
and other people she had telephoned until she had
left for her appointment with DIANE BRADY which
started at 1530 Hours in West Los Angeles. ARNOLD
further indicated that he had let in a heating man to

Unit #66, and according to other investigators and their conversations, it was unsure if any work or workers had been at that location on 30 May 89.

On 07 JUN 89 at 1000 Hours Detective CONLEY, Sgt. McKENNA and I returned to Unit #66 at the apartment complex. We entered into Unit #66 and, again, went over the layout of the crime scene. At this time, I, Detective LANDER, was approached by ARNOLD who was working at the complex. I asked ARNOLD again if he would tell me what took place on Tuesday, 30 May 89. ARNOLD stated that he had been told by his boss DAN BLACK to open Unit #66 at approximately 1300 Hours on 30 May 89 so that a heating man could come in and work on the unit. He stated he did open Unit #66 at 1300 Hours by use of his passkey where he unlocked the front door, entered Unit #66, went downstairs and opened the automatic garage door opener, at which time a workman he described as a large man was present and began work on the unit. At this time I again noted the conflicting statement in that victim TERRI HORGAN had been at her unit at 1300 Hours due to the fact she had telephoned her mother at that time. She further informed her mother she intended to stay at the location for a while doing chores until she was to leave for her appointment with DIANE BRADY. ARNOLD then continued and told me that he had left the unit and returned at approximately 1500 to 1530 Hours, at which time he noted that the gas man had left. He also stated that at 1300 Hours when he opened the unit there was a new white BMW parked in the garage of Unit #66 and that this same vehicle was still parked in the garage at 1500 to 1530 Hours when he re-secured the unit. He stated that at that time he lowered the garage door, exited the front door utilizing

his key to lock both locks on the front door. At this time a co-worker who was standing by mentioned that no gas man had worked on those units on Tuesday, 30 May 89. At this time I noted ARNOLD to appear confused and again stated, "Yes, there was a man there, I let him in. He was the large man who I saw in your trailer yesterday." The worker that ARNOLD was speaking with was not introduced to me, however, refer to Detective CONLEY's supplementary report for his identity.

Following the above conversation concerning the confusion between if or if not a worker had been at Unit #66, along with the reported newer white BMW being there, I requested that the construction crew search for the individual who was described as the large man. A few minutes later a Safeway Plumbing and Heating truck arrived at Unit #66 and upon driving up, subject ARNOLD stated, "That's the man. That's the guy I let in on Tuesday." I then contacted a workman by the name of BROWN, BUDDY, employed by Safeway Plumbing and Heating. Mr. BROWN was asked if he entered Unit #66 on Tuesday, 30 May 89, to which he stated no. He then gave the following account for his actions on 30 May 89. He stated that on 30 May 89 he worked on four other units, three of which were across from #66 and the last being on the same side as #66, however at the extreme south end of that four unit building. He stated that at no time on 30 May 89 did ARNOLD open a door for him nor did he recall seeing any white BMW at the location. BROWN stated that all of the units and log times are kept by him and that he could provide a sheet or ledger showing which units he had worked on that day. He stated after lunch on 30 May 89 he was at the end unit which is owned by a secretary employed

by of the construction company. He had worked on this unit the entire afternoon until it was time to quit. BROWN stated on 31 May 89 he was working in a unit directly across from Unit #66 at which time he recalled in the morning hours a request was made by DAN BLACK to borrow his ladder so an air conditioning man could get up to the attic in Unit #66. He stated that later in the morning he began working in the garage area of Unit #66 and was aware that BLACK was still inside of the complex doing last minute painting. He recalled that the victim's mother had arrived at the location and that shortly thereafter BLACK had run into the garage area and appeared very shook up, stating that something had happened to the victim. BROWN stated that he did enter Unit #66 after the victim's mother had discovered the body and he entered momentarily into the upstairs bedroom where he checked the victim prior to paramedics arrival and it was obvious to him that she was dead. He stated he immediately returned downstairs and remained at the location until he was subsequently contacted by one of the initial investigators (refer to the investigative follow-up reports).

In our investigation we observed that a FBI rap sheet indicated that DON ARNOLD had served a prison sentence for burglary in the state of Texas. On the morning of 07 JUN 89 Detective CONLEY telephoned Texas to request further details of his arrest and sentencing. I noted also on the report that DON ARNOLD had been arrested in the state of Arizona on 01 AUG 81. I called Sheriff's Department in Winslow, Arizona, and spoke with Detective PYLE. PYLE, upon view of his records, advised me that DON ARNOLD had been arrested by his agency on 01 AUG 81 for a violation of parole out of the state of Texas.

He stated that ARNOLD remained in their jail for twelve days and was subsequently released to Texan authorities on 13 AUG 81 and he had no further record or information concerning this subject.

On 07 JUN 89 Detective CONLEY and I drove to Saugus in an attempt to verity the alibi of DON ARNOLD. Upon arriving at the location we observed no one was home at his apartment and subsequently contacted the Assistant Manager of the complex BRENDA WARD. BRENDA WARD stated that she knew DON ARNOLD and his wife CONNIE. She stated that she recalled during the week, unknown 30, 31 of May or 01 June 89, she observed DON ARNOLD to be driving home from work and appeared to be upset in that he was shaking his head and running his hands over his face. She recalled on Saturday, 03 JUN 89 that he (ARNOLD) came to her office along with his wife, at which time she asked if everything was okay. ARNOLD made a statement indicating that everything was not okay, that during the week he had been working at a house at work in an upstairs bathroom when he observed a dead body in a bedroom next to it. He stated that the body was that of a female and that it had been mutilated, indicating that her fingers and toes had been cut off. He stated that he had thrown up and then dialled 911, notifying authorities, at which time he had to throw up again. He stated that the body was face down and shortly after the discovery a co-worker or his boss came to the location, at which time he threw up upon viewing the victim. He indicated that he was very shook up over this, at which time his wife had added that earlier in the week DON (indicating ARNOLD) had been so upset over this that she had to take him to the hospital for medication to calm him down. In re-questioning BRENDA WARD

she was not exactly sure if ARNOLD's wife stated she had to go to the hospital for him and get him medication or if, in fact, she took him to the hospital. In reference to ARNOLD's alibi on 30 May 89, 1 asked BRENDA WARD if the tenants in the building that ARNOLD lives in wash their own personal cars at the location. WARD stated that there was no exterior water outlets there and that she had never seen anyone utilize or wash their cars around that particular building. She stated there was an outlet at the front of the complex, however, she stated the occupants normally just went down the street to a carwash.

On 08 JUN 89 at 0750 Hours I again spoke with Mrs. GANDY on the telephone. I asked her to again go over her actions and the actions she was aware of TERRI doing on 30 May 89, the day prior to the discovery of her body. Mrs. GANDY recalled that TERRI was home in Hollywood Riviera until approximately 10 a.m. on Tuesday, 30 May 89, at which time she had left to run errands and practice golf. Mrs. GANDY recalled that TERRI called her at approximately I p.m., 1300 Hours on 30 May 89 and told her that she was home, was going to stay there for a while until she had to go to her appointment with DIANE BRADY. I asked Mrs. GANDY at this time if anyone in the family or anyone they knew who had been to the location, meaning TERRI's apartment, owns or drives a newer white BMW, to which she stated no.

On 19 JUN 89 at approximately 1140 Hours, Det. CONLEY and I had a second interview with DON ARNOLD; the interview was tape recorded, with the tape being retained as evidence (SEE TRANSCRIBED INTERVIEW.)

On 12 JUN 89, I contacted the County Crime Lab and set up a polygraph appointment for DON

ARNOLD. The polygraph was to take place on 14 JUN 89 at 1100 Hours. On this same date (12 JUN 89), I spoke with ARNOLD via telephone and advised him of the meeting on the 14th and advised him I would pick him up at the sales office, 3200 Alder Street, Lomita at 1000 Hours.

On 13 JUN 89, I was advised by the County Crime Lab that the laser used on victim TERRI HORGAN's purse was unable to turn up any fingerprints.

On 14 JUN 89, this being the date for ARNOLD's polygraph, I was advised at 1000 Hours by his co-workers that he had failed to show up for work. I was subsequently advised later in the day that ARNOLD did, in fact, show up for work at approximately 1130 Hours and told his supervisor that he had had car problems and was, therefore, late for work. Due to this fact, the polygraph was cancelled for that date.

On 14 JUN 89, I telephoned the apartment manager of ARNOLD's apartment complex in Saugus, who advised me that ARNOLD's car had been in his carport parking spot between the hours of 0830 and 0840. The manager checked ARNOLD's carport at approximately 1120 Hours and reported to me that his vehicle was no longer parked there.

On 14 JUN 89 at approximately 1245 Hours, Det. CONLEY and I contacted ARNOLD at the construction site. He explained to us that his car alarm on his vehicle had malfunctioned and he subsequently had repaired it himself. He further stated he had left his house at approximately 0830 Hours of the morning of the 14th and had arrived at the work site at 1000 hours. When I explained to him that we were also at the work site at 1000 Hours and had been advised that he had not shown up for work, ARNOLD then

stated that he had arrived at approximately 1030 Hours. Previous to this contact with subject ARNOLD, we spoke with his supervisor, DAN DARNELL, who advised us that ARNOLD had telephoned him at approximately 1125 Hours and told him he was 45 minutes away from work on the freeway. When I advised ARNOLD of our earlier conversation with DARNELL regarding his (ARNOLD) making a telephone call, ARNOLD denied ever calling DARNELL.

On 15 JUN 89, Det. CONLEY and I collected head hair and pubic hair samples from subjects DON ARNOLD and DAN BLACK. On this same date, these samples were taken to the County Sheriff's Crime Lab for comparison against fibers and hairs recovered at the crime scene.

On 15 JUN 89, I received a criminal history on ARNOLD from the state of Texas.

On 16 JUN 89, I was advised Criminalist HARRY BURNS had started working on the hairs and fibers collected from the crime scene regarding this homicide investigation. BURNS is employed as a Criminalist by the County Sheriff's Crime Lab.

On 16 JUN 89, I advised ARNOLD that a second polygraph had been set up for him, to be taken on the morning of 20 JUN 89 at 1100 Hours. ARNOLD was again advised that I would pick him up at 1000 Hours and transport him from his place of work for that test.

On 20 JUN 89, I was advised that subject ARNOLD had failed to show up for work and further learned that he did not report to work for the entire day. I was later advised by subject ARNOLD that an unknown suspect had stolen tools from his vehicle on the night prior to 20 JUN 89; therefore, he was unable to show up for work.

Prior to 27 JUN 89, I set up a third polygraph for subject ARNOLD with the Sheriffs Crime Lab. This polygraph was set up for 27 JUN 89, again at 1100 Hours. Subject ARNOLD was not advised of the pre-arranged polygraph and on the morning of 27 JUN 89 at 0950 Hours, Det. CONLEY and I contacted ARNOLD at the work site at 3200 Alder Street, urban. At this time, I advised ARNOLD that we had an opening at 1100 Hours and that his absence at work had already been granted with his immediate supervisor, BRAD BOLES. ARNOLD immediately appeared extremely upset-and in substance, stated that he could not take the polygraph; first - due to the fact that we had not previously informed him of it and, secondly - due to the fact that he had been drinking the night prior. I informed him that a small amount of alcohol more than 12 hours previously consumed would not affect the outcome of the polygraph, at which time, ARNOLD informed me that he refused to take one at this time, meaning 27 JUN 89.

On 28, JUN 89 at 0820 Hours, Det. CONLEY and I contacted subject DON ARNOLD's wife, CONNIE ARNOLD at her residence in Saugus. An interview was conducted among Mrs. ARNOLD, Det. CONLEY and myself and this interview was tape recorded. The tape was retained as evidence (SEE TRANSCRIPT).

On 28 JUN 89, Det. CONLEY and I collected head and pubic hair samples from subject SAMMY BATTLE.

On 29 JUN 89, Det. CONLEY and I collected head and pubic hair samples from subject JODY WILLIAMS.

On 29 JUN 89, the samples collected from BATTLE and WILLIAMS were taken to the County Crime Lab.

Prior to 06 JUL 89, a fourth polygraph was set up with the County Crime Lab. On this date, Det. CONLEY and I contacted subject ARNOLD, who stated he was willing to take the polygraph on this date. Subject ARNOLD was transported to the Crime Lab where the polygraph was administered by Sgt. WILLIAM CUSIK. CUSIK administered a test four separate times to subject ARNOLD and after completing the polygraph, advised us that the readings were indecisive. In further explanation, he stated that the graph shows that the person is neither lying nor telling the truth and had no responses on his chart indicating to him (CUSIK) if the subject responsible for the crime or not. Another test was administered to ARNOLD on this date, which included numerous items; one of which was the ligature used in the murder of TERRI HORGAN. During this test, CUSIK advised Det. CONLEY and me that ARNOLD did not show any response to any of the possible murder weapons, stated to him one of which was the correct one. CUSIK advised us that it was his opinion that ARNOLD did not know what item was used to commit the homicide.

On 18 JUL 89,1205 Hours, I interviewed:

PIZARRO, MATEO, WMA, BROWN, GREEN, 5-10, 145# of Compton, California, Age 25. Subject PIZARRO first met TERRI HORGAN when he accompanied TERRI and DAN BLACK on a walk-through at her condominium. At that time, HORGAN made arrangements with PIZARRO to finish sealing her tile. PIZARRO stated that while HORGAN was away for a week playing golf, he completed the tile work requested. PIZARRO was paid by HORGAN for his work on 21 May 89 and that was the last time he was inside Unit #66.

On Tuesday, 30 May 89, PIZARRO worked at the complex and completed his day at 1530 Hours. PIZARRO drove home and later went to his girlfriend's house for the evening.

On 31 May 89, PIZARRO heard of HORGAN's death while at work.

On 01 JUN 89, PIZARRO was eating lunch with a fellow worker, DON ARNOLD, at which time ARNOLD stated that HORGAN had been beaten and cut about the chest and face area. ARNOLD also stated something about HORGAN inheriting the money to buy the condominium. This is the only conversation that PIZARRO could recall any of the workers making in reference to the HORGAN murder.

Upon request, PIZARRO submitted his fingerprints to me for elimination purposes in the investigation. It should be noted that this is a synopsis of the interview. The interview was tape-recorded with the tape being retained as evidence.

On 25 JUL 89, I received a report from the Sheriff's Crime Lab, dated 25 JUL 89. Included in the supplemental report, Criminalist BURNS wrote the following results and conclusions:

"The two hairs found on the victim's shirt (GB-6A), were found to be dissimilar to the pubic hair standards from JODI WILLIAMS. Two of the four hairs found in the vacuum debris from the victim's bedroom (GB-8C), were found to be similar to the pubic hair standards from Mr. WILLIAMS. These two hairs could have originated from this person."

On 31 OCT 89, I was advised by Identification Analyst WALDO SCOTT, that he had made a Cal I.D. "hit" on the TERRI HORGAN homicide. I was advised by SCOTT that a fingerprint from the window screen frame, found inside the victim's front door, was iden-

tified through Cal I.D. to a JODI WILLIAMS, SID Number A0000475.
ON 31 OCT 89, DET. ED NORMAN and I contacted Parole Agent MONICA PEOPLES. Agent PEOPLES advised me that she was the Parole Officer for JODI WILLIAMS and further provided me with a photograph of subject WILLIAMS. Upon viewing the photo, I verified that her parolee, WILLIAMS was the same JODY WILLIAMS that fellow officers and I had previously contacted at the condominium site. I was provided an address where JODI WILLIAMS was reported to be living at.

31 OCT 89, I received a copy of fingerprints from Beverly Hills Police Dept. on a previous booking of JODI WILLIAMS. These prints were subsequently transported back to our Police Department where they were again analyzed by Identification Analyst SCOTT and were confirmed as being the same person who had left the fingerprints on the screen inside the victim's apartment.

Based on the recently received evidence, I wrote and obtained a Ramey Warrant for JODI WILLIAMS, dated 02 NOV 89 and signed by Judge JULIUS PIKE.

Officers of the Crime Impact Team set up a surveillance on 1438 West 137th Street, Watts, California, attempting to locate suspect JODI WILLIAMS.

On 6 NOV 89 at approximately 1345 Hours, officers of the Impact Team observed suspect WILLIAMS to exit a car and approach his father's residence at that address. Suspect WILLIAMS was taken into custody without incident and transported to our Police Department for booking.

On 06 NOV 89, Det. CONLEY and I interviewed suspect WILLIAMS while in custody at the Police Department. Warning and Waiver Card, provided and

stated he understood same and would wave his rights and talk to us concerning his arrest. This interview was tape recorded, with the tape recording machine being in plain view of subject WILLIAMS. This interview was approximately one hour and forty minutes in length and I inadvertently, upon filling Tape One, sides A and B, removed Tape One and mixed it up with Tape Two; thereby placing Tape One back into the recorder and copied over Side A and a small portion of Side B. Included in Side A was the advisement and waiver, given by myself to WILLIAMS, which was witnessed by Det. CONLEY. During this interview, WILLIAMS admitted he was working at the job site, 2300 Hours, 30 May 89 to 0600 Hours, 31 May 89. WILLIAMS stated he was wearing a blue security guard uniform and black Adidas tennis shoes. WILLIAMS admitted to meeting victim HORGAN on two or three brief encounters away from her condominium, while he was working on the job site, prior to her death. WILLIAMS repeatedly stated he had never been in HORGAN's condominium, #66 and denied any involvement in her murder.

On 07 NOV 89, Det. CONLEY and I had a second interview with WILLIAMS. It should be noted that WILLIAMS had contacted Jailers and requested our presence prior to this second interview. The second interview was tape recorded, again, with the tape recorder being in plain view of WILLIAMS. WILLIAMS was asked if he had previously been advised of his Rights (indicated 06 NOV 89), to which he stated he had and he further still wished to waive his Rights. Due to the fact that the previous tape had accidentally erased his Miranda Advisement, I re-advised WILLIAMS a second time, to which he again stated he understood his Rights and waived them. A sec-

ond interview was consistent with the first in that WIL-
LIAMS was questioned concerning his duties while
employed as a security guard at the condominium
site. SEE TAPES BOOKED INTO EVIDENCE FOR
COMPLETE TRANSCRIPTION OF INTERVIEWS.

Chapter II

SUPPLEMENTARY REPORT

I/O: JOHN HUNTER
CRIME: 187 PC, Murder
VICTIM: HORGAN, TERRI
DES: WFA, 26 Yrs.
RES: 3200 Alder Avenue, Unit #66,
Urban

INVESTIGATIVE SUMMARY:

On 31 May 89 at approximately 1220 Hours, I responded to 3200 Alder Avenue, Unit #66, at the request of Sgt. K. McKENNA, regarding a homicide investigation. Upon arrival, I was contacted by Det. LANDER at the front door of Unit #66 and he informed me of the circumstances; that being, a lone female adult, who appeared to be the victim of foul play, was deceased and lying on the floor of an upstairs bedroom.

Det. LANDER and I walked to the upper landing of the stairway (second floor) and through the open door of a bedroom located in the northwest corner of the townhouse, I observed the victim, face down, in the middle area of the bedroom. I also observed one white tennis shoe along the north wall, near the cen-

ter line of the bedroom floor. I further observed the
following:

A clock along the north wall, which was plugged
into an electrical socket and appeared to be func-
tioning.

Black scuff marks in the northeast area of the
bedroom that were located along the baseboard.

That the mirrored sliding door for the closet door
was off its lower tracks and noted a spot of mud
or dried dirt along the upper portion of the mirrored door.

Looking along the south wall, I observed a scuff
mark in the center area of the south wall, at a
height of 5 to 6 feet.

Upon entering the room, I observed the victim
had several large abrasions on her elbows (left
and right) and what appeared to be small abrasions on her fingers.

On closer examination of the victim, Det.
LANDER and I were able to determine that it appeared that the victim had been strangled, as
there was a dark purple line around her neck,
which was indicative of some form of ligature.

Det. LANDER and I then exited the bedroom as
C.S.I. Officers DIAMOND, IRELAND and V. H.
MURPHY were in the process of completing photographs and the recovery of other items, which might
have been of evidentiary value.

As this was being done, I left the second floor of
the townhouse and proceeded to the garage and
made a search of that location to determine if the
victim had possibly been assaulted as she was parking her vehicle, which was parked and all four doors

were locked; the garage floor and a storage room. Upon completing the search of those locations and the vehicle, I did not observed anything that was unusual or indicative of a struggle, which would have caused the injuries suffered by the victim.

While at the location, I was directed by Sgt. McKENNA to contact and interview a subject by the name of HAROLD NOLAN, who is president of Statewide Security Systems and whose company provides security for the construction site, which is adjacent to the occupied townhouses. Upon contacting Mr. NOLAN, spoke with him about security officers employed, who might have been on duty during the time period that the crime would have occurred. NOLAN then provided me with applicant cards, which are completed by the security applicant and which has a photograph, fingerprints of the subject, which is forwarded to the Dept. of Consumer Affairs for confirmation as to whether or not this subject is qualified for employment. NOLAN advised me that subject LEO PHINNEY was employed on Tuesday, 30 May 89 between the Hours of 1600 and 2300 and subject LUMUS WILLIAMS was employed from 2300 Hours on 30 May 89 until 0600 Hours on 31 May 89. NOLAN stated that another security officer had been scheduled to work on 30 May 89 from 1600 until 2300 Hours; however, because of complaints received from occupants from the townhouses, he had been removed from the schedule, replaced by Mr. PHINNEY and had on 31 May 89 at 1330 Hours, met with NOLAN, discussing his future employment with the company. Upon making inquiries to NOLAN about this subject, who identified him as SAMMY BATTLE. He stated this subject had arrived for work on 30 May 89 at 1600 Hours, but was contacted by 'phone and

advised to go home; that he was being re-scheduled because of complaints from some of the residents in the occupied townhouses. NOLAN went on to state the complaints indicated that BATTLE was being forward with some of the occupants and making people uneasy. I asked NOLAN about the meeting he had had with BATTLE at 1330 Hours on 31 May 89 and he indicated the meeting was very agreeable; that subject BATTLE had continued to show interest in his work and was making further inquiries as to his employment. NOLAN went on to state that BATTLE was not uneasy during the meeting and did not appear to be nervous and NOLAN did not recall observing any injuries to BATTLE'S hands or arms.

I inquired of NOLAN as to the type of equipment security officers at the construction location carry on their person and he indicated most of them carry a small flashlight, no weapons of any type and do not have any keys assigned to them that would allow them to enter any of the townhouses. At this time, I advised NOLAN that the investigators from the Police Department would like to maintain custody of the applicant cards, which contained the photographs and fingerprints and upon it being determined they were not of any evidentiary value, they would be returned to his company and he agreed to this. The interview was then completed, as he indicated he needed to return to his office.

I then informed Sgt. McKENNA of the information I had received and the fact that some of the occupants of the townhouses within the Paradise West complex had complained about one of the security officers being somewhat aggressive and at times, making them feel uneasy, along with the names of the other security officers who were assigned to that

construction site and it was determined that the sub-jects should be contacted as soon as possible to obtain statements from them. Sgt. McKENNA, at this time, assigned Det. L. MIZELL and I the task of locat-ing the employe of Statewide Security Systems, SAMMY BATTLE and upon responding to 1608 Narbonne, #6, we were able to determine that BATTLE did, in fact, live there. Det. MIZELL and I then responded to that location and upon knocking on the door, were contacted by a female subject who identified herself as the sister of subject BATTLE and she informed us that he was at that location and was currently sleeping on her bed. Subject BATTLE was then awakened by his sister, who advised him we were at the front door and he then responded and stepped outside with us so we might speak with him and not interrupt the activities occurring inside the small apartment (small children were watching the t.v.).

Det. MIZELL and I identified ourselves as Inves-tigators with the Police Dept. and we then asked BATTLE what his activities were at his place of em-ployment on 30 May 89. Subject BATTLE stated he arrived to work at approximately 1600 Hours, but was informed by security officer PHINNEY that he was not scheduled for work on that day. BATTLE stated he was informed to call the office, which he did and they told him he was not working on 30 May 89; that sev-eral complaints had been received about his activi-ties at the construction site and the townhouse loca-tion and that they wanted to speak to him the follow-ing day at 1330 Hours. I then asked BATTLE about what he did after receiving that information and he indicated he spoke with security officer PHINNEY, who's a white male, nearly eighty years of age and

that after speaking with him for only ten minutes, he left the construction site, walked to the corner of Sepulveda and Alder, where he caught Bus #6, almost immediately and continued home. BATTLE indicated to us that he spent approximately 15 minutes at the construction site. During our conversation with BATTLE, he was asked by Det. MIZELL if he knew the lady who lived in Unit #66 and he stated that he did and Det. MIZELL then asked if he was aware that the lady in that unit had complained about his behavior and he stated she might have been one of the people complaining about him and Det. MIZELL then asked if he was aware what had been said; BATTLE stated "one of the security guys told him, but he didn't pay any attention because he didn't give a shit." I then asked BATTLE if he had ever been inside Unit #66 and he stated that he had helped the lady who lives there by carrying a t.v. into her unit and on another occasion, he had talked with the worker near the driveway or inside the garage. I asked BATTLE if he had ever been inside the upstairs portion of the townhouse and he stated: "No." and I, once again, confirmed that statement by making the same inquiry and he stated he had never been upstairs. Det. MIZELL asked BATTLE the last time he saw the lady in Unit #66 and he indicated that he last saw her either when he helped her with the television or a day later, when she was driving her car past him; she might have waved and he returned her wave. Det. MIZELL then asked BATTLE if he was aware that the lady in #66 had complained about him because he had been responsible for her watch being lost the day he had helped with her television and he stated he knew she was mad, but he was just trying to help. Det. MIZELL and I then asked BATTLE what type of

clothing he wore when employed at the construction site and he stated a uniform with patches and at this time, we asked if he could obtain it for us and he walked back into the apartment, returning a short time later with a uniform jacket, shirt and pants on a hanger, which he let us look at. Det. MIZELL and I observed no evidence of stains or damage to the clothing. As Det. MIZELL and I were looking at the clothing, BATTLE maintained control of it and as he was doing so, I visually checked his arms and hands and observed no obvious injuries.

Det. MIZELL and I spoke with BATTLE for several more minutes, confirming our previous conversation, at which time, I presented BATTLE with a business card, requesting that he contact either myself or Det. CONLEY on 01 JUN 89, as Det. CONLEY may have some additional questions for him. The interview was then concluded.

Chapter III

CONTINUATION REPORT

(Urban Police Department)

Date: 31 May 89
Bonner, Douglas, WM 30
3200 Alder #65
Urban, California
Bonner, Helen, WF 35
Same as above

Interviewed by Det. D. Diamond, Urban PD.

Details: The Bonners arrived home approx. 1800 and at that time told me the following:

Mr. Bonner said he could see into the victim's condo and remembers see(ing) her about 2230 on the 30th. She was wearing a green sweatsuit appearing to be cleaning. They had just met the victim a few days ago and was aware she was just moving in. He did not believe she was staying over night at the condo. But a very short time later he said the lights were out and he figured she had left although he had not heard a car leave.

Both Bonners said they were concerned about a security guard who Mr. Bonner said was "5150"

(walking crazy). The guard was described as a WMA 20, black hair.

Mrs. Bonner said the victim had express(ed) concern about the weird actions of the security guard, that the victim said she felt very uneasy about him being around. She said the victim told her on Saturday 27 May 89 in the early evening that when she was receiving the delivery of her television the security guard was in her condo helping the delivery men. Mrs. Bonner said the victim told her she felt very strange. The guard also took out the trash for her.

Chapter IV

SUPPLEMENTARY REPORT

I/O: J. CONLEY
CRIME: 187 PC, MURDER
VICTIM: HORGAN, TERRI
RES: 3200 Alder Avenue, Unit #66, Urban
DATE & TIME: 31 May 89, approximately 1150
Hours

DETAILS:
On 31 May 89, I was advised by Sgt. McKENNA to respond to the above address re a homicide. Upon arrival at approximately 1325 Hours, I was contacted by Det. LANDER, who briefly informed me of the circumstances and advised that he and I would be conducting the investigation. Officers DIAMOND and IRELAND were assigned to the Crime Scene Investigation Unit and Officer HALL was assigned to the D.B.R. and crime report.

I completed a walk-through of the crime scene and noted the victim was lying in the northwest, upstairs bedroom. I did a preliminary check of that room and then advised Sgt. McKENNA I felt the Sheriff's Office laser should respond to assist us in the recovery of any latent prints that may have been in that

upstairs bedroom. I also located some hair and fiber throughout the unit and collected same (SEE PROP- ERTY REPORT).

At approximately 1500 Hours, the coroner's rep- resentatives arrived: DAVID JACKSON and LARRY McHENRY. Coroner's Representative JACKSON stated lividity was fixed and rigor mortis was full; he noticed an abrasion on the left elbow of the victim; also, ligature marks on the victim's neck. It appeared that the victim had been struck to the right side of her eye. Victim also had an abrasion on her right elbow. The victim was dressed in a pinkish-colored t-shirt and a blue pajama-type bottoms. She was lying face down in a southwest direction. Mr. McHENRY recov- ered a hair on the left inner elbow of the victim; also a hair on the right, outer elbow. Mr. McHENRY also completed a sexual assault kit, #926, and took samples and nail clippings from the victim.

At approximately 1615 Hours, I contacted: LEO PHINNEY, age 79, Security Guard, Statewide Secu- rity Company.

This individual was the security guard on duty on 30 May 89 from 1600 to, 2300 Hours. PHINNEY indicated there was no unusual activity in or around the victim's unit and noted no unusual circumstances. He indicated to me that he had been relieved by Se- curity Officer WILLIAMS at approximately 2240 Hours on 30 May 89.

On 01 JUN 89 at approximately 0830 Hours, Det. LANDER and I drove to the victim's parents residence, located in Hollywood Riviera. We contacted the victim's mother, MARY GANDY; the victim's father, JOHN GANDY and the sister KATE GANDY. We learned that victim HORGAN had been at her sister KATE's residence on 30 May 89 between the Hours

of 1700 and 1730. She indicated that the victim had a group therapy session to attend from 1800 to 1930 Hours and that she used KATE's residence to change clothes. She indicated her normal activity would be to attend the meeting and then go to a location known to her as Willie's Cafe in West Los Angeles with the group for coffee after the session. She also indicated to us that victim HORGAN was very security minded and that her normal habits would be to go to bed early, due to the fact that she was an early riser; she would wake up between 0500 - 0530 Hours and do a regimen of stretching exercises to improve her golf.

We further learned through the parents and the sister that the victim, more than likely, had more than fifty dollars cash in her possession and the possibility of more like $100.00. We asked the parents if the victim had any problems with anybody and the only problem that TERRI did have recently was with a security guard, who works for the Statewide Security, SAMMY BATTLE.

Mrs. MARY GANDY indicated that on the night of TERRI's walk-through (a walk-through of her new condo unit for orientation and to see if there was any problems that needed fixing). They returned to the unit and while walking toward the unit, they were followed by this security guard. Mrs. GANDY indicated that it was a "very creepy feeling" due to the fact that this security guard was asking questions to the effect of: "Where's your husband? What are you doing here?" Mrs. GANDY further indicated that her daughter had informed her she would be sleeping in the small bedroom of the unit on comforters and that she would be using the small bathroom due to the fact that it was more private and she had not entirely moved in yet.

On 01 JUN 89 at approximately 1015 Hours, I was contacted by DON DARNELL, who is a Director of Construction for Dunn Homes and is in charge of the Paradise West condominium complex. He indicated to me that during a manager's meeting, he was informed by two other owners that they had lodged a complaint about the security guard. DARNELL further indicated that he had contacted Statewide Security and informed them of the complaints and asked that this guard be removed from the grounds.

DARNELL further stated that on 30 May 89, when security guard BATTLE reported for work, he was told by security guard PHINNEY that he was not scheduled to work and told BATTLE to call Statewide for further information. Apparently security guard BATTLE went to the sales office at approximately 1530 Hours and used the telephone to call his office. Shortly after that, he was seen leaving Paradise West Complex at approximately 1545 Hours.

On 01 JUN 89 at approximately 1310 Hours, Det. LANDER and I attended the autopsy of victim HORGAN, which was performed by Dr. ROONEY. Upon examining the body, we noticed a bruise on the left hand, abrasions on both the right and left elbows; that the victim did receive a blow on the right eye; that it was swollen and most likely done while the victim was still alive. Also noticed abrasions to her nose and scratches on her face. There was pitikial hemorraghing in both eyes and we noted that the victim had three ligature abrasions around her neck. The upper-most ligature measured 3/8 inches thick by 3 1/2 inches in length; the lower ligature was 3/8 inches in width by 6 1/2 inches in length and a small ligature abrasion on the chin area of the victim. Dr. ROONEY also informed us that the victim had bruis-

ing inside of her lip and that she did receive a blow to the top of her head. Dr. ROONEY also informed us that the ligature was applied from the back and it was sort of a garotte applied from the back and it was sort of a garotte-type movement; it appeared that the suspect would be pulling the victim's neck back while attempting to strangle her. Dr. ROONEY stated the cause of death was ligature strangulation.

On 01 JUN 89 at approximately 1500 Hours, Det. LANDER and I contacted security guard SAMMY BATTLE at his residence. (For details, see Det. LANDER's supp).

On 01 JUN 89, when we returned to the station, we were contacted by Det. RICCI, who indicated he had been working some residential burglaries which were occurring at Porto Bello, which is a complex owned by DUNN, also under construction. He indicated in his investigation, he learned that an employee of Dunn Industries, DON ARNOLD, had been arrested in Texas for burglary. With this information, we called DAN DARNELL and attempted to set up an interview with ARNOLD on 02 JUN 89 at approximately 0830 Hours.

At approximately 1620 Hours on 01 JUN 89, I had a telephone conversation with HAROLD NOLAN, Supervisor, Statewide Security, who indicated to me that on Tuesday afternoon, he had received a call from Dunn Industries, requesting that Security Guard BATTLE be removed from the Paradise West job site. He further indicated that when BATTLE reported for work on 30 May 89, he was informed to call dispatch. He indicated that BATTLE did this and at that time, was told that he was being removed from the post and was further instructed to report to Statewide Security Office on 31 May 89 to discuss the situation.

NOLAN stated that BATTLE did come to the office on 31 May 89 at approximately 1330 Hours and NOLAN discussed the problems that had arisen at Paradise West with BATTLE. NOLAN stated he asked BATTLE if he had been in any of the units; BATTLE indicated that he had not after anyone had moved in.

On 02 JUN 89 at approximately 0700 Hours, I conducted an interview with JODY WILLIAMS, age 23, Statewide Security Systems, the security guard who was on duty on 30 and 31 May 89, from 2300 to 0600 Hours. I asked WILLIAMS if he was employed by Statewide Security, working at Paradise West on 30-31 May 89 and he indicted to me he was and had reported to work at approximately 2240 Hours and relieved security guard PHINNEY. WILLIAMS stated he noted no unusual activities during his tour of duty. I asked WILLIAMS if he had been informed that an individual had been murdered at the Paradise West Complex; he stated he was aware of that. I asked him if he knew the victim and he indicated he had met her once and that was on a Sunday morning at approximately 11 or 12. He indicated he observed the victim going through a trash container in the complex and that he approached her to see what she was doing. She indicated to him about the problem she had with the other security guard, SAMMY BATTLE and that she was searching the trash due to the fact that a watch was missing. Mr. WILLIAMS stated he jumped up into the trash can and found a bag, which the victim indicated was hers and in looking into this bag, the watch was located. WILLIAMS stated that the victim was very pleased in finding her watch and appeared to be very happy. He stated that was the only time he had spoken with the victim. I asked WILLIAMS what the victim had told him regard-

ing the other security guard; he indicated that on Saturday, the victim had received some deliveries of furniture and that the security guard, BATTLE, had helped the delivery men move her furniture in to her unit. He stated the victim felt this was very strange when she observed the security guard standing in her living room.

Security Guard WILLIAMS stated he reported to work at approximately 2230 Hours and that the main gate on Paradise West was secure, but the secondary gate was open. He indicated he closed this gate but it can't be secured; you merely have to push on it and the gate will open. He further indicated that nothing unusual occurred on his tour of duty and that he was visited by his supervisor during his shift. (FOR INFO ON WILLIAMS's SHIFT, SEE HIS DAILY LOG).

On 02 JUN 89 at approximately 0035 Hours, Det. LANDER and I conducted a taped interview with SAMMY BATTLE, age 24. (For details, see taped interview).

On 02 JUN 89, at approximately 1050, Hours, Det. LANDER and I conducted an interview with DON ARNOLD at the Police Department and the interview was taped. (For details, see taped interview).

On 02 JUN 89, at approximately 1410 Hours, I had a telephone conversation with Mrs. MARY GANDY. I was trying to ascertain the number of unit keys which were outstanding. She indicated to me that TERRI had one key on her key ring and that she had the remaining seven keys at her residence. She further indicated to me that all the deliveries to TERRI's unit were made on Saturday, 27 May 89. The deliveries came from Pacific Sales, who delivered a refrigerator and a washer and dryer, the Contemporary Styles on Sepulveda Boulevard delivery was made

of oak furniture and a television was delivered from Kyle Cramer Co. at approximately 1700 Hours.

On 02 JUN 89, I contacted DAN DARNELL of Dunn Homes and requested a list of all persons who had master keys to the Paradise West project. He indicated he would supply this as soon as possible.

On 05 JUN 89, Det. LANDER and I responded to the County Coroner's Office, picked up all evidence that the Coroner had collected and transported this to County Crime Lab. We Were also informed by Sgt. McKENNA that no latent fingerprints were developed in the northwest bedroom of the victim's condo by the Crime Lab.

On 06 JUN 89, approximately 0900 Hours, we attended a briefing with fellow detectives and compared notes.

On 06 JUN 89, approximately 1130 Hours, I was notified by DAN DARNELL that he had completed a list of all the employees who had keys and all recent move-ins to the Paradise West Complex. (For details, see the recent move-in list of employees with master keys).

On 06 JUN 89, approximately 1145 Hours, I contacted the Contemporary Styles regarding the deliveries (there was some confusion on the dates that the deliveries were made; we had received information from Mr. ARNOLD that a delivery was made on Tuesday afternoon. I contacted NEIL BRIDGES, owner of Contemporary Styles, who indicated that a delivery was made to the victim's unit on 27 May 89 at approximately 1130 Hours and that the victim, TERRI HORGAN, had signed for the deliveries. The two delivery men were BUD WILSON and BILLY JETT.

At approximately 1150 Hours on 06 JUN 89, I had a telephone conversation with the president of

Dunn Homes, DICK PERKINS, who indicated to me that DON ARNOLD had missed work on 05 JUN 89 and that he did not call his immediate supervisor. PERKINS further indicated that this was out of the ordinary for this employee, due to the fact that he had a pretty good attendance record and if he would miss work, he would always call in. PERKINS further indicated that the employee who had discovered the victim in her unit on 31 May 89 was a "basket case;" that he had not been back to work since and that he is feeling very guilty about not opening the bedroom door and discovering the victim sooner. PERKINS stated this employee was going to be going to counselling.

On 07 JUN 89, 0940 Hours, Det. LANDER, Sgt. McKENNA and I made a final check of Unit #66. I did observe and collected one brownish hair fiber from the northwest bedroom, which was in the corner, below the black scuff marks (See property report). We also had C.S.I. Officer DIAMOND complete additional C.S.I. work (For details, see Officer DIAMOND's report).

On 07 JUN 89, approximately 1330 Hours, Det. LANDER and I drove to Saugus in an attempt to contact the wife of subject DON ARNOLD for an interview. This was met with negative results. We did contact the assistant manager of the apartment complex, BRENDA WARD. (For details of this interview, see Det. LANDER's supplemental report).

On 08 JUN 89, 0940 Hours, I had a telephone conversation with customer service supervisor BRAD BOLES, who indicated to me that he had received information, through his field supervisor ROBERT SMITH, that subject DON ARNOLD had been having domestic problems and that his information was that ARNOLD had split up with his wife. He further indi-

cated the problem arose over money that his wife had removed from an account and that she did not inform him of this. BOLES further indicated that ARNOLD had a very good attendance record up until the victim was discovered and until that point, he was late one day (the day he was to meet with Police Department investigators). He also missed Friday and was sick on this date (08 JUN 89). BOLES indicated to me that for further information, I should contact his field supervisor, ROBERT SMITH, who has daily contact with ARNOLD.

At approximately 1000 Hours, I contacted ROBERT SMITH, age thirty years. I advised SMITH of the conversation I had had with BOLES; he stated that he had received this information from SMITTY LYMAN, also a customer service representative. SMITH stated that upon receiving this information, he immediately called in ARNOLD and had a conversation with him regarding his personal problems. During this conversation, ARNOLD had advised SMITH that everything was okay at home and everything had been taken care of. SMITH indicated to me that on this date, ARNOLD had called in sick and left a message on the answering machine. I asked SMITH if he had noticed any abnormal behavioral pattern in ARNOLD and he stated that ARNOLD seemed a little up tight and he had seemed concerned over talking with detectives. SMITH stated that seemed to bother ARNOLD.

At approximately 1145 Hours on 08 JUN 89, I had a telephone conversation with DAN DARNELL of Dunn Homes, who indicated on 07 JUN 89, ARNOLD had been at the corporate office for Dunn Homes and at that time, had a conversation with DARNELL about receiving some time off from his work.

On 09 JUN 89 at approximately 1140 Hours, Det. LANDER and I conducted a second interview with subject ARNOLD. This interview was taped and was conducted at the design center of the Paradise West Complex, 3200 Alder Avenue. (For details see transcribed taped interview).

During the second interview of subject ARNOLD, he indicated to us that the victim was not sexually assaulted and that he could not figure out a motive. When we questioned ARNOLD about how he knew of this information, he indicated he had received it from BRAD BOLES on the day that the victim had been discovered.

On 09 JUN 89, approximately 1230 Hours, I had a telephone conversation with BRAD BOLES. I informed him of the statement made by ARNOLD and BOLES stated he could not remember making that statement to ARNOLD immediately after the discovery. He did indicate that he could recall later that that was a topic of conversation, but he does not recall making it to subject ARNOLD. BOLES did state that after his attending a meeting with other supervisors, did put out a statement to his field units, ROBERT SMITH, that it did not appear that the victim was sexually assaulted, due to the fact that she was fully clothed when he saw her.

At 1240 Hours, 09 JUN 89: BOLES called me back and stated that he did remember seeing ARNOLD on the day that the victim was discovered. He indicated that ARNOLD was coming from the opposite closed end of the complex and that BOLES was walking with the landscaper. BOLES stated ARNOLD asked him what had happened and BOLES stated to him that a woman was dead; BOLES stated he did not elaborate at that time regarding any sexual

assault or how she died. I asked BOLES if he knew the day that ARNOLD was transferred from Porto Bello to the Paradise West Complex; he indicated this was done on 08 May 89.

Chapter V

SUPPLEMENTARY REPORT

TODAY'S THE FIRST OF JUNE, 1989. IT'S 0918 HOURS. THIS WILL BE AN INTERVIEW CONDUCTED BY MYSELF, DETECTIVE A. CAMPBELL AND DETECTIVE B. HUNTER, WITH MR. DAN BLACK, REPRESENTATIVE OF DUNN HOMES, WHO WAS PRESENT AT THE CRIME SCENE YESTERDAY AT 3200 ALDER AVENUE, UNIT NUMBER 66. OKAY, AND THIS'LL BEGIN THE INTERVIEW:

> LEGEND: "C" = DET. CAMPBELL
> "H" = DET. HUNTER
> "B" = DAN BLACK

C: Okay, Mr. BLACK, basically, what I want you to do for me is go ahead like yesterday when we had our interview, as far as what time you arrived at the location; basically what duty you performed within the location up until the time the deceased was found and also, if at all possible, some type of sequence, if you could also at least give us, if not the names, the other individuals who were there; either sub-contractors or people who were there and approximately what time they were there.

B: Okay. I returned a 'phone call that I had received the day before on the thirtieth, stating that Terri wanted her locks de-mastered; it was an electrical problem in the garage, the garage door would not operate properly without the storage light being on and a yellow stain in the master bathroom, on the window and on the window frame. Stated that she wouldn't be there on the 30th but would be there most of the day on the 31st. I called around 7 o' or around eight o'clock, give or take a few minutes on the 31st to see if anybody was home; had no response on the 'phone; went over there a little after eight; knocked on the door, rang the doorbell. Opened the door. Announced myself, I, which, just for standard procedure in case somebody's upstairs, never, you don't want to surprise them. De-mastered the locks, proceeded to go upstairs. Announced again that, as I went upstairs in case somebody was still upstairs. Got no response whatsoever. Went, proceeded to go into the master bedroom to look at the problem, at the window, over that toilet area.

C: Can I interrupt this for one second? Can you recall when you first went to the residence and you used a key to enter the residence, was the door locked; could you tell if the deadbolt was locked in the actual lower lock?

B: To be honest with you - no . Because the way the locks are on the master system, some are tighter than others and there's, it, if I can recall; I don't think the deadbolt was locked because that was real easy. Just went, put it in and it turned. I mean, it seemed that it was not locked.

C: So what you did was a free turn?

B: Free turn; no resistance; nothing there. The

passage lock, down below, I know because I heard the click.

C: Okay. And that's the one that takes the finger to hit the little thing on the inside of the doorknob?

B:That's, on the in-door, close the door behind you.

C: Another thing before we go further on it - when you first arrived at the location, could you tell, even though it was daylight, when you entered, were there any lights left on anywhere in the house that you might have turned off? Anything at all that you can think of like that?

B: No.

C: There were no lights on whatsoever?

B: Not that I recall. I, downstairs, I noticed that screen in the entryway as I walked in and I wondered, you know, what that was doing there. I mean, you know, she have problems getting it out trying to clean a window or something; I don't know. You know, it was there; didn't recall any lights downstairs on. I went upstairs. We have the skylights. Don't recall the hall lights being on. I know I opened the master bedroom door; one door was opened. I opened the other one so they were both open as I walked in and there's no lights in there at all. In the bathroom area, there were no lights on.

C: Okay. We'll go back where you were, going up to the master bedroom where the bath, I think it was. And you said you entered the premises, what, about eight o'clock, I think that you were there?

B: Little after eight.

C: Okay.

B: Eight, eight-fifteen, somewhere in that time span. Went upstairs. Started, like I said, I looked at the window and the cleaning crew uses a yellow

substance sometimes turns the dry wall mud and leaves a yellow residue of some sort. So I proceeded to take the screen out, took the window out and went downstairs, through the garage, opened the garage door, got some of my tools out, masking paper, tape, my paint and came back upstairs, started cleaning everything up, getting ready to paint and the gas man, I noted, he had knocked on the door and needed to come in to work on the furnace, so I said, "Well, c'mon up. It's in the master bedroom." you know, "It's upstairs."., he says, "Well, I don't have a ladder."; he went and got the ladder from a sub-contractor, Safeway Plumbing and Heating. I had gone downstairs to meet him in the garage. We walked back upstairs together and I showed him where it was. He started to work in the attic. I went back in the bathroom to continue doing the work on the window, came back and asked him how it was going and he says: "Well, there's no electrical outlet up here." I proceeded to go upstairs with him; looked around; found the electrical outlet; plugged the furnace in; couldn't get it to fire. But, there was gas going to it. So, he left, dropped the ladder back off with the Safeway Plumbers; I went over and talked to the plumbers to verify that they had come over and test out the furnace why it wasn't working. I was told to leave it in the 'on' position to see if it would eventually come on. Went back upstairs, finished around the window; painting that; put the window back together, came out and on the walk-through, I had noticed that a small stain on the linen cabinet that the homeowner didn't notice; thought, well, I'll just clean that up; take care of it.

C: Where's the linen...

B: That's where the clothes were, the ...

C: That's the upper landing?

B: That's the upper landing. That wooden rail that goes around and then the wooden cabinet. The wooden...

C: Yeah, where that little...

B: Where that, I don't know, box of blankets or whatever was ...

H: Yeah.

B: ... on top that I picked up and I had moved over to the clothes. It looked like somebody, after they had put the varnish on it, had rubbed a cloth over it or somethig, so there was a residue in the finish, that it wasn't done by the houseowner and like I said, I had noticed it on the walk-through; I didn't say anything, 'cause we like to try and get perfect walk-throughs, it just makes everything look better and then they have a chance to fill out request for service, thirty day type things.

C: I have a question. When you first came up, obviously the door to the one bedroom where the victim was located was closed?

B: Correct.

C: When you first came up with the other workman, you had already been upstairs a couple of times ...

B: Correct.

C: ... for different things, you noticed the clothing that was laying on the rail? Is that correct?

B: That was there, correct.

C: Okay, and did you also, was the door open to the small bathroom?

B: Yes.

C: And did you notice the wallet and personal belongings kind of thrown across the top area there?

B: Everything was there, 'cause I know that I had

gone in; after I had done the other bathroom, I had gone in to check around the other window above the other toilet and I had checked out the bathroom just and I looked down and I saw her I.D. and I did pick up her license and check it and go, you know, she's 27 years old, she's ten years younger than I am. It's kind of young to be, you know, such a nice place and being . . .

C: Did you think it was unusual that her purse and everything; it looked like to me when I saw it like it, maybe somebody had been, had gone through it, everything was laying there and you could think that there might have been somebody home at that time, especially with the door closed?

B: No. I'd been in so many units working and people leave things in different, in such a way when they're moving in that their coming and going and with the car in the garage and I had met her mother the week that she was gone playing golf. I thought, well maybe she was over there staying and that they were going to come back together or something to that effect. it really didn't, nothing triggered. I mean, I don't think that way.

C: Nothing raised any suspicions in your mind?

B: No, I mean, I, nothing at all.

H: The driver's license. Where was it found?

B: Okay. As you go into the number two bathroom...

H: Right.

B: . . . the left sink; it was on something. There's two sinks in that bathroom.

H: Yes. Uh huh.

B: Okay. There was a lot of stuff throughout. I mean, just, you know, different things and it was sitting on something just to the right of the left sink. So, it was totally out in the open.

H: Okay.

C: It wasn't sitting on top of the wallet that was kind of open there? It was like it was picked out and set aside by itself with everything else . . .

B: Well, there was a license was here, the couple credit cards.

H: Some credit cards. Yeah.

B: You know, there was just all kind of, I mean, now that you, you know, you start to think about it, you know, it looks like, you know, somebody could have just been flipping through type stuff, but I didn't really think anything of it because I've seen, in other places as people are moving in, just things are disarrayed so much until they get organized; so I didn't think anything of it.

C: Did you ever knock on the door that was closed?

B: No.

C: Once you were in?

B: I didn't even, it didn't even dawn on me to even open that or even to think about going into that room. I mean, I just never . . .

C: Okay. So after you've refinished that landing or the cabinet in the landing?

B: Yeah. Well, I had been in and out of the unit. The gas man had left; I talked to the heating guys. I needed to get an electrician back in because as we were up in the attic, the gas, there wasn't a cover for the electrical outlet in the attic access that we provide a light up there and I didn't have that, so I went to look for the electrician and have him come over some time to put that in during the day. The elect, the gas man said he was going to come back so I was in the unit; I started to come downstairs; the mother came into the house.

H: What time do you think that was?

B: I would say that was some where in the vicinity of eleven fifteen to eleven thirty.

H: Okay.

B: And asked where her daughter was and I said: "I don't know. I haven't seen anybody here."; I said: "There is a door closed upstairs. Could she be sleeping?" and she said; "Yes. She's a real sound sleeper." I said: "Well, . . .", mother started to go upstairs, I followed her. She got to the doorway, she opened the doorway, said: "Terri" and that, just, you know, I figured she was asleep so I just walked out. Okay. I didn't want to, you know, she got up. I came back in and . . .

H: Where did you walk to?

B: I walked out the front door, walked down . . .

H: So you walked downstairs?

B: Went downstairs and out of the unit.

H: Yeah, okay.

B: I figured, well, if she's gonna get up, give her a few minutes to herself type thing.

H: Yeah.

B: Came back in, knocked, announced again as I was coming back in.

H: So just a couple of minutes has gone by?

B: Yeah, just a few minutes. I'd gone to my truck for something. You know, to get something or other. Or put something back or whatever. I really don't recall. I came back in; the mother was on the 'phone. I looked, I could tell by the look on her face that something was wrong. I walked over to her and she could hardly talk. I helped her sit down on the sofa, I took the 'phone and said this is, you know, I told her, I think I said: "This is Dan, Customer Service, can I help you?" And the voice said, "Are the ParaMedics needed?" I said: "I don't know. Just a minute." I put

the phone down; I went upstairs and I saw her laying on the floor. I picked up the blanket to look and my first instinct was well, should I try mouth to mouth? Dropped the blanket back, went downstairs, got on the 'phone and said: "Yes, the ParaMedics are needed. Immediately, please." and they just re-confirmed the address and they said yes. Hung up the 'phone, got on my radio and my supervisor, Brad Boles, was out on the project doing landscape.

H: What's his name again? B: Brad Boles.

H: How's his last name spelled?

B: (spells:) B-O-L-E-S Boles.

H: Okay.

B: Boles. I think you've got his business card.

H: Okay.

B: I said: "Would you please come over here. I need you here at the unit." also, by that time, the sirens were already in the air; you could hear 'em. I said: "You need to see this." he went upstairs. He, you know, tested her pulse and at that point in time, I also, you know, try to see if I could feel anything on her neck. The body was cold. We went back downstairs, tried to keep everybody out. Dan Darnell, you've got his name. He's the director of construction. I think it was at that point in time we took the screen out of the master bedroom to yell down to get the vehicles out of the way.

H: Okay. For the emergency vehicles?

B: For the emergency vehicles, if they were going to come in, they were going to have clear access.

H: Yeah.

B: And that's when I think I took the screen out.

C: And the window was open?

B: Yeah. Well, I opened the window when I was painting.

C: Okay.

B: To let some ventilation in. And we took the screen out; this is in the master bedroom. And then the ParaMedics came in. I mean, they just kept filing in and I kinda just . . .

H: How many ParaMedics do you think there were? Firemen?

B: I'll be honest with you. It just seemed like there was, you know, just, they just kept coming.

H: And they all went up the stairs?

B: They all kept going up. Every, I mean, I just stood there on the stairwell and I just kept watching this; I'm going "What's going on? Is this reality?" I mean, just, I started to loose it at that point in time. I mean, I just, I'd never dealt with anything like that and they just said no. You know, they shook it, one guy just shook his head and then just asked everybody to leave and I guess the police, then the police were called and then you guys were called and I mean, just everybody kept coming and coming at that point.

H: Going back to the room, when you walked in, you said there was a blanket on her? Do you recall the color it was?

B: It seemed like a greenish something or other. A green color.

H: Did you leave it over her or . . .

B: I picked it up and I dropped it. You know, after I, when I went back downstairs.

H: Okay.

C: That was the comforter?

B: Whatever that, I don't know. It almost looked like a quilt.

H: Yeah, there were a couple of them up there. I'm just wondering which one.

C : When you picked up the blanket, or, when you went back the second time and you touched for the pulse, what position was she in? Was she lying on her stomach?

B: She was lying on her stomach, it seemed like her hair was over her face; she had one arm here and one arm . . .

H: Okay, so you're indicating the left arm's extended over her head?

B: Yeah. It was over her head.

H: The right arm is down alongside beside her?

B: Down beside her.

H: Yeah.

B: And Brad, you know, my boss, he tested her left arm and that's when I tried to feel her pulse on her neck; if I could get anything at that palm.

H: Okay, so the left arm's extended palm down? The right arm's along her side, palm up?

B: Uh,

H: More or less?

B: More or less, I don't know. The right, the left hand was out.

H: Okay.

B: This arm was back. I don't know if the palm was up or if it was down. I don't recall.

H: Okay.

B: I just recall,

H: You just recall it was that position.

B: I just remember it was that position and I remember looking at the feet and the feet were yellow and that's what freaked me out.

H: Okay.

C: Okay. Unless we missed it in the initial part of this interview, there was one other individual and I think he was the gentleman who worked for the air

conditioning or the heating; he also went up those stairs with you, did he not?

B: Okay. I went down into the garage to call.

C: This is after you discovered?

B: After I had discovered, after I had gotten off the 'phone with the ParaMedics and after I had seen the, seen her laying on the floor. I had gone downstairs to try and get him on the radio. I did not want to say that in front of the mother. To put any more f ear. I said it: "Would you please get here? It's an emergency.". He . . .

H: This would be Brad Boles.

B: Brad Boles. Yeah. and then the Safeway guy was working on the air conditioning; the (unknown word) which is in the garage. He ran upstairs. I was not with him when he went upstairs. But then he came out and he wasn't in there for any length of time.

H: Did he say anything to you when he came up?

B: I don't recall.

H: Okay.

B: I don't have much, I don't have a whole lot of recollection, really, on that.

H: Okay. When you're, just to get back to the scene upstairs; when you're up there doing the touchup work, were there any other employees assisting you?

B: No.

H: So you were the lone (unknown word) . . .

B: I was in there basically by myself ...

H: Okay.

B: . . . other than the gentleman from Southern Gas Company and then . . .

H: Air conditioning.

B: . . . air conditioning guy, when he, yeah.

H: Okay.

C: That's Mr. Brown, I think.

B: Correct. Buddy. I believe his first name is Buddy.

C: One other thing. Somewhat important. What did you observe on the exterior of the closed door and what were you doing?

B: Okay. There was a, looked like just a shoe scuff mark on the lower left hand corner. Like someone may have kicked it if they had their arms full or something. And then in the middle of the door, halfway up in the paint, could tell that after it had been painted, somebody had just kinda run their hand over it, like to test if it was dry. And so what I had done, with the paint, since I already had it out and we do a lot of times, we just go and touch some place up for the homeowners just to help 'em out and I just, I had done the paint touchup on the outside of the door, without all painting the door; painted the upper middle section and then tried to paint over the scuff mark.

H: When was the last time you were in that unit? Do you remember?

B: Prior to that?

H: Yes.

B: I had been in it earlier the other week when I, Terri's mother had come over to the unit and I did not know who she was. I went over and said, asked if I could help you and she said "Well, I'm here to meet so and so; I'm Terri's mom." and that may have been Wednesday, the prior, the week earlier and I don't even think I walked in. I may have walked in the front door; I don't know.

H: Okay. So around the 24th of June (S/B May) would be the only other time or, you know . . .

B: Yeah, and then, the only, prior to that would have been the original walk-through.

H: On the original walk-through, were any of those, on the door, were any of those scuff marks noted?

B: The black scuff marks was not noted. I would have noticed that. I did not notice it.

H: Okay.

B: That . . .

H: Yeah, it would have really stood out when you walk up the stairs and saw it.

B: Yeah, you could just see that. The other one, I didn't see until I started working on it. It was more, you had to be more of at an angle to see that and that is something typically would not be caught on a walk-through. I mean, they take about an hour, an hour and a half and you are trying to get through rather quickly and show 'em the lights and . . .

H: How things are . . .

B: introduce them to their house.

H: Yeah,

B: More of an introduction type thing. The scuff mark would have been noticed and would have been taken care of at that point in time because I have couple guys from the production end, our quality control guy said if the homeowner sees anything that they're unsatisfied with, they take care of right then on the spot, so that's how we get clean walk-throughs.

H: Okay. Anything else, Campy?

C: We discussed yesterday and then we couldn't come to a conclusion; what I'm going to try to do, maybe you can think again; you didn't at any time whatsoever go near the sliding glass door . . .

B: No.

C: . . . Down in the room area?

B: I never went into that room, the gas man never went into that room and the heating guy had no reason to go in there, either. So,

C: We, so as f ar as we know, none of the workers had unlocked that door?

B: Correct.

C: How well did you know Terri? You were talking about that she played golf last week; that, you talked to her a few times?

B: I talked to her, what day did I talk to her? After the walk-through, I had talked to her once when she was at the unit and she had mentioned that, you know, she was a golfer. It may have been on the walk-through, the original walk-through when we were talking, 'cause I'm dating somebody that plays, you know, trying to play some golf and trying to pick up some golf tips from her. But, she just had mentioned that she was going to be gone on a tournament the following week; that, if somebody could come in and do some of the work; grout, she wanted somebody to seal her grout on her tile. So, I don't do that but some of the guys do do work on the side for the homeowners; you could talk to them. So.

H: Do you know if she ever contacted anybody regarding that?

B: Yeah, she did. Gentleman by the name of Matt. And I don't even know Matt's last name. I just call him "Wookie" on the radio.

H: "Rookie"'?

B: Yeah. Well, we all have different handles on the radios so it's, uh . . .

C: 'Cause there's a receipt for a guesstimate, or an estimate for that job; I think Will has it, we took it yesterday amongst her paperwork.

H: Oh.

C: Did you at any time when you talked to Terri the one time, I guess, you know, in your duties around that area, did you ever see her with anybody else?

B: No. I've never, I come in about 6:30 in the morning; I clock in about quarter to seven. I actually go to the job site 7:30 to 8 o'clock to drive and from my construction trailer. We don't go into units, people's homes until 8 o'clock unless we have permission, prior permission. I leave around 3:30, they've cut our overtime so I basically leave right on time, as often as I can and since I'm out in Orange County, I go sit in the parking lot going home.

C: Okay. One last thing real quick: prior to de-coding the deadbolt lock . . .

B: Okay.

C: . . . how many people have access to passkeys that would open that particular lock? That worked within the company? And any knowledge you have of numerous people who possibly could have been past employe(e)s and still have those in their possession? Do you know anything about that or should we talk to somebody else about that?

B: Okay. I know that some of the sub-contractors have a builder's key. Which ones, I do not know. You have the builder's key, you have the knock-out key, you have the homeowner's key and then you have the master key. I usually use the knock-out key after the homeowners have moved in; that way, if a finished trade needs to go back in and do any little things, they can. Sometimes construction has sub-contractors go back in and have things on order for a particular unit. An example, the unit right across from hers, the bathroom window, the one I was working on at Terri's unit, in the opposite unit doesn't fit quite right. Well, they just dummied one in there that, until the new one came, which was ordered by construction. So, construction still has access, but they always, once a homeowner's moved in, always

ask me and I let them know whether or not it's been de-mastered or not. So, I don't know how many keys are out.

H: Once the lock's been de-mastered, the only key that works is the homeowner has?

B: The homeowner has and then my master key. And then there's three of us that work the project and I don't know if all three of us have a master to phase two. I know there are at least two out there; I think there's three. Don Arnold. I believe you have his name down and another gentleman by the name of Tom Green, who's on vacation this week.

H: Okay. Anything else?

C: No, nothing I can...

H: Okay. That'll conclude the interview. It's now 0946 hours. Thank you,

TAPE ENDS.

Chapter VI

URBAN POLICE DEPARTMENT

SUPPLEMENTARY REPORT

I/O: Det. JIM CONLEY
CRIME; 187 PC, Murder
VICTIM; TERRI HORGAN
RES: 3200 Alder Street, #66, Urban.

On 02 June 89 at approximately 0700 hours, I conducted an interview with:
JODY WILLIAMS
DOB: 27 June 65
BUS: INTERSTATE SECURITY SYSTEMS
the security guard who was on duty on 30 and 31 May 89, from 2300 to 0600 hours. I asked WILLIAMS if he was employed at Paradise West on 30-31 May 89 and he indicted to me he was and had reported to work at approximately 2240 hours and relieved security guard PHINNEY. WILLIAMS stated he noted no unusual activities during his tour of duty. I asked WILLIAMS if he had been informed that an individual had been murdered at the Paradise West complex; he stated he was aware of that. I asked him if he knew the victim and he indicated he had met her once and that was on a Sunday morning at approximately 11

or 12. He indicated he observed the victim going through a trash container in the complex and that he approached her to see what she was doing. She indicated to him about the problem she had with another security guard, SAMMY BATTLE and that she was searching the trash due to the fact that a watch was missing. Mr. WILLIAMS stated he jumped up into the trash can and found a bag, which the victim indicated was hers and in looking into this bag, the watch was located. WILLIAMS stated the victim was very pleased in finding her watch and appeared to be very happy. He stated that was the only time he had spoken with the victim. I asked WILLIAMS what the victim had told him regarding the other security guard; he indicated that on Saturday, the victim had received some deliveries of furniture and that the security guard, BATTLES, had helped the delivery men move her furniture in to her unit. He stated the victim felt this was very strange when she observed the security guard standing in her living room.

Security guard WILLIAMS stated he reported to work at approximately 2230 hours and that the main gate on Paradise West was secure, but the secondary gate was open. He indicated he closed this gate but it can't be secured; you merely have to push on it and the gate will open. He further indicated that nothing unusual occurred on his tour of duty and that he was visited by his supervisor during his shift.

Chapter VII

While playing Hide and Seek with his four and a half year old sister, three year old Sammy Battle was hiding in the closet of their parents' bedroom. This was a forbidden place as Mommy and Daddy had always told both of them not to enter that room without permission. Sammy knew this was a perfect hiding place because Lilly, being an obedient little girl and scared to death of their parents, would never look for him there. He left the door open a crack so he could see out, just in case Lilly broke the parental rule and did come in.

Sammy heard his daddy's car stop in the loose gravel driveway and heard his parents as they clomped into the house, screaming and giggling. He knew they had both been drinking by the noise they made. He also knew that one or both of them would head straight for the bedroom. He did not have time to get out without being discovered, so he cringed farther back into the closet, shaking with fear.

He saw both of his parents enter the room. They both got naked quickly; his father, Rodney, down to his socks and his mother, Nell, down to her garter belt and hose. They embraced and felt of each other for a little bit and then his father pushed his mother backwards onto the bed, Sammy watched them hav-

anyone what they were doing; that it was "grownup stuff"; that Mommy and Daddy would get mad and whip them if they found out. Daddy had shown them the horsewhip that was among the "bondage" equipment he and Mommy kept in their bedroom. As they grew, neither Sammy nor Lilly was taught anything about sex, sexuality or sexual mores by their parents or anyone else; consequently, they continued in the activities they found enjoyable as young children. Lilly continued with her father. Sammy became more bewildered as his penis grew and strange feelings connected with his groin area manifested themselves by those strange but pleasurable nocturnal emissions and a growing need to masturbate whenever his inexplicable sexual fantasies took hold of him. The sight of almost any girl could trigger them. Although the subject of sex was a conversational taboo in the family, Sammy and Lilly continued to experiment with each other and, keeping their secret from their parents, they grew emotionally closer to each other, finally culminating in sexual intercourse. Sammy was then eleven and Lilly twelve and a half. By that time, Lilly found out it was wrong for Daddy to "do it" to her but he had been "going all the way" with her since she was nine, so she knew how to teach Sammy. She tried to get her Daddy to stop but his insistence on continuing the incestuous relationship, accompanied by a few subliminal threats of embarrassment to her if the word got out, caused her to keep quiet.

Of course, at that time, Lilly told neither Nell nor any of her friends or playmates about her and her Daddy nor about her and Sammy. She did, however, become her male schoolmates' "punch board." Rodney and Nell knew that Lilly was not a vivacious

nor outgoing personality - in fact she was somewhat introverted, due to her lack of identity with a social peer group. They never "snapped" to why Lilly received numerous telephone calls, always from boys, nor to why she did not have a single female "best friend," as almost all girls do. She was very popular among the pubescent boys but none of them wanted to be seen with her except in a "gang bang" situation - that usually taking place in a nearby grove of trees on an old, discarded divan after school. By the time she was well along in High School, Lilly was a thoroughly miserable person but kept up her promiscuous sexual activities because they constituted her only true identity - her only sense of self-worth. When once asked by one of the older boys, who tried to befriend her, why she consented to have sex with just about anyone, she replied, I trust you, so please don't tell anyone but I just feel that if my Daddy can do it to me, why can't the other guys?" That boy did not tell on her and continued to speak to her as they passed each other in the hallways at school. She liked him but felt nothing for the other boys.

As Sammy continued to grow, Rodney and Nell would sometimes be gone for several days at a time, leaving Sammy and Lilly to more or less fend for themselves. Due to their dysfunctional family life, neither of the children learned many social skills. Sammy spent a good deal of his time at a nearby playground, kicking soccer and footballs. He did not acquire any of the technical skills or theory of either game; however, but did develop an uncanny ability to kick a ball an incredible distance with almost laser accuracy. It was always place-kicking with the football, using the straight-on toe kick and the soccer-type kick. He and the playground supervisor, along with some of the

other playground kids, rigged up a net and two sets of wires, one about five feet above the other with the lowest one about as far off the ground as a regular football goal's crossbar. On the top wire, they hung two used tires, spaced eight feet apart. On the bottom wire they hung three tires, one near each end and one in the middle of the wire. Then they marked off lines representing different distances from the "goal" they had set up. Sammy then did his kicking. He practiced endless hours, every time he got a chance. As time went by, crowds gathered to watch this kicking phenomenon. Word finally got to the small High School's football coach, who was, incidentally, gay. He came to watch.

The school was so small that virtually every boy who could walk had to be used for its athletic teams; consequently, Sammy made the football varsity with no problem. After the first scrimmage, the coach was satisfied that Sammy had no athletic skills save his kicking ability, but his eye-foot coordination was so nearly perfect it was unbelievable. Also after this first scrimmage, in the shower room, the other members of the team discovered that Sammy had a member half again as long as any of them. Since it seems that every member of an athletic team, if he is accepted by the other members, has to have a nickname, Sammy's team dubbed him "The Snake," which quickly abbreviated to simply "Snake." The coach salivated. He had to figure a way to get this phallic Adonis alone so he could seduce and enjoy the possibilities of that colossal appendage.

During the entire football season, the coach did not use Sammy in a single game, until the last one. To begin with, there never was a place-kicking situation, except for the kickoff and he was not about to

use this star talent for such a mundane part of the game. Instead, he made Sammy and his unique talent a part of the half-time show, setting up the necessary equipment crossfield at the fifty yard line so that all spectators could have a "ringside seat." Sammy wowed 'em at every game. His work also intimidated opposing teams.

Sammy's self esteem had been growing steadily, what with the approbation and praise heaped upon him by his teammates and by that world class appellation they had hung on him: "SNAKE! Oh boy, wait'll I tell Lilly about this," he thought. "She'll probably claim some of the credit for it." His self confidence remained several steps behind, however, due to his lack of all-round athletic ability and the fact the coach had not used him in a game all season. But, all in all, Sammy was on Cloud Nine, having been included in all of the locker room bull sessions with the guys, bragging right along with them about how much pussy he had had and with which of the girls at school, when actually he hadn't had any and was deathly afraid of girls, except for his sister Lilly.

The coach had always been kind to Sammy, telling him what a fine looking young man he was and that he had a nearly perfect athlete's body. He couldn't tell Sammy often enough how he wanted to put him in a game but that the opportunity just hadn't presented itself yet. "You'll get your chance though, Sammy. Our offense has been so good this year that we've been able to win with just running and passing. Today's game is for the championship so I'm really going to keep an eye open for an opportunity to use you. And by the way, if you're not too busy, I'd like to see you in my office after the game. I might have a pretty good offer for you."

"Gee, coach, what's it about?"

"Let's wait 'til after the game, Sammy, Okay?"

"Sure, coach, I'll be there."

SITUATION: Last game of the season; One game away from the championship; Playing the most hated traditional enemy; The whole town was in the stands; The game had been savagely played and the score was seven to six in favor of the visiting team; Sammy's team, the home team, had the ball. The ball was on the eighteen yard line; It was fourth down and nine yards to go for first and ten; The handwriting was on the wall and only one time out left; The coach called it with only twenty seconds to go in the game; The coach was beside him self with anxiety. He didn't know what to do.

Suddenly a low roar was heard coming from the home grandstand, rapidly growing into a crescendo, as the crowd chanted, "SAMMY - SAMMY - SAMMY - SAMMY . . ."

"Get in there and kick the fucking ball," screamed the coach.

Sammy couldn't believe it but, rocketing off the bench where he had spent so many lonely hours, into the huddle he sprang. The quarterback called for a field goal.

Then disaster struck!

The ball was hiked. The holder held the ball steady. And Sammy stood there and wet his pants.

The crescendo from the stands changed. Now the chant was "KILL HIM -KILL HIM - KILL HIM - KILL HIM . . ."

The home fans poured from the stands and went for Sammy. His teammates followed suit. Sammy had to be rescued by uniformed security men and hustled

away to a safe place. As he removed his football uniform, showered and put on his street clothes, the security men talked to him and tried to comfort him, refraining from any teasing or criticism. He never forgot that. He was escorted home, where he was comforted by Lilly. They made love again and all was right with his world. Sammy and the coach both forgot all about their tentatively scheduled after-the-game meeting in the coach's office.

For the first couple or three years after graduating from High School, Sammy had a series of menial jobs; flipping hamburgers, clerking in discount stores and other no-future jobs paying entry level wages, but he never forgot the kindness of the security officers who had helped him. He started hanging around those people whenever he got the opportunity. They had been the only ones in his miserable, inadequate life who had ever shown him any mature compassion. He wondered if it would be hard to become a security guard - or maybe even a policeman.

Meanwhile, Rodney was reported for sexually molesting Lilly and went away to prison for a long stretch. Nell had seen the inside of the jail in a nearby city several times, mainly for vice activities; not only for prostitution but also for steering "marks" to crooked gambling games. She had tried to "turn out" Lilly into that kind of life, telling her she was "sitting on a million dollars" and making other remarks designed to make Lilly believe she could make lots of money selling her body. Lilly wanted none of it. The memory and disgrace of Rodney's abuse of her was too fresh and lasting in her mind. She did not need any more Rodneys in her life. She left home, got a job and moved in with a friend from work, keeping in touch only with Sammy. Earlier, she had complained

to her mother about her father but Nell's only response had been to give her a stinging slap in the
face, cuss her out and call her a damned liar.

Lilly's only strength came from her relationship
with Sammy and a few friends she had made after
High School, who showed her there was a different
way of life than she had experienced and who knew
nothing about her family or her sexually promiscuous past.

One day a security guard friend showed Sammy
an ad in a city newspaper offering employment to
qualified security guards. Sammy told his friend that
he didn't know if he was "qualified," but the friend
told him to "go for it" anyway. He did so and because
he was a healthy, strapping young man with a good
attitude, an obvious great desire, a High School Di-
ploma and no criminal record, he was snapped up
almost immediately, after submitting an application,
by a large, prestigious security conglomerate, as a
Trainee. Although his prior employment record did
not show a particularly strong work ethic, his new
employers believed that could be corrected with the
proper training and motivation. As a breaking-in ex-
ercise, Sammy was assigned to an older, experienced
guard and for two weeks they walked various posts
at different venues and on different shifts together,
with the older guard making daily written reports on
Sammy's progress. Sammy did well. He was then
put out on his own, assigned to a large, new
townhouse and condominium complex being built,
on which Statewide Security Company was the con-
tract guard service. Sammy was on his way, still as
ignorant of the ways of women as he was in High
School.

Chapter VIII

URBAN POLICE DEPARTMENT

SUPPLEMENTARY REPORT

Legend:　"L" = DET. R. LANDER
　　　　　"J" = DET. J. CONLEY
　　　　　"B" = SAMMY BATTLE

TODAY'S DATE IS SECOND OF JUNE (1989). IT'S APPROXIMATELY 0740 HOURS IN THE MORNING. WE'RE IN THE BAY OF THE URBAN POLICE DEPT. DETECTIVE DIVISION. PRESENT IN THIS INTERVIEW IS DETECTIVE CONLEY, MYSELF, DETECTIVE LANDER AND MR. SAMMY BATTLE.

B: Battle.
L: How do you spell your last name, SAMMY?
B: No "S"
L: (spells:) B-A-T-T-L-E?
B: Correct.
L: Sammy Battle. (Spells:) B-A-T-T-L-E. Sammy you understand you've come here freely and voluntarily? Is that right?
B: Correct.
L: Okay. And you haven't been threatened or intimidated?

B: Correct.

L: Okay. And you're just here to give a statement of facts as to your actions or what maybe you've seen in and around the condominium complex due to the fact that we're doing the investigation of a homicide of Terri Horgan? That correct?

B: Right.

L: Okay. You start, Jim, if you want.

C: Did you know Terri?

B: Vaguely.

C: Vaguely. Why don't you tell us how you met her.

B: Well, just coming in and out the complex.

C: What unit did she live in?

B: 66.

C: 66? Were you employed by somebody over there?

B: By Interstate Security

C: Okay. So you met her while you were working?

B: Correct.

C: And, have you ever been inside her unit? Her condominium complex?

B: Only in the kitchen. That's when I helped one of the movers.

C: What were they moving in?

B: Moving in a television set.

C: Do you remember what day that was?

B: That was approximately two weeks ago.

C: Two weeks ago during the week or on the weekend?

B: During the week. Think it's Thursday.

C: Thursday?

B: Right.

C: And, did you happen to go anywhere else in that unit other than the kitchen?

B: No.

C: Did you take some trash out or something?

B: Yes.

C: Was there a...

B: Just being a nice guy.

C: Yeah. Was there a problem with you taking the trash out? Did you find out at a later time?

B: I found out later that she lost a watch or something. Somebody told, another guard told me she'd come up to him and said she had lost her watch, so he jumped up in the there and dumped it out, found her watch.

C: Did you have any further conversation with Terri after that incident?

B: No.

C: Okay. Did you, were you on the job site on Tuesday, the thirtieth of May?

B: Yes, I was. Around two-thirty.

C: What was your activities on the job site on that day?

B: Well, I was just waiting until time to start. 'Cause I always get there, you know, at least an hour early, 'cause I have to walk.

C: Okay. So you got there about two thirty and then?

B: Started about four. When I walked around the office. Called in. They told me I wasn't working today.

C: Who did you talk to at the office? This is your office? Interstate Security?

B: Correct.

C: Who did you talk to?

B: Paul.

C: What's his last name?

B: Fuller.

C: Fuller? And what did Paul tell you?

B: He said that they're trying to change the schedule.

C: And that you weren't scheduled to work?

B: And I wasn't scheduled to work.

C: On the thirtieth. Okay. About what time did you leave the Paradise West complex?

B: About four fifteen.

C: And where did you go?

B: To the bus (sounds like:) park on Sepulveda and Alder.

C: Caught a bus?

B: Caught the number seven bus to Pacific Coast Highway and Wilmington Avenue, transferred to number three and caught it on over to Lomita. My home.

C: On Lomita Boulevard?

B: On, yeah, Lomita Boulevard. Lomita and Cabrillo.

C: Lomita and Cabrillo?

B: Right.

C: That's where the bus dropped you off?

B: Yes.

C: And then you walked on . . .

B: On home.

C: On home To?

B: Well, actually, I stopped off at the doughnut shop to pick up my check and my glasses, my cap.

C: What doughnut shop?

B: Dunkin' Doughnuts.

C: Dunkin'

B: Doughnuts.

C: Where's that at?

B: Lomita and Cabrillo. The new shopping center.

C: Oh, that new place. How come your hat and coat were there?

B: Because it was too hot to wear.

C: Oh.

B: That day.

C: So, you asked, you somebody who works there?

B: Yeah, I know all, I know the family.

C: Then you went on home . . .

B: I've known them for two, three months.

C: You went on home to . . .

B: Take a nap.

C: . . . the apartment on Lomita Blvd.? Who was there when you got home?

B: Lucy Duran.

C: And who else?

B: And her kid.

C: How many kids does she have?

B: Three. Four. Well, three at home. One's with her mom.

C: Once you got home, what were your activities for the rest of the day or night, or . . .

B: Went home, took a nap.

C: How long did you sleep for?

B: About an hour. 'Til the detectives came.

C: Uh huh.

B: Then that woke me up. The two detectives, that is. "Want to talk to you."

C: Did you talk to 'em?

B: Yes.

C: What did they ask?

B: They asked me if, questions about the job site.

C: Okay. Then after they left, what happened?

B: I went back in and laid back down.

L: Wait a minute. I think we're talking about the wrong . . .

C: No, we're talking about the right date.

L: Okay.

C: How 'bout, that was Wednesday 2 detectives came over?

B: Right.

C: I'm talking about Tuesday, the day you left the job site. When they told you you weren't working.

B: Oh, I went home and went to bed.

L: You skipped and afternoon and night, Sammy. What detective Conley here is trying to know, after you left on Tuesday and you took the bus home, you stopped off at the Doughnut shop? Is that correct?

B: Right.

L: Okay. And then you went home. This will be the afternoon of the day prior to the Detectives coming over. Okay?

B: Right.

L: He just wants to know your actions for that afternoon and nighttime. That's all. Do you understand which day he's referring to now?

B: Yeah. Tuesday.

L: Okay. Go ahead and . . .

C: No Detectives came to your house on Tuesday. . . .

B: No.

C: . . . They came to your house on Wednesday.

B: They came on Wednesday.

C: Okay. So what happened on Tuesday, after you left the job site; you were informed that you weren't working that night, that there was a mess-up in the schedule?

B: That's when I caught the bus home.

C: Okay. Caught the bus home and you got home about what time?

B: That was around, oh, wait a minute, I stopped

off at another place. I got off the bus, the bus I got on. Just got off at Dolores and Carson, went to burger shop, played a couple games of Miss Pac Man; stayed there for, 'til 'bout six, seven. Then got home about eight.

C: Think you got home around eight o'clock, Tuesday night?

B: About eight. Yeah. And I stayed home the rest of the evening.

C: Was anybody else with you at the, at your house?

B: Lilly.

C: Was she there the whole time?

B: She was there the whole time. With the kid.

C: That's on Tuesday.

B: That was on Tuesday.

L: At any time on Tuesday night after you got home, did Lilly leave the house to go to errands or go see anybody or anything?

Or . . .

B: She went to the bar to have a cup of coffee and then she went on over to Manny's, talk to her husband.

C: That's Manny's Cafe?

B: Right.

L: Okay. Do you know when she returned from Manny's

B: 'Bout two, I think. Quarter to two.

L: Quarter two in the morning?

B: Right.

L: Okay. And during that time she was gone, do you remember about what time she left to go to Manny's.

B: Twenty minutes 'til nine.

L: Twenty minutes 'til . . .

B: Or, ten. Twenty minutes to ten.

L: Twenty minutes to ten? Okay. Then we're talking in the nighttime? Right?

B: Right.

L: Okay. And then she returned a little bit before two a.m. in the morning?

B: Correct.

L: And during that time, you were in the house...

B: I was in the house, watching the kids.

L: Watching the kids.

C: Watch any t.v. that night?

B: Yes.

C: What was on?

B: Uh, or did I? I don't remember if I did or not.

C: Okay. Once you got home Tuesday, you did not leave? B: I didn't leave. I stayed . . .

C: Stayed.

B: . . . right there. My attitude, I was the only one there, there was nobody to watch the kids.

C: You don't have a car?

B: I borrow a car right now.

C: Uh huh (affirmative).

B: 'Cause I gotta drop off some way and getting, pick up some stuff.

C: Whose car you driving today?

B: My friend, Bud Tubbs (?) I was gonna bring the bus, but they said, but they asked me to go ahead and take the car so I could stop off and get some stuff.

C: Okay. We have some reports that you were seen in the complex on prior occasions, going up and knocking on people's door and talking to them. Can you explain to me the reasoning behind all that?

B: Well, the only time that would have been is to ask people if their car is parked on the (unk word) and if it was, I'd ask them to move it.

C: How 'bout when . . .

B: It's not supposed to park there.

C: How 'bout occasions where the people were getting deliveries? Would you show up at somebody's door?

B: No.

C: No?

B: Not that I recall.

C: Are you still working for Interstate?

B: As far as I know.

C: Uh huh (affirmative). You haven't worked since when?

B: Monday.

C: Monday?

B: Six o'clock p.m.

C: What is your duties over there at Paradise West?

B: To watch over the construction site and make sure nothing out of the ordinary comes around; nobody is not supposed to be there, come and, out.

C: Have you ever been arrested or anything, Sammy?

B: Only for traffic warrants.

C: Just traffic warrants? How long have you been in California?

B: Nine years.

C: What's your date of birth, Sammy?

B: 7-21-65.

L: Seven, twenty-one, what?

B: Sixty-five.

L: Sixty-five? Previous to living in California, where'd you come from?

B: Oregon.

L: That's where your family was from?

B: No. That's where my dad been. Me. My sisters. No, my father passed away. I had to come here. I was only fourteen.

L: Do you know which family, do you have your, L.A. area?

B: My mom, my step-father, my half brothers, sister, my two half sisters.

C: Oh, you've got a lot of them, huh?

B: I've got three sisters and two brothers.

C: Do you remember about a week or so before this tragedy happened with Terri? You come up and you knocked on the apartment one night, about ten o'clock in the evening, you talked to Melanie, she works over there? Do you remember that?

B: Yeah.

L: Yeah. She said it was about ten o'clock at night. She's a rather small, dark-haired, attractive young lady and she recalls you knocking on her door one night and asked her if she smelled a skunk?

B: Oh, yeah.

L: Do you remember that? Was there any reason, I mean, were you just trying to make friends with her or what?

B: Well, it's boring out there. It's like kinda scary, too. Felt like, my first week out there, so scary place by yourself. So boring.

L: Were you attracted to Melanie?

B: Not really. I never, it was the first time I saw her.

L: Well, of all the people that lived in the complex, why did you pick her unit to knock on the door?

B: Why, she was, that's her apartment, it's right there.

C: It's close to where your patrol is? or . . .

B: Yeah.

L: Did you see Melanie before and knew she lived in this particular unit?

B: No.

L: Did you know that there was a female that lived in that unit?

B: No.

L: When you knocked, went up to Melanie's door and knocked on it, you didn't know who lived there at all?

B: No.

L: You just knocked . . .

B: I seen the husband out, or the guy on the garage one time. Washin' his car. I guess that was the husband.

L: Has this occurred at other units where you got bored or whatever? Had you gone up to other units during . . .

B: No.

L: . . . the time when you're working there and knocked on the door, have somebody to talk to?

B: No.

L: You sure?

B: I would only talk 'em, that's to come out and walkin' their dogs or something.

L: Okay. But on this particular night, then why did you go up and knock on the door at ten or after ten at night, on Melanie's door and engaged her in a conversation about I think it was over movies that you liked and things like this?

B: I don't know. I just, the light was on.

C: Did you see her walkin' around in her unit?

B: No.

C: No? Had you been lookin' in the window or anything?

B: No. I'm not that way.

L: Okay. You don't remember knocking on any other doors and initiating other homeowners in a conversation other than this one time with Melanie?

B: No.

L: And, had information that you've talked to quite a few people there; mostly ladies or teenage daughters that you've engaged them in conversation and not about security work but about other matters. Do you, is this true?

B: About, uh (unk word).

C: Do you know Carrie in Unit 209? The red-headed girl?

B: (No response).

C: Do you know her?

B: No.

C: Have you ever knocked on her door, had a conversation with her?

B: No.

C: No? How 'bout the owner in 104? Name's Betty?

B: Oh, yeah. I know her. She's the, she works in there. She works in the office.

C: She does? Do you ever knock on her door

B: I . . .

C: Talk to her?

B: (No response).

C: No? How 'bout a elderly lady that lives over there? Remember having any contact with her?

B: Only if she lives, that's the one walkin' her dog. She's the one who walks her dog a lot of times. That's the only time I can catch her.

C: She lives in 124? Mrs. Borden?

B: No.

C: No?

B: She had a big, black dog. Then I know her.

'Cause I only know 'em if they walk the dogs or if they're out for a midnight stroll or whatever.

C: 'Kay. The day that you were in Terri's unit, helping the movers bring the t.v. up? Did the movers ask you to help 'em?

B: Not really. They didn't disagree.

C: Was Terri there? Did she ask you to come in?

B: No. She didn't disagree, either.

C: She was there?

B: She was there.

C: Were you in your security . . .

B: Security . . .

C: . . . guard uniform?

B: Yeah.

C: And you just came up and the two guys were helpin', you was helpin' 'em carry up the t.v. or were they carrying it up? Or did you just follow them . . .

B: One guy was inside explainin' to her how to hook it up and everything.

C: Uh huh (affirmative). Did she tell you that she didn't want you in her unit?

B: No.

C: Did you have any conversation at all with her?

B: No.

C: 'Kay. And you said you took it upon yourself to carry the trash out? Did she ask you to carry the trash out?

B: No.

L: Were you aware that because of the trash and the mix-up with the watch, that Terri had complained? Were you told by your supervisors that there was a complaint by Terri?

B: Nobody told me that. The other security guys told me about it. That she walked up to him, started complainin' to him.

L: Did that make you upset?

B Not really.

L: Or you were there to, just to be a nice guy and then she was complaining about you. Did that kinda irritate you or . . .

B: Well, I've had things like that before.

L: There at the job site or just . . .

B: No, other places where I used to work.

L: Where was that at?

B: People were always complaining about me and I don't know why.

L: Where did you work before at, Sammy?

B: Before this job? For Interstate? I worked for Thrifty's for 'bout December to about February.

L: Which Thrifty is that?

B: I was hired at the one on Hawthorne Boulevard but worked mostly at Aviation and Artesia and at South Bay store. On Hawthorne Boulevard.

L: Hawthorne and what?

B: I don't know if you'd call it Artesia or 182nd.

C: That's end of, up there by Galleria and . . .

B: Right.

C: . . . South Bay Bowl and all that? How long did you work there?

B: For 'bout December to about February, March.

C: You said people were complaining about you on that job? What . . .

B: Well ...

C: . . . type of complaints?

B: I don't remember.

C: Don't remember? Do you have a problem with women?

B: No.

C: No? Well, you mentioned some complaints.

Obviously, you must know what type of complaints they were because you said . . .

B: Well, it is not, they didn't tell me why. I'm doing what, don't mess with this, take care of the customer. That's it.

L: What was your job at Thrifty's?

B: Well, I was a cashier at one store and I'm (unk word) handy at that other, ice cream or another.

L: Speak up a little bit, Sammy. I couldn't . . .

B: I was a cashier at one store and ice cream at another store.

L: One store you were the cashier and the other store you managed the ice cream section?

B: Correct.

L: Going back to Terri, after she had complained to the other guards though, did you talk to her again about this? Or, uh . . .

B: No.

L: . . . did you have any other conversation with her after that?

B: No. Just that, just the day when she come out. Monday? I waved to her; she waved back.

C: That was Memorial Day? The holiday?

B: That was just last Monday.

L: Other than that one time that you entered the house when they were putting in the television and you took out the trash, had you been in her unit any other time before or after?

B: No.

L: Have you ever been in any other part of her unit 66 other than the front room area?

B: No.

L: Have you ever been in the upstairs portion of Unit 66?

B: No.

L: So there'd be no reason, no possible way that your fingerprints or anything like that could ever be found in the upstairs portion? Right?

B: No.

L: Okay.

C: Did you ever have a key to anybody's unit?

B: Nope.

C: What type of keys did your company supply you with when you're working there?

B: Uh . . .

C: You are in uniform?

B: Yes.

C: What type of uniform do you . . .

B: Just a regular guard uniform.

C: Guard uniform? What type of shoes do you wear on the job out at . . .

B: Black.

L: Are you wearing black shoes now? Are these the same shoes?

B: That's the ones. These my own.

L: These are the same shoes you been wearing? For how long?

B: Two, three years.

C: Okay.

L: Okay. You don't have another pair? These are the ones that you always use?

B: That's it.

C: What's the soles look like?

B: What's the soles look like? You don't want to see 'em.

C: Oh sure, show them to me. Well, I can't see them. It's too dark.

B: Aw, yeah, yeah.

C: Back up and stick them up in the air here. Okay. Um. You can come closer now.

B: Yeah.

L: Can you explain why you're staying with, uh . . .

C: Lilly.

L: . . . Lilly?

B: 'Cause I have no where else to stay. (Three words covered).

L: How 'bout, you have so many brothers and sisters?

B: 'Cause they're in Artesia.

L: Okay.

B: And 'til I get a car, I can't stay on my own. Even after I get a car, obviously. I'm going to move back home with my mom as soon as I get a car (rest of sentence covered).

C: Did you know Terri was murdered?

B: Not until I talked to my boss.

C: When was that?

B: Ew, yesterday.

C: Yesterday afternoon?

B: Yesterday afternoon.

C: Is that when I talked to you while you were in the office there?

B: Yeah.

C: I asked you to come down? How did he tell you she was killed?

B: He said: "You're aware there's been a homicide?" and I said: "What? You're kidding?", he said: "No."

C: Did he tell you how she was killed?

B: No.

C: Do you know where she was killed?

B: No.

L: Why do you think she was killed, Sammy?

B: Well, I don't know.

L: Did you ever see her with any guys or any other people around her unit?

B: The only two that I've ever seen her was a couple that she always come in and out with. Whenever she come in with them, she'd go and leave in her own car. Either (two words covered).

C: Can you describe that couple?

B: or, the lady was short, stocky and the guy was . . .

C: Older couple?

B: Yeah. About older couple.

C: Think it was her mom or dad?

B: No, I think it was more like a (two words inaudible). The very first time I met her was 'bout a week before she moved in.

C: Did you think she was nice?

B: Yeah, I thought she was nice.

L: She attractive?

B: Pretty much so.

L: Were you attracted to her in any way?

B: In a sense. Probably.

C: Did you take that to try to be friendly with her because you wanted to get to know her a little better or . . .

B: You might say that.

L: How do you think . . .

C: But you didn't kill her?

B: Ten four on that. I would never do that. I would never do something like that to anybody. That would be the last thing on this earth I'd do.

L: You know in the complex, and been there in the construction and all that. Maybe you could help us out. If a burglar was gonna get into one of those units, what would be the best way to get in? How do you think he'd get in there?

B: Uh, got me. Man, such a good, quiet neighborhood, nothing like that, you wouldn't think something like that would ever happen.

L: Well, I'm asking you to make believe that you had to get into a unit. Okay? Put yourself as a burglar. This is only make believe. Okay? And you were gonna break in to one of those units, how would you do it? Maybe you could help us to look at how the guy that did this, maybe we're, you know? We're not sure how he got in, . . .

C: Yeah.

L: We're not that familiar with the units. If you had to break in to one of those units, how would you get in?

B: Probably through a window. Or, there is those side doors.

L: If you had to go through a window, how would you get in? How would you get the window open?

B: I don't know.

C: You know any of the employees over there? For Dunn. Like customer service guy? Dan or Don? Do you know them guys?

B: I met one guy yesterday. Was it yesterday, yeah, yesterday afternoon. He was driving a BMW. Black BMW.

C: Oh, that's Ben Barry?

B: I guess, I didn't even say his name. He just says, just told me and the other guy that the other guard is on duty that to "I want that gate over there locked at all times, I don't want, no way for anybody in or out." That's the site . . .

C: You were back over there yesterday?

B: Talking to 'nother guard.

C: Which guard were you talking to?

B: Doug.

C: Doug? You were on the grounds yesterday?

B: Yeah.

C: Did your boss tell you that they didn't want you over there for a while.?

B: No.

C: No?

B: Just I wasn't going to work there anymore. I had to pick up something.

C: Can you, you can't think of any way to get into those units other than through a window or maybe that sliding door?

B: No.

C: Do you know that Terri had moved in to that unit?

B: I knew she was movin' in . . .

C: But you didn't know if . . .

B: . . . I didn't know if she was completely (TAPE ENDS)

Chapter IX

URBAN POLICE DEPARTMENT

SUPPLEMENTAL REPORT

I/O: R. LANDER

THE DATE IS JUNE 7, 1989; THE TIME IS 1050 HOURS. THIS WILL BE AN INTERVIEW CONDUCTED AT THE URBAN POLICE DEPT. TAKING PART IN THE INTERVIEW IS MYSELF, RICK LANDER, MY PARTNER, JIM CONLEY. WE WILL BE INTERVIEWING MR. DON ARNOLD.

LEGEND: "L" = Det. R. LANDER
            "C" = Det. J. CONLEY
            "A" = DON ARNOLD

C: Okay, Don, just for the tape, Could you give me your address on the tape?
A: It's (Illegible) 31st Avenue, Number 203.
C: And what city is that in?
A: Saugus.
C: Saugus? How long have you worked for Dunn?

A: I worked for Dunn about a year.

C: About a year? Prior to that, where were you working?

A: I was working for Acme Builders.

C: What city would that be in?

A: Ventura Boulevard.

C: The valley? Maybe?

A: Right.

C: How long have you been in the State of California?

A: Five years.

C: Five years? And prior to that?

A: Texas. Amarillo, Texas.

C: Amarillo, Texas. Okay. What is your job function or duties over at Dunn Homes? Over at Paradise West?

A: I do customer service. The homeowners fill out a request for service forms and send them to the office and then they send them out to us and we do the work that's on the list.

C: So, your job duties - you would be, have a special unit go into and repair anything that the homeowner . . .

A: As requested.

C: . . . is not satisfied with?

A: Right.

C: Did you know the victim in this case, Terri Horgan?

A: No, I didn't.

C: Had you ever met her?

A: No.

C: Okay. How 'bout being inside of her condo unit specifically? Have you ever been inside there?

A: The day before, I went in to let the heating guy in.

C: Mm hmmm.

A: Went through the front door, downstairs and opened up the garage.

C: About what time was that?

A: 'Bout eleven, I guess.

C: That's the only time you've been in the...

A: Right.

C: . . . unit, so to speak?

A: I've only working in Paradise West for about two weeks.

C: Okay. Where did you work before Paradise West?

A: Phase Two.

C: Phase Two?

A: Right. They transferred us over there. Because Phase Two's about done.

C: I see. So you was only in her unit that one day and that was? Can you remember the date?

A: It was the day before the accident which was Tuesday.

C: Tuesday?

A: The first?

C: Tuesday the first? About what time?

A: I would say about eleven.

C: About eleven? Were you present when some furniture was delivered?

A: On Wednesday?

C: No. On Tuesday.

A: Yeah. Right.

C: Tuesday afternoon?

A: I had to, brought the heating guy in all those units out there.

C: Okay. Heating and air conditioning guy. Do you know his name?

A: No, I don't. They interviewed him, though.

C: Okay. So you opened up her front door and

then went down to the garage and opened up the garage door?

A: Right.

C: And then left the unit? Did you secure the unit when you left or did leave it open?

A: When I left. Because he had to do all those units.

C: Uh huh. Okay. What time did you secure that unit?

A: About three-thirty, quarter to four.

C: And how did you secure it?

A: I shut, no, let's see. I shut the garage door and went out then deadbolted it and locked the door on it.

C: And exited out the front?

A: Right.

C: And that's the only time you personally had been in there?

A: Yes.

C: Okay. So you were not upstairs at all?

A: No. I was never upstairs. No.

C: When the furniture was delivered, how did the deliverymen get in? Do you now?

A: Through the garage.

C: Through the garage?

A: Uh, she was home.

C: She was home?

A: Yes.

C: 'Bout what time was that?

A: I saw 'em about two, two-thirty.

C: Two or two-thirty? And you did see her . . .

A: Yes.

C: . . . in the unit?

A: I saw that. They were talking to her in the garage.

C: Okay. Do you remember the delivery service that delivered the sofa?

(some lower toned conversation with detectives - inaudible)

A: I didn't really pay any attention to the truck.

C: Okay.

A: Because you see 'em all the time.

C: But when you came back, she had left and the unit was wide open, so to speak?

A: Yeah, the garage door was open.

C: Was her car gone?

A: No.

C: Did you see it in the garage when you . . .

A: There was a white car in the garage.

C: You mentioned you came back and locked everything up when you came back the second time around. Was the car still there?

A: Yes.

C: The car was still there.

A: Mmm, hmm. Delivery truck wasn't.

C: Okay. What kind of car was it?

A: Like a white BMW or something.

C: All white car?

A: Yeah. Newer model.

L: That was approximately three forty-five in the afternoon when you secured her unit? Unit 66?

A: Right.

L: There was a newer, white?

A: Parked in the garage.

L: A newer one?

A: Well, you know, it's an early model. I don't know what year.

C: It's just a white car?

A: Yeah.

L: But it was still there when you secured?

A: Right.

C: And you did not see her when you locked up?

A: I didn't see her at all.

C: Okay. Go through how you locked up her unit for me. One more time.

A: Close the garage door. Went upstairs. Went out the front door. Well, I pushed the button on the knob where it was closed and then did, lock.

C: Did you check the sliding door off the patio?

A: No, I didn't go through that.

C: Do you know if that particular door was locked or unlocked at that point?

A: No. But those doors are so easily (unk word).

C: Yeah. So you only met her one time and that was on Tuesday when you saw her talking with the delivery man?

A: Right.

C: Did she speak with you personally or any-thing?

A: No.

C: And how did you find out about what hap-pened, say, Tuesday, early Wednesday? You came?

A: Through Ben Bolton.

C: Ben Bolton? Who is he?

A: He's in customer service.

C: Supervisor?

A: Yeah.

C: What did he tell you?

A: Wanted me to go to the sales office and get addresses to all the units for the Fire Department or somebody and then when I came back with that, he told me she was dead and I said: "Who?" and he said: "The lady upstairs."

C: Did he tell you anything about it?

A: No.

C: Do you know anything about it?

A: 'Cept what they said. She was dead upstairs.

C: Okay. Who said that?

A: Ben Bolton.

C: Ben Bolton?

A: And Gary (inaudible).

C: Did you talk to the detectives on Wednesday?

A: Yeah. I talked to one of them; I don't know what his name was.

C: Do you remember what the conversation went like? When you talked to him?

A: I was telling him a story (rest inaudible).

C: Did you mentioned to him something about a security guard?

A: Right.

C: What did you relate to him about the security guard?

A: He went up to the mover guys and asked them if they needed help.

C: Which was Tuesday?

A: Right. And they say you'll have to ask the lady of the house. Apparently, she was in the garage and she said she had to call somebody first. Apparently, she went in to call the sales office. She called earlier that week about him.

C: So you were present when the security guard came over and asked the movers if they needed help?

A: Right.

C: They say: "Well, you'll have to ask the owner of the property." or whatever?

A: Right. He didn't have access to the unit.

C: Uh huh.

A: And I seen him standing in the garage. And then when I left, he wasn't there. And I went around the tract 'cause I heard a lot of homeowners say he was kinda weird.

C: Uh huh. Had you ever personally met him?

A: No.

C: Do you know his name?

A: Mm mmm (negative).

C: But you did see him there Tuesday about three, three-thirty?

A: Right.

C: Or was it earlier than that?

A: Time is so hard.

C: Well, you said you secured the place about three-thirty, three forty-five, so . . .

A: Right. And then I drove around the tract, because I wanted to see if that guard was around. And then I left. They usually leave about, usually try to get out by three-thirty.

C: Is that the person we're talking about; I'm showing you a photograph of the individual. Do you recognize him as being the security guard you're talking about?

A: Could be. I don't know. Just got flashes of the guy.

C: Yeah. Was he in uniform that day?

A: Yeah. I could . . .

C: Interstate Security guard?

A: Right.

C: So, basically, this gentleman asked the movers if they needed help?

A: Right.

C: And, so, well, "Ask the lady . . . ? . . .

A: The lady of the house.

C: So she says: "Well, I'll have to call . . ."

A: She said: "I'll have to call somebody first." is what she said. I assumed it was the sales office. She talked to . . .

C: Did you see the movers or the delivery man move a sofa in?

A: (no audible response)

C: To your knowledge? When you came back to secure everything . . .

A: Mm hmmm.

C: Terri wasn't there, the owner of the unit wasn't there?

A: I didn't see her.

C: Didn't see her.

A: Could have been there or upstairs or somewhere or maybe . . .

C: You indicated there was a car in the garage?

A: Right.

C: The garage door was opened. You shut it. Did you use the garage door opener or did you have to manually shut it?

A: I pushed the door, I mean, the button. Yeah.

C: You came up out the front door, pressed the button, secured the deadbolt with your passkey?

A: Right.

C: Is that a grandmaster or just a . . .

A: Just a master key.

C: And then you left and notified the next day about her death?

A: Right.

C: And you know anything about how she died or have you heard anything about how she died?

A: Just from Gary.

C: What did Gary say?

A: Said she was strangled or something.

C: Did he say how or what or anything?

A: No.

L: After you secured that about three forty-five in the afternoon, when did your workday end that day?

A: Right after I did that. After I secured ...

L: That would be the last duty for the day?

A: Yeah. I usually leave at three thirty. I was a little (unk word) that day.

L: Okay. So after you secured that, why don't you tell me what you did the rest of the day and that night?

A: The rest of the day? I spent three hours on the freeway to get home and then went and had pizza. My wife and kids.

L: Do you know where you had pizza at?

A: I think it's Shakey's

L: That was in . . .

A: Saugus.

L: In Saugus?

A: Yeah. On Saugus Avenue. Then I washed my truck.

L: And then?

A: Went home. Showered. Then went to bed about eleven o'clock. Eleven-thirty. About eleven-thirty. It was after the news.

L: When you and your wife and kids had dinner at Shakey's, did you go alone, did you go with a couple, a group or anything like that?

A: No, it was just me, my wife and our youngest son. And we got it to go. Two large pizzas.

L: Okay. So you went to Shakey's, got a go and you went back to your house?

A: Right.

L: Had dinner?

A: Right.

L: Then you washed your truck?

A: Mm hmmm, (affirmative)

L: Okay. And, just stayed home?

A: Showered. Went back home, showered and then went to bed.

L: Okay. And that was sometime after eleven o'clock?

A: It was after, about eleven-thirty because it was after the news.

L: Did you get up for any reason that night and have to go any place?

A: No. My alarm goes off at three-thirty.

C: Long way to drive, huh?

A: Yeah. L: And do you and your wife share the same bedroom?

A: Yeah.

L: Do you have double beds or single bed you both sleep . . .

A: Single bed, yeah. It's a twin-sized mattress. And each boy has his own room. It's three bedroom apartment.

L: So then, all that night, you were home asleep? And the alarm went off at three thirty and it was 'prepare for work as usual'?

A: Yeah.

C: What time did you get to Paradise West on Wednesday morning?

A: 'Bout eight-thirty.

C: Eight-thirty?

A: I get to the trailer about seven.

C: Where's the trailer you're speaking of?

A: It's in between Phases One and Two. It's like an open field.

C: Check in there with anybody?

A: No. We just come in, get all our paperwork ready for the day. And then we start. Because we can't get in the units until eight.

C: I notice you have some tattoos. Could you tell me what those tattoos are on your right forearm?

A: Yeah, the kid and Sandra (Next sentence inaudible). Sandra was a girl I went with.

C: Okay. And doesn't mean anything now? Sandra's not your wife?

A: No.

C: Okay. What's your wife's name?

A: Connie.

C: Connie? Does she work?

A: No, she's, she worked for Lucky's and then she, they don't know; some steam thing they set up there in Saugus, they said she sold to a minor. So, she's been through Court for about a year now.

C: Alcohol? Something like that?

A: Yeah. It's an older guy and a younger guy at the, uh, it's a big ordeal. But now she's got 16 days community service, she's doing it, Palmdale, High Desert Hospital. And that's over with.

C: Okay. Do you have any injuries on either of your arms or hands?

A: No.

C: Could we look at 'em real quick?

(no audible response) Okay. Do you want to turn them over this way?

A: Just scars from my cat.

L: Do you have any scratch marks on your chest or upper arms?

A: No. I don't. Well, I got this from my motorcycle.

L: That's a little scar.

A: Yeah.

C: Any recent scratch marks or anything like that?

A: No.

L: For the tape, I'm unable to observe any bruising, scratch marks or any other injuries. You've had a couple days to think about this. Is there anybody that pops into your mind as, you know, being around

there, knowing the people? Anybody that pops in your mind as a possible suspect?

A: No. As I say, I worked in Phase Two four (or 'for') years. I don't know anybody in Paradise West.

L: Did you, were you told when you were in that unit on Tuesday, were you informed by the owner, the victim, Terri, did you have knowledge that she was going to spend the night there?

A: No. From what I knew, nobody had lived in any of the units 'cause Dan had just walked those units. And most of 'em weren't lived in.

L: And, why don't you go over, unless you did while I was out of the other room, the fact that the key,

A: So you have what they call a "knock out key;" when they're building the units, the builders have the key. And after the walk-through, they put in what they call a "knock-out-key" and their keys no longer work. Ours and the homeowners does. And that was done apparently Wednesday morning.

C: By Mr. Black?

A: Dan Black.

L: Okay. Did he do it with you or did he tell you he did it on Wednesday?

A: He told me.

L: Okay.

A: That wasn't in the (inaudible - possible "walk").

L: The tumblers were turned and the knock out key was used on Wednesday after, some time Wednesday after the body's been discovered?

A: No, Wednesday morning 'cause Dan working in there Wednesday morning.

L: I see. Wednesday morning, before the body's been discovered, that's when the key was used?

A: Right.

L: How many master keys or whatever you refer

to, after the knock out key's used, okay, the home-owner has a key . . .

A: And Dan Black has a key.

L: Okay.

A: I have a key. And Jones has a key.

L: Okay. And these three keys, would they fit any unit in the complex?

A: Yes. Unless they changed their locks.

L: So it's a basic master key?

A: Right.

L: Even for the units that are occupied?

A: Right. You have a key for each phase.

L: Okay.

A: A master key for each phase. You only have one key fits all the houses.

C: On Wednesday when you used the knock out key, were you present anywhere in the unit?

A: No. I was working in the models. We have a list every week that comes Out of the models.

C: Okay. I don't have anything further at this point.

L: I don't either. I have a question and it's, uh, I'll do it when the tapes not on. But it really has no pre-cedent in this investigation. We're gonna terminate the taped portion of this interview. Again, just for the tape, Don, You're advised before the interview started and that, you come here freely and voluntarily in this interview and this interview is open and you're not being coerced or anything?

A: Yes.

L: Okay.

(TAPE ENDS).

Chapter X

URBAN POLICE DEPARTMENT

SUPPLEMENTARY REPORT

THE DATE AND TIME IS 6-9-89, IT'S 1140 HOURS IN THE A.M. THIS'LL BE A SECOND INTERVIEW WITH DON ARNOLD. IT'S TAKING PLACE IN THE DESIGN CENTER OVER AT THE COMPLEX AT 3200 ALDER STREET, THAT'S WHERE DON WORKS. PRESENTLY IN THE INTERVIEW IS MYSELF, DETECTIVE LANDER, MY PARTNER, DETECTIVE CONLEY AND MR. ARNOLD.

LEGEND = "L" = DET. R. LANDER
         "C" = DET. J. CONLEY
         "A" = DON ARNOLD

L: Mr. Arnold, this is the second interview. We've come over to where you work so it'll take up less time and inconvenience; you don't have to come to the station. Is that okay?

A: That's fine.

L: Okay. And you understand you're not under arrest?

A: Right.

L: And you're not being detained forcefully or anything like that?

A: Right.

L: Okay? You're just assisting us with our investigation into Terri Horgan's homicide?

A: That's right.

L: (beeper going off at this point). Okay. The tape's back on again; there's a short interruption there for the telephone call. Don, we've gone over everything up to this point and there's a few things we need to just make sure.

A: Okay.

L: We're going, I Just want to ask you again if you've had time to think about it in connection with Tuesday, the thirtieth, the day before Terri was found.

A: Right.

L: Okay. You said in a couple of interviews and when I talked to you the other day that you let a gas man or a furnace man into Terri's unit, number 66 on that morning approximately 11 o'clock.

A: In the garage.

L: Into the garage.

A: Yes.

L: Okay. Now, when I talked to you the day before yesterday, you indicated it was the big man, name unknown . . .

A: Yeah.

L: Now, you were with me when we talked to him.

A: Right.

L: . . . He says he never went in to Unit 66.

A: Right.

L: Could there be any days that you're getting mixed up as to when you were in that apartment or do you still, sure it was Tuesday?

A: Still sure it was Tuesday.

L: Okay. When you opened the door for him, did you personally see him go in?

A : No.

L: You just opened the garage door?

A: Right. And two units up at the same time. That one 'n the one next to it.

L: Okay. And then when you came back and secured the unit later on that afternoon?

A: Mm hmmm (affirmative).

L: That was about what time?

A: 'Bout three-thirty. Between three and three thirty.

L: Was the front door, then, still unlocked?

A: Right.

L: Okay. It's our information, and this has been verified, that Terri was home on that day; she got home at one o'clock.

A: Mm hmmm (affirmative).

L: We're wondering is, if the man had not gone in and did any work, as he said he didn't and that apparently has been verified by his work schedule.

A: Right.

L: The units that he worked on . . .

A: Min hmmm (affirmative).

L: . . . why wouldn't Terri secured her own apartment when she left because, according to her mother and her schedule, she had no idea or information that anybody was to do any work in unit, in her unit on that day.

A: I don't know. There was a different car in the garage.

L: Well, okay. We have, that's another question that we still can't, you know, find out who possibly would have owned a newer, white BMW.

A: Right.

L: We've, but my question which I'm that's got us stumped right now is, we know Terri was home at one o'clock in the afternoon on Tuesday.

A: Okay.

L: We know that she left somewhere around two or two-thirty and she drove to West Los Angeles because she had, she did attend a meeting that started at three-thirty in the afternoon. That's been verified.

A: But the repair guy had no reason to go in the unit. He's only in the garages.

L: Okay. If the repair guy had no reason to go in the unit, then why did you leave the front door or the apartment unlocked. Why don't you just open the garage door?

A: I go through the front door.

L: Yeah?

A: I come out the garage. I didn't go back up through the front door and lock it.

L: Okay. But now you've just said again when you came back at three or three-thirty in the afternoon, the garage door was still open?

A: Right.

L: And the front door was still open? A: Right.

L: Which would be inconsistent with Terri's actions. She was security minded; she would have first questioned "Who is this white car in my garage?"; the family doesn't own a white car.

A: Mm hmmm, (affirmative).

L: There is no newer BMW known to anybody that she associates with or is related to. I mean, common sense would tell you she is, "Whose car is this in my garage?" Right?

A: Right.

L: And if she went in the house, coming home at

one o'clock and found her garage door open, a strange car parked in her garage and the front door unlocked, I think she would have called her mom or mentioned it to her mom at one o'clock when she telephoned her mother. Don't you think that's reasonable?

A: I do, yeah.

L: Is there any explanation you have for this conflict in what seems reasonable and what you remember occurred on that day?

A: Well, unless the times were different than what I thought they were.

L: Well, you told us this before . . .

A: See, I know where I was because I break out a lot and my wife got me this band yesterday.

L: Uh huh (affirmative).

A: But, I normally leave around, between three-thirty and four.

L: Okay. If you se . . . , that you remember securing Unit 66, Terri's unit, before you left that day? ·

A: That and about six other locks.

L: Okay. But you secured Unit 66?

A: That's right.

C: See, that is inconsistent because Terri left about two o'clock and secured her own unit. There was nobody there.

A: (First two words possibly: "No it") . . . wasn't because the front door was opened. I went through the front door, it wasn't locked.

L: Well, if Terri had came home, which we know she did . . .

A: All right.

L: Okay. We have a telephone call made to her mother. One o'clock.

A: Okay.

L: I think she would have noticed there's a car in her garage 'cause that's where she parks.

A: Mm hmmm. (affirmative).

L: So, that doesn't jive.

A: Doesn't jive, yeah.

L: She would have been concerned about the front door being unlocked because first of all, she had no scheduled repairs for that day.

A: Right.

L: Second of all, she had already requested that that lock be de-mastered. And while there might have been a confusion as to when it was gonna be de-mastered, she was of the opinion the lock had been de-mastered prior to Tuesday.

A: Well . . .

L: She had asked the week previous to have that lock de-mastered.

A: However, when she called her mother, did she mention that the house was un . . . that the house was open?

L: No, she didn't.

A: Well, it was. (Start of another sentence covered, stops).

C: You told us also that when you opened that garage that morning, that white car was there.

A: Right.

C: And when you closed it that afternoon, that same white car was there.

A: Well, it wasn't that morning when I, it was later.

C: Oh.

A: You know, after lunch.

L: It was, okay. One time you said eleven.

A: (Inaudible word).

L: And then I think another interview, you said it was more like one. It was before lunch or after?

A: Mmmmm . . .

L: Do you remember?

A: Uh, I'm sure it was after one (or: "lunch") be-cause they, the other guys were down at that end unit that he said he was in and one of their vans was there and I said: "Are they still working the unit?", she said: "No, they went to lunch.".

L: Terri said that to you?

A: No, uh, Dunn, Dunn's personal secretary. Couple units at the other end of that same building.

C: So you never saw Terri on Tuesday? When you opened it up or when you closed it?

A: No. And that wasn't the car that was in the garage.

C: That one we looked at the other day?

A: No. That was not the car that was in the ga-rage. I'm sure of that.

L: How 'bout on a, you went home that night after you left work and why don't you tell us again what you did that night?

A: Okay. My wife and son was up at the pizza place, ordering a pizza to go. Two pizzas. So I went up there and, uh, sat with her for a little while (clears throat), then I went and washed my truck.

L: Where did you wash your truck at?

A: Right next door to pizza place. Where you do it yourself.

L: Okay.

A: And then I went home, showered, ate, went to bed.

L: And what time did you recall getting up?

A: My alarm goes off at three-thirty (last word inaudible; possibly: "five").

L: And what's your normal when you get up at

three-thirty? Is anybody in the household get up with you or 'cause of that hour, you're alone?

A: No. Nobody else gets up.

L: Okay. So, you got up three-thirty on Wednesday morning and what's your normal, what took place that morning?

A: Well, I eat a light breakfast and then I take off. 'Bout four o'clock.

L: 'Bout four? You drive from your house in Saugus here?

A: To the tract, to the trailer.

L: To the trailer. What time do you arrive here 'bout?

A: 'Bout six, little after.

L: And you normally start work at what time?

A: Uh, eight. I sleep for an hour or two. We can't clock in 'til seven.

L: Okay. And why do you leave at four to get here to sleep?

A: The traffic.

C: The traffic? Okay. So what time do you remember getting to work on Wednesday morning?

A: 'Bout six o'clock.

C: Six? It took you two hours travel time?

A: It takes me two hours. If I leave any later than that, it takes me three. That's why I leave at (inaudible).

L: Do you know how many miles that is from your house? Have you ever just paced it for the hell of it?

A: It's eighty six miles one way.

L: Eighty-six?

A: Yeah.

L: Okay. We drove out to Saugus the other day. We left here in the afternoon and drove moderate, semi-heavy traffic. We made it from Urban Police

Department to your apartment complex in an hour and ten minutes.

A: Mm hmmm (affirmative). What time did you leave?

C: 'Bout one thirty in the afternoon.

L: Thirty or two in the afternoon.

A: Yeah. Then, I usually make it then 'bout an hour, hour and a half.

L: Okay.

A: (Sounds like:) It's a long fucking drive.

L: We went out there to try to talk to your wife and that just to verify your story but apparently, I, we weren't able to get a hold of her.

A: She's at home.

L: Well, at the time we went out, it wasn't there, but we talked to some of the people in the apartment complex and they told us a story that you told to Mary Brown? Do You know Mary Brown?

C: Nora Brown.

L: Or Nora Brown. The assistant manager out there? A: Oh, Nora? Yeah.

L: Okay. Can you, do you recall what you told Nora? Last Saturday?

A: No.

L: When you and your wife, apparently you went to the office and she asked you how you're feeling because she noted, she told us that she saw you earlier and you appeared to be upset? Do you remember having a conversation with her?

A: I just told that we had a death up here on the tract.

C: Did you tell her that you had discovered her? The body?

A: No. I said that Dan Black, the guy I work with, discovered the body.

C: You didn't tell her you personally discovered her?

A: No.

L: Did you tell her that the body had been mutilated?

A: Mutilated?

L: Mut-il-lat-ted.

A: No.

L: Did you tell her that you were the one that was working in the bathroom and you found the body in this mutilated condition and because it was such a horrible sight that it caused you to vomit?

A: To vomit? No.

L: Did you tell her that you're the one who personally dialed "911" for Paramedics?

A: No.

L: Why would she make up all ...

A: I told her that Dan did.

L: . . . these stories?

A: I don't know. Maybe my wife told her all this junk.

L: No, she said you told her.

A: I did?

L: Uh huh (affirmative).

A: All's I told her is we found the body in the unit and, uh, my partner that I work with is, uh, out on, sick you know, from it.

C: Did you tell her that you had to go out to the hospital and get a tranquilizer?

A: Well, I did.

C: You did?

A: Yes.

C: When was that?

A: That same night, I believe.

C: Which night? Can you be more specific?

A: Wednesday night.

C: Wednesday night?

A: Oh, no, Thursday night. The next night. 'Cause we had to take our son in to, uh, he has a problem or . . .

C: Which hospital did you go to?

A: Um, Saugus Medical Group.

C: And what type of tranquilizer did you get?

A: Uh, he gave me Tylenol with, a, codeine.

C: Why did you need that?

A: I was all wound up anyhow.

C: From what?

A: From all that was going on around here.

L: But, you never saw the victim, did you?

A: No, I never saw the victim.

L: If you've had, if somebody was to die in the next complex over there, would that upset you, if you never saw it? You told us earlier you never even met Terri.

A: Mm hmmm.

L: Why would her death have upset you to the point where . . .

A: It wasn't her death, it was all that, you know, I'm getting questions thrown at me.

L: But we talked to you same as we talked to fifteen other people in and around the complex.

A: I know, but, I get nervous. I couldn't stop.

L: Okay.

A: It's just me.

C: How 'bout, what has caused you so much grief over this incident? Prior to this, you had a pretty good attendance record, but within the last couple of weeks, you've been off work two days, late one day?

A: Mm hmmm (affirmative)

C: Can you explain anything?

A: A lot of it was the Tylenol codeine. I can't come to work on it. I can't drive on it. It was all due to my ankle, basically.

C: What's the matter with your ankle?

A: I twisted my ankle chasing some guys that were trying to break into my truck.

C: When was that?

A: A week prior to that.

C: Was it here in Urban or . . .

A: No. At home.

C: In Saugus?

A: Yeah. I got a doctor's report.

C: Did you report that to the Saugus Sheriffs or . . .

A: Mmm, no. Unless the apartment notified them.

L: We found out some other information which we're wondering why you told us what you said and that is: you brought up, or we mentioned to you we were aware that you had an arrest down in Texas.

A: Yes.

L: For burglary.

A: Right.

L: Do you remember what you told us concerning that arrest?

A: Yes, I told you that I had ran away from a children's home and it was snowing, cold and I went into a vacant apartment to get warm.

L: We have telephoned and talked to the people in Texas who have pulled the reports and that doesn't jibe with what they're tellin' us took place.

A: That, that . . .

L: That is not the circumstances of your conviction down in Texas.

A: Well, what was it then?

C: You know what was?

A: I know. But what are they sayin'? That's what happened. That's why I got . . .

L: According to us and they're mailing us off the reports, it should be here, according with the court documents . . .

A: Mmm hmmm (affirmative).

L: that you entered a occupied unit with a female during nighttime hours and was discovered by her in, on her bedroom floor while she was in bed, sleeping.

A: No, that wasn't. Before, okay, I was in one children's home, in Amarillo and our dad stole us. And they took us back and in between taking me from that children's home to this one, they put us in a foster home.

L: 'Kay.

A: Me and one of my brothers. And, uh, that woman there, after they put us into there, when I ran away, I was going to Charlie, their son. To use his car. And, uh, went through his bedroom window. And I went in to ask his mother where Charlie was. I knew her. I lived with 'em for a year and a half, and, uh, she gave some stupid story to the cops. But that isn't why I got put in.

L: That's not why you got put in?

A: No. It is not.

L: Didn't you steal a car down there?

A: 'Cause I ran, no. I took my brother's car.

L: Well . . .

A: After that, okay . . .

L: You're telling us that they sentenced you, right on the rap sheet it says "a burglary, second count, inhabited", which means . . .

A: Okay. That count you were just talking about was reported. But nothing was done. 'Cause I was

working for her husband. Well, they were going through a divorce, in construction in Lubbock.

L: But. Okay. We've just been told this over the 'phone. We have it and it's enroute the mail; we haven't had a chance to personally read the court documentation in that, but you're tellin' us again that they sentenced you for two, for six years . . .

A: They gave me probation for that first one.

L: Which one?

A: The one with the woman you're talkin' about.

L: Okay.

A: Uh, Mullins.

L: Okay.

A: And then, the girl I was runnin' away with wanted to go back home, so I seen her back home. Children's home wouldn't let me back in. So I slept two nights in a bus. And then on the third night, I went into an apartment. There was no one living in that apartment. It was a vacant apartment. I slept on the closet floor in the, gotta be the master bedroom.

L: Okay. And that's the offense that they sentenced you on?

A: Right.

L: Okay.

A: That next morning, they came up and had guns all drawn around when I was in the closet.

L: Now, how old were you then?

A: I was sixteen. Just about to turn seventeen, which in Texas, you're concerned . . .

L: What year was that?

A: 78

L: You're born in what?

A: 60.

L: 60 or 61?

A: 61, excuse me (next few words inaudible).

L: 'Cause if you're born in 1961, I think and the conviction was in 1979 . . .

A: 79?

L: Okay?

A: I turned 17 in the County Jail.

C: Did you get arrested in Arizona? Once?

A: Yes.

C: What was that for?

A: Um, I hit a motorcycle with a car; fell asleep at the wheel and I was a parole violator. And they took me back.

C: What year was that, if you recall?

A: I couldn't tell you for sure.

L: Do you understand our problem, Don?

A: Yeah.

C: What do you think?

A: About what?

C: Our problem. And we're looking at you.

A: I don't know. But you're not looking at me at this problem.

L: Well, we're looking at everybody, but, everybody else's stories and that have basically, up to now, have basically panned out. They jive with somebody else's observations and yours don't. Your's make no sense. I mean, it can't be verified by anybody; the part that could be verified has been denied by other workers, that that took place or that occurred and common sense wise, it doesn't make any sense because we know Terri was home on the afternoon of Tuesday. She would not have left her apartment unlocked; she would have not have called or made mention to her mom because her mom and Terri talked about every damn thing, from which napkin to put in there to, I mean they talked to each other eight ten times a day.

C: Plus she had property in there. She had her television in there and her sofa. She wouldn't walk off and leave everything open.

A: I don't know I just, that's what happened when (unk two words); I know that.

L: Did you come to work early on Wednesday and go to Terri's apartment?

A: No, I didn't.

L: Early in the early hours of the morning?

A: No sir, I didn't.

L: And you never been upstairs?

A: No.

L: In Terri's apartment?

A: No sir.

L: Well . . .

A: My wife can verify which time I left.

L: She was up?

A: Well, I kiss her good-bye every morning. So she knows when I left.

L: You left at three thirty? There's no traffic, or quarter to four or four o'clock. You could have been here easily by five ten, five-fifteen.

A: No, I go through...

L: Which goes well within the time of death period.

A: I go through...

L: If Terri had been killed at five-thirty or six o'clock, the condition of her remains when she was found at eleven-thirty would be consistent with the time of death at that time.

A: I go through Bokay Canyon, mountain road. I take my time. I'm in no; that's what I do every morning.

L : So, Miss Brown out there is hallucinating when she tells us that you said that concerning the circumstances around the body that you found?

C: This is what Nora told us. She said she saw you pull in a couple days last week. She was out walkin' her dog and you just shook your head like "Man, I've had a tough day."

A: I do that every day.

L: Okay.

A: Everybody does something like that all the time.

C: Then she says you showed up either on Saturday or Monday to pay your rent and during that time, she told us that you said you were working in a unit, you had a terrible week; "I found a body; I rolled her over. She was face down. Her fingers were cut off, her toes were cut off; I immediately vomited."

A: Well, she's stretchin' at that.

C: Well, what did you tell her?

A: I told her that a body, we had found a body. In a unit. That had been apparently strangled or whatever. It said we, there's no motive to it. I said there was no rape, there was nothin' stolen. And I told her it sound to me like family dispute or something.

L: Who told you there was no rape?

A: Ben.

L: Ben Bolton.

A: Bolton.

L: Where did he get this information?

A: I don't know.

C: We haven't put that out to anybody.

A: He said she hadn't been murdered, I mean, uh, (sucks teeth, unk word) she hadn't been, uh, robbed or raped.

L: And who, Ben said she hadn't been robbed or raped?

A: Yeah. Said there's no motive. He came down

and said: (Affects different voice tone:) "She's dead."
Said: "Go in to . . ." . . .
        L: When did Ben tell you this?
        A: Wednesday. I pulled up and . . .
        L: So when you pulled up to the complex, not even
knowing what had taken place there with Terri. . . .
        A: I was . . .
        L: . . . you were talkin' with Ben? And at that time,
he said she'd been murdered but she hadn't been
raped or robbed?
        A: Right. What I did that morning when I started
work was I went to the sales office, which is right here
and got the model list, with a model maintenance and I
started on the models. And, I'm not sure what time it
was, it, Dan got a hold of me on the radio. Dan Black.
He said: "I want you to open up some . . . ," um, we're
talkin' about Wednesday now, right? So, I went over to
find Dan. Wednesday morning. And Ben, there was a
fire truck out there and Ben came out. He was all up on
the stairs, so was Dan and (sounds like:) Ellen. He said:
"Go to the sales office and get addresses to all the units.
All the phases." And he said: "She's dead." I said:
"Who's dead?" He said: "The girl up there." And he
said that it seems funny they weren't robbed or raped.
        C: This is Wednesday? Right after the incident?
That's when he told you?
        A: Ben told me.
        L: Okay. Check out Ben.
        C: Well, we'll talk to Ben.
        L: Uh. . . .
        C: Earlier in our conversation, I think you men-
tioned that, taped interview, you said something to
the effect of it was that her death was an accident?
        A: Accident? (first two words slurred; sounds
like:) think I said that; I don't know.

L: On Wednesday morning, did you go into Terri's apartment and she, for whatever reason and she confronted you and was there a struggle?

A: No sir, I hadn't even go in her apartment at all.

L: You're not responsible for Terri's death?

A: No sir.

C: And you've never been upstairs in her unit?

A: No sir.

C: So, if we tell you we find your prints up there, how will you explain that?

A: I don't know. My prints shouldn't be upstairs.

C: How 'bout any hair or fiber off of clothing?

A: No sir. I hadn't been upstairs.

C: Never?

A: No sir.

L: Well, because there is the problems in as far as the vehicle; if it was there, if it wasn't there; Terri, she left the apartment unopened and that, would you be willing to take a polygraph if we set one up for you?

A: Sure would.

L: And if all the hair fibers and that, that were collected from the upstairs apartment are not all traced back to the victim, would you be willing to give a small couple of pieces of hairs, a hair sample as comparison?

A: I would. I would, yes sir.

L: Okay. The reason, like I said earlier,
(TAPE ENDS ....)

(TAPE BEGINS ON SECOND SIDE)

L: Okay, the tape had stopped, so I'm going to go back over two questions real quick, 'cause I'm not sure if they were recorded on the other side: uh, I'll just ask 'em again, okay?

A: Okay.

L: Because of the circumstances surrounding some of the facts as stated, mainly the fact that the problem, if or if not there was a white, newer BMW in that garage the fact that we believe or know Terri was at home at one o'clock and do not understand why she would have left at two or two-thirty and not secured her own house because of her valuables in it and items like this, would you be willing to take a polygraph?

A: Yes I would.

L: And again for the tape, at no time had you ever been on the second floor of Unit 66?

A: No sir.

L: Okay. We did collect hair fibers and some other items on the second floor of that unit. If some of these hair fibers are not traced back to the victim, would you be willing to give a sample of your hair for comparison?

A: Yes sir, I would.

C: Is there anything you want to tell us, to get off your chest?

A: No sir.

C: Nothing at all?

A: No (second word inaudible).

C: Reason that this has got you all shook up, that requires you to go to the hospital to get tranquilizers is just . . .

A: It was my wife's idea.

C: And the reason you've missed work was basically because you'd taken the tranquilizers and couldn't drive in?

A: Right. And my supervisor told me not to come in. (Few other words inaudible).

C: That's Mr. J.

A: Yes.

C: Do you normally, what type of attire do you normally come to work in?

A: This.

C: This?

A: Mm hmmm, (affirmative).

L: For the tape, that's soft shoes, blue jeans and a Dunn blue customer service, short-sleeve pullover polo type shirt.

A : Right.

C: Have you ever taken a polygraph?

A: No sir.

C: Do you know what they are?

A: No sir.

C: It's a machine that measures your heart, pulse rate, beating. You're hooked up to it and they ask you key questions to see if you're being truthful or not truthful.

L: If we do set up a polygraph, one of the things we'll advise you well in advance is that you cannot be taking any medication for at least 48 hours prior to the test. No alcohol for at least 24 hours prior to the test.

A: (Inaudible)

L: You're not currently under any heart medication or you don't take Librium or Valium or something prescribed on a regular basis?

A: No sir.

L: Okay. Because they will ask you that in the beginning and it will register if you're trying to deceive . . .

A: Yeah.

L: The polygraph operator, 'cause that's key question they ask you. Okay?

A: (First words covered) in advance . . .

C: They will also advise you of your constitutional Rights, prior to administering that test..

A: 'Kay.

L: Okay, Don, I appreciate your coming over again. Like again I stated, we're talkin' to other people; the reason we have to recontact you is for the problems we've just discussed.

A: Yes, sir.

L: We can't figure out why Terri would have come home, found the house in that condition, found a strange car in her garage, not reported it, first of all to her mother.

A: Right.

L: And sure to the people, at least your office, because . . .

A: (Inaudible possible only one word).

L: she wasn't that type of person. I mean, she was security minded somewhat; she was very alert. She knew what was going on around and she always locked her items, you know, as best she could and that doesn't, something's wrong.

A: Yeah.

L: It doesn't fit there. I don't know what happened. Hopefully, we will some time. And again, you know, if something happened that night, if, were you seeing Terri or anything? Was there any relationship between the two?

A: No sir. I've never even seen the girl. I've never even met her.

L: Okay. And as far as you're concerned, the assistant apartment manager out there where you live then is probably just blowin' her part of the story. . .

A: Yeah.

L: . . . up to make it sound better?

A: Yeah. (Three words inaudible). Nora's that way.

L: Okay. She wasn't trying to lay you out. You don't, you know, you don't have to go back and have any. . . .

A: No.

L: Because she didn't know and we didn't say one thing to her. . . .

A: Yeah. Uh . . .

L: When we showed up, she goes: "Yeah, I heard about it."

A: Yeah.

C: "He told me what happened."

A: I've heard some . . .

L: So she wasn't surprised or nothing like that. Okay?

A: Yeah.

L: Okay. So you don't have any problem there with Nora anymore, right?

A: No.

C: And your wife's at home now? We could give her a call?

A: She should be back by two o'clock.

C: Back home?

A: Yeah.

L: Okay.

A: (Sentence too low).

L: Okay. I appreciate again your cooperation. I know it's inconvenient; at least we did it here at work so you can go right back to your, the bosses are being very considerate. They know we have to talk to other employees off sites to talk to them, too, so, you know, you're not the only individual that we're talking to.

A: All right.

L: All right? Thanks again, Don, for your cooperation.

TAPE ENDS

Chapter XI

URBAN POLICE DEPARTMENT

SUPPLEMENTARY REPORT

THE DATE IS JUNE 28, 1989. THE TIME IS 0820 HOURS IN THE A.M. THIS WILL BE AN INTERVIEW WITH MRS. CONNIE MAE ARNOLD AT HER RESIDENCE IN SAUGUS. PRESENT IN THE INTERVIEW IS MYSELF, DETECTIVE LANDER, MY PARTNER, DETECTIVE CONLEY AND MRS. ARNOLD.

Legend: "L" = DET. R. LANDER
    "C" = Det. J. CONLEY
    "A" = CONNIE MAE ARNOLD

L: When did you first become aware that a murder had taken place? When did Don first tell you about it?

A: He came home that night and told me that, you know, a horrible thing that happened at work.

L: That was from the thirty-first? On Wednesday?

A: (laughs) That's what I'm a little, I remembered the date.

L: Okay. What, well, do you remember it was a work day?

A: Yes. Uh huh (affirmative).

L: Okay. Do you recall what he told you?

A: Just the lady had been murdered and it was awful.

L: What did he tell you about it? I mean, what do you remember . . .

A: There was blood all over that him and his friend had gone upstairs and the guy that was working with him. And discovered the body.

L: Where did he say the body was at?

A: Upstairs in the bedroom.

L: What did he describe about upstairs besides "upstairs in the bedroom?"

A: He's, there's blood all over the walls and he thought maybe she had just injured herself or hit her head or something like that where he turned her over to see if he could, you know (laughs) resuscitate her or something like that. He, before, had found a girl that took a drug overdose and called the ParaMedics. You know, so, he was just thinking (laughs). Just trying to help her, I guess.

L: Did he describe what the victim looked like?

A: He just said that he threw up when he saw her. When he turned the body over; that it was grotesque. There was blood all over and that her neck was cut. There was blood all over; he just said it was terrible.

L: So he, did he say how she she died?

A: He just said, you know, that she was murdered. He didn't know, you know, what weapon was used or what. He just said it was a horrible, he was really shook up.

L: You could see in his demeanor that he was shook up that night?

A: Oh, yeah, See, Don never, he couldn't believe another human being could do that to somebody.

We didn't talk too much about it. It was just, he was really upset about it.

L: Okay. So he said he was, did he say he was working in this unit or he just went there?

A: Yeah , he was working downstairs.

L: Uh huh (affirmative). And then he went up and found the body?

A: He went up with Dan Black? I think that's his name?

L: Okay.

A: And then they found the body together.

L: Okay. Did he say who notified the authorities?

A: I think he said he called the "911" or whatever.

L: Oh, okay. You recall him saying that there was blood on the walls and that her throat had been cut?

A: Uh, I can't remember the details; all I know is he just said he turned her over and it looked like her throat had been cut and she looked awful. And he was just really upset about it. He's never seen anything like that before.

L: Did he say anything else about her physical condition?

A: That she was cut, you know, looked like she had been cut up. And he just didn't want to talk about it. It was horrible.

L: Did he say if she was wearing clothes or not?

A: Let's see. I think he said she was half dressed or? I can't recall the conversation.

L: Uh huh (affirmative). Did he know the victim's name?

A: No. huh uh (negative). He just said he had seen her before. You know, that she was really nice, like, he'll talk to a couple of people that live down there and he won't, lot of times they're new and he

won't know their names or anything; but he didn't know her that well. And he had just, you know, once or twice before, something like that.

L: But, that day kinda stands out in your memory 'cause you come home, he told you about this tragedy. Right?

A: Yeah.

L: Okay. Going back to the night before, you can recall when he got home and what took place here with your family that night before?

A: I think when he got home, oh jeez, I don't know about the time. I think we were, we met at the pizza parlor, we were having pizza that night. My two sons. Up at Dante's Pizza.

L: Okay. And then after you had pizza, what went on the rest of the night?

A: Well, he came home. Usually takes a shower and we go for a walk and then usually it's about nine-thirty or ten or something like that. He has to go to bed pretty early 'cause he has to get up at three. You know. So I usually walk (laughs - covers rest of conversation) or he's sound asleep.

C: He usually leaves the house every morning real early?

A: Well, between three-thirty and anywhere from four-thirty if he oversleeps. He attacks the alarm clock when (laughs) he gets up. I have to put it across the room.

L: To the best of your recall on the morning that he left for work, that would have been a normal time for him?

A: Yeah.

L: And that would have been three-thirty or four o'clock?

A: Yeah.

L: 'Bout that (talking to Det. Conley, very low, inaudible). Since this has happened and it's been some time now, has he said anything more about it?
A: No. He's just, you know, hopes they catch whoever did it. He just thinks it's awful. (One word covered)
L: We became aware that he's missed several days at work. Is there any . . .
A: (Laughs). Um, he had all of his tools stolen. In the back of his truck. This is a bad area. And . . .
L: When did they steal his tools?
A: They broke into his truck. And they took twelve hundred dollars worth of tools; the power tools and stuff.
L: When was that?
A: Uh, let's see. Last Tuesday. I can't remember it. He had called the, yeah, and reported it and then had to go down to the insurance company, then we went to Sears to see if we could get the prices on it, each item. (Two words slurred; unknown if from this subject). You know, bought 'em over a period of three years.
L: Sure.
A: And then one night, he was chasing away a carload of, I don't know, they were in their twenties and fell in a hole and he sprained his ankle and this is like at two o'clock in the morning, he has to get up at three, three thirty which he, and he was just watching, he heard some noise . . .
L: Mm hmmm.
A: . . . and usually the dog wakes us up if he hears anything, so we both run out there and I went back in the house and he stayed out there and got the license number of the car and then he (laughs) followed them on foot, I don't know why. I think he's very clearly when something like that's happening.

L: A couple weeks ago, did he have a problem with his alarm? On his truck?

A: Um. Oh yeah. He's (laughs) killed about two of 'em.

L: Did he ever tell you that he's one of the individuals because, you know, he works in the unit there where the victim was found; that we asked him to take a polygraph?

A: Oh yeah. Uh huh (affirmative), he told me that.

L: Did he say anything last night to you about the polygraph?

A: No, huh uh (negative).

L: What did he tell you about us asking him to take a polygraph?

A: He just said, you know, that you guys could do whatever you wanted with him, 'cause he didn't care.

L: Okay. Well, the first time we asked him to take a polygraph, apparently just so happened that the day he was supposed to do it, he was late to work.

A: That was . . .

L: Four, five hours.

A: . . . one of the times when I think he (laughs) killed his alarm clock.

L: Yeah. Okay, well next time we asked him to take the polygraph, he said he didn't come to work 'cause he said his car got broken into.

A: Yeah.

L: So that was last week?

A: Yeah.

L: Well, then we asked him yesterday, we had another time and he was at work and yesterday he refused to take the polygraph.

A: Oh yeah?

L: Is there any reason why he would do that?

A: Not that I know. He's real upset over his tools. I know that. And he did some side work for somebody and had the check bounced (laughs).

L: Yeah.

A: Things have been going . . .

L: Well, we don't care about the bounced checks or anything else. The only thing we're concerned about is a homicide. That's all.

A: Okay. Well, that's all . . .

L: I don't know why, kinda get the feeling that he's avoiding taking a polygraph.

C: Is there anything that you can think of that would help us out in this matter? Why would he be so hesitant to take a polygraph?

A: He never mentioned it. Mean, I'll bring it up today, to have lunch with him.

C: Are you?

A: And my son starts work there too. Cleans windows and stuff.

C: How 'bout any type of marital problems that you and Don have had in the past?

A: No, nothing.

C: We had some information that came from a rumor at work that you guys were separated for a while over a problem that you took some money out of a bank account, something (inaudible).

A: Um, they put his check in Home Savings, they put his payroll check, we had a big argument about it; he had to go down and find out about it, but they put his whole paycheck ('phone rings) . . . guy's account.

TAPE STOPS . . . . . TAPE BEGINS

C: Goin' again? Does goin'. Company put Don's check in the wrong account?

A: In Japanese guy's account and I thought he just (laughs) better not put anything . . .

C: Oh.

A: . . . and I was in the wrong because I, you know: "What did you do with; how could you lose your check?" and so I went down there and got it straightened out.

C: That's caused you to argue with Don?

A: Yeah. He was really (laughs) upset, he didn't do anything that . . .

C: Do you know anything about Don's background in the past, where he comes from or anything?

A: From Amarillo, Texas. He was in orphanage since he was like two and with his two other brothers. I think that, well, his father was an alcoholic and his father had ('phone rings) shot his mother.

TAPE STOPS AND BEGINS:

C: You mentioned one thing: "Don kills the alarm"? This is . . .

A: Well, he hits (laughs) just hit it and threw it across the room when he woke up.

C: Do you know if he has a problem with the alarm on his truck working or . . .

A: Oh yeah. We had to take it in to Magic Ford to get it fixed. A little, it's like a anti-theft thing and a little thing. He hit it with his knee and it popped in half and it was kinda hard to start it so, strange (laughs).

C: You don't recall when that was? In the last three weeks?

A: Uh, he hasn't had it that long, so, I don't know about time. About three weeks ago? I don't know. But we took it back last week and 'em put, had it put on the other side so if you needed it, I had to drive down with him just in case be longer than we thought.

L: What we're doing, like I explained earlier is that, you know, we're talking to a lot of people and then the people that are closer, just so that we can eliminate them and we're asking them to take polygraphs, so, I don't know if he has a problem; he said he didn't but then every time we bring it up, he appears that he is avoiding taking one and if you talk to him, can you just assure him that we're not going to ask him about any other crime or any other, you know, "Had you ever committed a theft in your life?", "Have you ever," you know . . .

A: Oh.

L: . . . We don't care about anything like that. So, if that's the problem that he has, you know, thinking well maybe something other than this might surface, maybe he shoplifted some time or that's bothering him . . .

A: Uh huh (affirmative).

L: . . . You know, we're not going to ask those type questions. We don't care about 'em. We just need to satisfy in our mind that' each person has absolutely no guilty knowledge . . .

A: Oh.

L: . . . Of this crime so we can eliminate them so we can go on with our investigation.

A: Okay.

L: Understand?

A: (Covered).

L: Otherwise, we're at a standstill. And we can't, at this time, we can't make or we can't eliminate him. So,

A: Oh, okay.

C: And from our perspective, Don is definitely worried about this polygraph.

A: Oh, okay. I'll assure him it's okay.

L: The only thing he said now, did he ever say what the victim was killed with?

A: No. Huh uh (negative).

L: We talked to one girl over here and she said apparently that she related, you and Don related to her one of the assistant managers? That the girl was dead and like she was mutilated? Or . . .

A: Yeah, he just said it was, you know, feet's cut up or, mu, you know, it was just horrible. So, I don't know. I don't remember anything other than him saying something about there's this blood all over (few words slurred). I remember.

C: And he told you he threw up?

A: Yeah. as (slurred)

C: You could see that he was very upset.

A: (Laughs) I mean, he was just, he would never say anything like that; he would just shut up or, you know. The whole evening and how do you pacify somebody like that? You know, I could imagine being a police officer and . . .

C: Did you take him to the hospital?

A: I took him to urgent care to ...

C: For tranquilizers?

A: Yeah.

C: Was that the same night?

A: Yeah.

C: That he came home?

A: Uh, I think it was the same night. I can look in the urgent care, the date on the slip.

L: Prior to this incident, Don's attendance at work has been pretty good.

A: Right.

L: He's barely missed work?

A: Um, yeah. He's been pretty good. Unless his

alarm (laughs), he's had a couple times that he's been like three hours late or two hours late.

L: Does Don have any problems? Any drinking problems?

A: No. He doesn't drink.

L: Not last night, but the night before, was he home with you?

A: See if maybe,

L: Yeah, night before last?

A: Yeah, he's been home.

L: Okay. And he was home that evening?

A: Yes.

L: Okay. Was he drinking with you all night, that night?

A: No. He had, once in a while his friend, Chuck, comes over, he goes over there and they have like one beer apiece; they don't drink very much. That's all they drink.

L: This was Monday night?

A: Um . . .

L: That's two nights ago.

A: Put the calendar, where it was (laughs)

L: Not last night, but the night before.

A: Let's see, I was with, I was volunteering at the hospital, I came home. Yeah, he was home. Then he went over to Penny's and Chuck's. I left work a little early. Well, I volunteer at the hospital.

C: Did you see him consume any alcohol in your presence that night? Monday night?

A: Well, he usually opens a beer and he'll have a, two sips and he doesn't finish it. I usually have to empty everything out. He doesn't really drink.

C: He went to bed normal time Monday night? With you?

A: Yeah, about eight-thirty. Nine. Something like that.

C: Have you noticed any change in Don since the discovery of the homicide victim?

A: Um, not, well, he doesn't want to really talk about it. He, you know, he just thinks it was horrible. I mean, it was just; he'd never say anything like that before.

L: Has he said anytime to you about why he thinks she was killed?

A: He hasn't, no, he just said that she, he had met her one time and didn't remember her name but she seemed like she was really nice.

L: Did he ever mention to you if she was sexually assaulted or not?

A: No, huh uh (negative).

C: There was basically blood all over and she . . .

A: Yeah.

C: What if I told you Don didn't find her?

A: (Laughs) I don't know. I'm just telling you what he . . .

C: What he told you?

A: Yeah.

C: Well, Don was not involved in the finding of her.

A: Oh, I didn't know that.

L: We're just wondering: why would he be so upset in this if, in fact, according to his story that he told us, he never seen her. He never saw her that day.

A: I don't think he saw her that day, 'cause he was working downstairs.

L: He told us he never saw her, he never discovered the body, he was never up there and why would he be so upset that he would need medication? If

he's saying that he's never been upstairs and he didn't discover the body?

A: I don't know.

L: We know for a fact that he didn't discover the body.

C: His partner did. But he wasn't even inside the unit. Never saw the body or nothing . . .

A: No, he didn't. I don't know why he would say that.

C: Is he the type of person that strives for some type of sympathy? From maybe his partner or his wife, tell this thing, to say "I just wanted you to feel sorry for me"? Or do you know?

A: I don't know. He's, I mean, I've never doubted him before, I mean, except for that bank thing.

L: You've been married for a year?

A: Yes.

L: And I understand you two lived together for a few, couple years before that?

A: Yes.

L: Okay. During that three or four years, whatever it is that you've known Don, is this the first time that you've ever heard of him coming in, seeing or being around a tragedy of this nature?

A: Yes. Uh huh (affirmative).

L: Is there anything in Don's personal makeup that, like my partner Jim was asking you here? That Don would make up stories?

A: I don't think so. I mean, he's never done it before.

C: You said something about his past, he came from a broken family or something? His father was shot or something?

A: No, his father was drunk and shot his mother.

L: Well, okay.

A: I don't understand.

L: We just have some questions. Obviously, you can understand we just need to clear up some items and if you can talk to Don and if you can impress upon him that we would appreciate it if he would take a polygraph. He does not have to take one. This is only on his own accord and we've already told him this. If you can assure him that we're only interested in this crime and no other crime, that's the reason that we want the polygraph. So, if he has no involvement in it, we would really appreciate it if he would take the polygraph so we could eliminate him.

A: Okay. Well, he isn't into trouble that I know of.

C: I just want to ask you about your financial situation. Are you guys pretty well . . .

A: Well, it's okay for now (laughs), I mean. It's about guy's check bounced on us and made us behind on our rent; we never had that before. So, I have to go down there and talk to the bank and see (inaudible).

(Low conversation between Lander and Conley - inaudible).

L: Why don't you go check?

TAPE ENDS

Chapter XII

SUPPLEMENTARY REPORT

This will be a taped interview at the Urban Police Department. The date and time is 8-22-89 and the time is 11:50 hours in the a.m. This will be in regards to investigation. Present in the room is myself, Detective Lander and Mr.Dan Black.

DETECTIVE LANDER = L
DAN BLACK   = B

L: Mr. Black, just for the record, will you state your date of birth?

B: 1-13-53,

L: Okay, Mr. Black, is it true that you came here on your own accord, you were not summoned, you were not subpoenaed and you came here to aid us in the investigation of a homicide?

B: Correct.

L: And you also know that you're not being detained, that if any time you want to get up and leave, you're free to do so?

B: Correct.

L: Mr. Black, you were previously interviewed by some of my assisting officers, Dets. Hunterand Campbell. This would have been following the

discovery of Terri's body. Do you remember that interview?

B: Yes.

L: So we don't have to go in complete repetition and go over everything that was in that interview. Now that some time has passed, do you still recall that morning when Terri was found?

B: Yeah.

L: Is it still pretty vivid in your memory?

B: I mean, to be honest, I can recall what day it was but I can recall basically the events, I mean that's . . .

L. According to my record it was May 31st. It was a Wednesday morning. Does that sound familiar?

B: Yes. Wednesday or Tuesday, yeah.

L: Okay. And on that day do you recall that Terri had purchased and was moving into unit number 66?

B: I go by lot numbers and I don't recall.

L: Okay.

B: Yeah.

L: Okay. If I refer to Terri Horgan, do you know who I'm referring to?

B: Yes.

L: Okay. As much as you can remember, why don't you go back and tell me first of all let's start off on the night, or the afternoon of Tuesday, the 30th. That would have been the day before Terri was found. Do you recall if you worked the day before?

B: I worked the day before because I think the Monday was a holiday and I was backpacking and I had a message on the machine when I got back stating that she wasn't going to be around on Tuesday but would be around on Wednesday to have some work done in her unit.

L: Okay.

B: So that's why I went over on Wednesday.

L: Do you have any recall of when you left work on Tuesday, the 30th?

B: I usually leave somewhere in the vicinity of three thirty because that's when we clock out.

L: Do you recall if you went or had any contact with Miss Terri Horgan on Tuesday the 30th?

B: None whatsoever.

L: You didn't go by her unit or speak to her?

B: I basically had no contact with her after my walkthrough. The previous, it would have been almost a week and a half.

L: By previous, you mean previous to the 30th?

B: Yes. I had no, other than the message that was on the machine, I had no communications, I hadn't even talked to her. I attempted to get hold of her that morning - that morning by phone to inform her that I had come over to do the work that she had requested.

L: Okay. You did the walk-through with Terri . . .

B: Correct.

L: . . . a week or ten days prior to the 30th.

B: The 30th, yes.

L: In between the walk-through and the morning of the day that Terri's body was discovered on the 31st, did you have any contact with Terri personally?

B: No.

L: Any contact with her verbally over the phone?

B: No. She said that she was going to be out of town due on a golf tournament or something so I really had no contact with her. I did meet her mother during that week cause her mother was helping her move things in, but that was the only contact that I had.

L: Looking back at it now, were you either told

by Terri's mother or any other employee or Terri herself of when she intended to move into the unit?

B: No.

L: Had you been asked to demaster unit 66 by either Terri or her mother, prior to that date?

B: She had left that message on the phone or she had left that on my answering machine to have her locks demastered.

L: Do you recall which message or when you got that message?

B: Yes. I got the message the day that I came in. I believe that was on Tuesday.

L: Okay.

B: And usually we like to demaster it with the homeowners there so that they see us doing it and due to the fact that she wasn't going to be around I waited till Wednesday to do that.

L: Okay. Did she leave something on your answering phone telling you she wouldn't be around or . . .

B: Yes.

L: Okay.

B: She would not be around most of the day.

L: Okay. Let's go to the evening now of the 30th, that's Tuesday after you got off work. Do you recall what you did that night or where you went?

B: To be honest I don't. Usually I just go home and I'm home usually by myself, just I either have dinner with friends or whatever, but that night I don't recall doing, I don't think I did anything that night.

L: Is your roommate Sonny Higgins is he usually home in the evening hours?

B: No. He comes in and out very frequent. He has several different jobs that he holds, so he's in and out.

L: At the time, that would have been Tuesday, May 30th, at the time were you dating anybody regularly?

B: No.

L: You can't recall what you did that night but then what would be your normal hours for getting up and coming to work on the 31st?

B: I usually go to bed sometime between ten and eleven. I get up somehwere in the vicinity of five o'clock. Leave the house somewhere between five-thirty and quarter to six. Because of the commute I don't like fighting the traffic both directions so I get in early. Some mornings I'll sleep once I get here until seven o'clock or some mornings I'll have like a quiet time with my bible, dependig on, I don't know, it depends on how I feel when I get to work.

L: Do you remember what time you got to work on the 31st, that particular day?

B: I would say approximately I got here six-fifteen, sixthirty probably. I mean that's the average that I pull in.

L: Okay. And when you come to work on a normal basis, where do you go first?

B: I go straight to my trailer.

L: Okay. And other employees that work with you, do they utilize the same trailer?

B: Correct.

L: Now on that morning do you remember if there was any other employees or other co-workers when they arrived at work?

B: Usually everybody else comes in seven to seven-thirty. Okay, since my commute is the furthest I get here the earliest. I'm usually here before everybody else gets in.

L: On that particular morning do you remember

if Donald Lee (Don) Arnold when he got to work that day?

B: I don't know. If there is anybody here before I am, he would be here. Because he lives out in Saugus and he has the furthest commute and a lot of times he's sleeping in his vehicle out in front.

L: Do you have any specific recall if you saw his car or when he would have been there that morning?

B: I don't have recall on that, I'm sorry. It's . . .

L: That's okay. So after you got to work then, working day started, when did you first go to Terri Horgan's unit?

B: I called a little before eight o'clock in the morning. I make my phone calls in the morning. I tried calling, I got no answer. I don't recall if she has an answering machine or not. If she did, I would have left a message, I'm coming over to do the work. I got over to her place a little after eight. The work that needed to be done had to do with demastering the lock and painting around her master bathroom window. There was a yellow stain of sorts in there and when I was working in there the gas man, the gas meter man came by and needed to get up in the attic and so, since I was working in the house I just let him in. The appointment was made by Terri herself and that was about eight thirty, I guess, when he showed up.

L: The gas meter man?

B: Yeah.

L: Okay. So you got there a few minutes before that?

B: I got there a little after eight and I started doing the work on the window.

L: When you got to the location, how did you make entry?

B: With a key, with a master key.

L: And through the front door?

B: Correct.

L: Okay. Thinking back, do you remember if both locks were locked, one lock was locked or the door was unlocked?

B: The bottom lock was locked for sure because you can't get in without going through that, that was locked. The deabolt, the way the key turns, you can't tell. Because of, you know, the tumblers and the whatnot so I don't really know if the deadbolt was locked or not. But I do know for a fact that the bottom lock was locked.

L: Okay. And at that particular time you hadn't had the opportunity yet to demaster it.

B: I hadn't before I had gone into the house. I demastered them at that point in time, when I went into the house. I just took the . . . and used the demaster key.

L: So that's one of the first jobs you completed then, was demastering the front door?

B: I demastered the f ront door as I went into the house, yes.

L: Okay. As you went into the door, did you notice anything right by the inside of the door?

B: There was a bent screen just to the right as you go into the house.

L: Okay, did you pick it up or handle it or do you remember?

B: I don't believe I touched it.

L: Okay. While you were working in the house that day did you find out or observe where that screen would have come from?

B: Later on in the day I did. It was the family room. The bonus room right off the kitchen.

L: And that window overlooks the garage doors. . . .

B: Correct.

L: . . . down into the . . .

B: Driveway.

L: . . . driveway?

B: Um hmm (affirmative).

L: Okay. Did have any chance to go out the sliding glass doors?

B: No, I did not go out there. Didn't even go into the living room. I know that for a fact.

L: Okay. As you were doing your work the gas man came, correct?

B: Correct.

L: Do you, by any chance, know that gas man by name?

B: No.

L: Was he in uniform?

B: Yes.

L: And he was with what company?

B: Southern California Gas.

L: Okay.

B: And I believe he was black.

L: Okay, and he needed to get into the upstairs attic?

B: Attic. Correct, which is in the master bedroom closet.

L: When he came up and knocked on the door or whatever, were you inside working?

B: I was in the bathroom and I didn't actually hear him knock. I saw him walking away and I kind of stuck my head out the window because I had removed the screens to do the work and I asked, "Can I help you," and he said he had an appointment to get in and do some work.

L: And that's the bathroom in the upstairs master bathroom?

B: Correct.

L: Okay. So you went downstairs?

B: And let him in.

L: Okay, so the door was relocked?

B: I don't know if it was relocked or not. I just opened the door and let him in.

L: Okay.

B: If I'm in the house I usually lock the bottom lock but I may not have at that point in time, I don't recall. But as soon as you reopen the door, the lock becomes undone anyway, so.

L: Okay. If you was to unlock the front door, walk in and close the door and then walk outI would that door automatically relock itself?

B: No.

L: Okay.

B: It has to be manually relocked.

L: Okay. But then on occasion, while you're inside working on a house you said sometimes you will throw the bottom lock.

B: Yeah, throw the bottom lock and sometimes even the deadbolt if I know that I have to get a lot of tools out of my truck I park in the garage and open up the garage door and I'd go in and out through the garage and the front door remains locked. That way I have to be concerned that anybody else is coming in and out of the unit.

L: Okay. On that morning did you have to open the garage door?

B: Yes, I did. We had to borrow a ladder 'cause the gas man didn't have a ladder. The air conditioning guys were working right across the alleyway and we

borrowed their ladder so that gas man could get up in the attic. So they went out through the garage.

L: So approximately how long was the gas man there, from eight-thirty?

B: I would say approximately half hour to forty-five minutes.

L: When he completed his work?

B: Yeah. He completed what he needed to do but it couldn't be done without the AC, the heating guys coming in doing their work, but his work was finished.

L: And did he leave the location?

B: He left.

L: Do you know if he left by the front door or did he go out by the garage?

B: I think he went out by the garage because he took the ladder back to the plumber, the heating guys.

L: Okay. When you went down and opened the garage door did you notice a vehicle in the garage?

B: There was a car there, a white something or other. I don't know what the make or anything was.

L: Was the car familiar to you?

B: No. I'm unfamiliar with the homeowner's vehicles unless I'm working a unit and they've been home. Most cars I wouldn't recognize.

L: Okay. So you demastered the lock. You let in the worker at about eight-thirty, the gas man, and you were painting upstairs in the master bathroom. What other work did you complete inside the unit?

B: Since I had the paint out I touched up some of the walls that had been scuffed. The baseboards, the flat paint that we use scuffs real easy and since I had the paint out I used that. I had the enamel out so I did go into the secondary bathroom, bathroom number two.

L: Upstairs?

B: Upstairs and I checked the bathroom window over the toilet area to see if that had any discolorations or anything on it also. It didn't. I had asked the heating guys to come over sometime. They were going to come over sometime that morning when they were finishing their other things so that they could get the heater working.

L: That's the people you referred to earlier, that you borrowed their ladder?

B: Correct.

L: Okay.

B: I did some restaining of the cabinets countertop, the linen cabinets up on the, upstairs and I did some paint touchup on the number two bedroom door that was closed.

L: That's the door that Terri was . . .

B: behind.

L: Behind. Okay, while you were looking in that area and checked the second bathroom to see if there was any staining, did you observe some of Terri's belongings?

B : Yeah. My first impression was, you know, this girl's going to be, you know, kind of a pig sty. There was clothes on the stairwell and it looked like makeup and a wallet and everything was kind of spread out over the countertop. To be honest I didn't think a whole lot of it because when people are moving in, you know, they're living out of suitcases and this and that, and so I didn't think much of it. You know, I just thought it was kind of careless way to be keeping things, you know, in a brand new house. But, according to everything else downstairs and everything was pretty clean so you know, I just figured, you know, this is the one room she's living

out of right now, the bathroom. Because the master bathroom, bedroom and bathroom had no curtains or anything and it just made sense to be using the number two bathroom if you were going to be changing and things like that.

L: Do you remember handling anything in the number two bathroom?

B: I may have lifted her license 'cause it was out and it was sitting there. I just, everything was spread out throughout and I may have looked at her license and put it down.

L: Would you have handled the vanity?

B: I'm trying to think if I moved things to look at the doors. I don't recall.

L: Okay. If the man got there at eight-thirty, stayed forty-five minutes. Okay, the gas man left nine-fifteen or maybe nine-thirty. When you continued, did you leave the unit or did you continue working in the unit until eventually Terri's mother arrived.

B: I was in and out of the unit. I had gone, got supplies and had come back to do different things. Tried to stay close there because the Safeway Plumbing and Heating guys were going to coming over to work in the unit. So I was in and out of the unit most of the morning. I was in her unit when her mother showed up, yes.

L: Prior to her mother showing up, and it's covered on the first tape, but do you recall calling out if anybody was in the unit?

B: When I go into the house, I always ring the doorbell and knock. I mean that's just a habit that I do. When I open the door I always yell "customer service." Sometimes people are upstairs, they don't hear or they've got radios on or whatever. Or you hear water running. As I went upstairs I yelled out,

"customer service" again, just in case, you know, but I didn't hear anything. I got no response.

L: Her mother arrived about eleven-thirty, eleven fortyfive. Sometime around in there.

B: Ahh . . .

L: Was it earlier?

B: It was around eleven because the paramedics showed up I think around eleven-thirty. It happened, it was before noon that they were all there, I mean. After the mother showed up, I think, somewhere around in the vicinity of eleven, eleven-fifteen, somewhere in that area and asked for her daughter.

L: And you were where when she showed up?

B: I think I had just came downstairs and I met her in the dining room area, okay, I was just coming down the stairs.

L: And then?

B: She asked for her daughter. I said well, I haven't seen her. I mean, she said she was going to be here, but I haven't seen her and she asked if that was her car in the garage and I said well, I don't know. It's not mine. I said there is a closed door upstairs. And I said, you know if she's a sound sleeper, I said we've had a couple of guys in the attic and I've been working here most of the morning. I followed, then she went upstairs and so I followed her. She opened the door and called out Terri, and went oh. So I thought I'd leave. I went downstairs and I went out the front door thinking well, if she's asleep she's going to want to get dressed, whatever. Then I came back a few minutes later and the mother was on the phone.

L: She was on the phone talking to who?

B: Well, I didn't know at the time. She was gasping for air and I went over and I sat her on the sofa and I picked up the phone and I said, "This is

Dan Black, Customer Service, can I help you?" and the voice just said "are the paramedics required?" and I said "I don't know." I ran upstairs real quick and opened the door 'cause it was somewhat closed and I opened the door and looked down and here she laying on the floor kind of like, you know, I mean, I pulled this blanket up and I could tell that one arm was here and this hand was like that and she was basically on her stomach, her feet were up. Her feet were yellow, discolored.

L: And then you come downstairs and whatever tell them?

B: Get on the phone and said, "Yeah, they're required immediately." I then got on the radio and called my supervisor, Brad Boles, He said well, I'm kind of doing a thing with the environment and I said that doesn't matter. Come over now. Well, talk to me. Tell me what. I said no, please come over and that's when he and Dan Darnell came over. And then we went back up and Dan tried her pulse and I put my hand here on her neck and basically the paramedics showed up a couple of minutes after that and then it was just, they took over and I was just kind of out of the picture.

L: Do you recall if the man from the heating company, Safeway, did he go up and also see Terri?

B: I think he did because I panicked. I mean I just, and I think he went upstairs also and saw her.

L: Going into Terri's death, since May 31st, have you heard any rumors or any comments from any other worker or anybody that seems unusual concerning her death?

B: It's, well afterwards the whole thing was, I ended up taking time off. After giving the story I was given both Thursday and Friday off. I had tried to

come into work on Monday and I really couldn't deal with it and they sent me to the emergency psychiatric, you know, for counseling type thing and the doctor told me just to take a week off and he says, you know, you've been through a traumatic deal. Just, it's going to take some time. And I was given a lot of, to be honest I felt work was not very supportive of me whatsoever. Dealing with . . . I was the only one that had, basically dealt with her on both sides, when she was alive and when she was dead. Sales only dealt with her when she was alive and my boss, Brad, only dealt with her when she was a body there, I mean , it wasn't really a person. I mean, he didn't know her. I didn't even really know her but, I just, I had done the walk through and you know, and personal contact and it was the first time I had dealt with anything like that other than suicides that I had when I was growing up in high school and my grandparents died, and that type of thing. I had never dealt with nothing like this before.

L: Do you know how Terri was killed?

B: Not really. I've asked some questions and nobody's really been giving me any answers. I asked if she was sexually abused or strangled or whatever and I was told, you know, that we're not at liberty to say that.

L: Have you read anything in the newspapers?

B: I have not read but I have heard stories, you know, that she paid, well, I knew that she had paid cash for the unit and this and that but nothing really, I have, personally haven't read anything, no.

L: You said you heard she was strangled or what?

B: I don't know if I heard she was strangled or if she was beaten or what. You know, just that it was violent.

L: Do you remember who would have told you this?

B: It may have been listenig to the paramedics while they were up, you know, because they said that she was dead. It may have been something they had said. I don't know.

L: Do you know if anything was taken that belonged to Terri

B: No, I have no idea.

L: Looking back or trying to remember now, when you went into that bathroom and you saw her purse because there was paramedics and people in there afterwards, do you remember if you were able to see any currency in plain view?

B: I didn't see any, I saw credit cards. But I don't remember seeing any cash. No.

L: Jewelry?

B: I don't remember if there was any jewelry out at all. I'm trying to think if she had any jewelry on when I did the walk through and I don't recall anything. There wasn't anything spectacular or that stood out. You know, a lot of times women will have rings on, or earring or something that will, you know, just flash, but I don't recall anything.

L: Being an overseer for the properties and kind of knowing what's going on around here, to your nowledge had there been any break-ins or reported thefts in and around that complex prior to this?

B: The only one that I really know about that happened in phase one. Somebody complained about a stereo being taken or something being taken out of his garage. But we reversed the locks so one lock will allow you in from the garage but you can't get all the way in from the house either so one lock works one way, the other lock works the others so

they're working against each other. And that way people can store things in their garages without having access, you know, if workers are still doing work in the units, that's the only one that I recall. I know when we first started building phase two they had some appliances that were attempted to be stolen and that was . . .
L: Phase two is which complex?
B: Paradise West.
L: Paradise West.
B: I mean I'm talking . . .
L: Strictly about Paradise West?
B: Strictly about Paradise West. We have three phases. Terri lives in phase three. That stereo, whatever it was, was in phase one and I didn't hear anything. And we started building phase two which is around in front of the sales office. We had like, they tried to break in and steal some of the appliances out of the units and then nothing other than that. I mean, I've heard that they've had some problems over at Porto Bello but nothing in Paradise West.
L: Thinking back, can you think of any reason why somebody would have killed Terri?
B: I have no idea. She seemed like a nice young gal. She was just, you know, it appeared to me that things were going great for this lady. That you know, here she pays cash for this thing and she's starting a pro career in golf, you know and she was just really, you know, that's where she was headed. She was very positive, at least, in dealing with her it seemed like, you know, she, you know, had what it took to get where she was going.
L: Do you now recall anybody maybe voiced an opinion of jealousy or anything because of her young age that she was able to purchase an expensive home like that?

B: No.

L: No other workers or nobody ever heard anything?

B: Most of the workers don't really know that she pays cash for it. I, because I'm (Side one of tape ends, side two begins) dealing with the home owners I like to get a little insight on, you know, how they are through sales, you know, how picky they are so I can get, 'cause some of the home owners are very pleasant with sales and some of them are just real picky with sales and they have to be pampered all the way through. And I went in and asked about her they said, no, she paid cash for it. It was an inheritance or something like that.

L: Going back now let's try to visualize Terri's unit on the day you're in there working. Is there anything other than her purse being in a state of disarray in the bathroom, is there anything else about the unit that seemed unusual or caught your eye?

B: Well, in the linen cabinet area where I was working, I mean I didn't think it was too unusual but there was some clothes there. The way they were, just bundled up here. There was no furniture in the master bedroom. She had a new sofa down stairs. I think she had a tv, a stand, some type of stand for it, a refrigerator, you know, it looked like she was just in the process of trying to get the furniture moved in. It really, it just . . . no.

L: I think I asked you earlier, but refresh my memory. When you went in that morning to do the painting and that, when was the last time previous to that when you were in that unit?

B: I may have been in there on Monday with the electrician, no wait a minute.

L: The would have been the holiday.

B: That would have been the holiday. Okay, it would have been Tuesday then, because she said that there was a garage, she couldn't work her garage door without the light being on in the storage closet. The switch was off in the storage closet of the garage door and so I had the electrician in there.

L: That would be Tuesday though?

B: That would have been the day before.

L: That's the day she left the message on your phone.

B: That she wasn't going to be home.

L: Tuesday.

B: Correct.

L: Didn't you tell me earlier the reason you didn't go there Tuesday is because she wasn't home so you set everything up for Wednesday.

B: For Wednesday. But the electrician wasn't going to be back on Wednesday and he was there that day doing some work.

L: Okay, so this work that would have been done on Tuesday would have been in what section of the house?

B: In the garage.

L: So you would have, what, made entry through the front door?

B: Locked it up. Went through the garage, locked the garage door and went into the garage.

L: And would that have been Tuesday morning or Tuesday afternoon?

B: I believe it was Tuesday morning.

L: Tuesday morning. She was home twice on Tuesday. Do you recall seeing her at all that day?

B: No. I had heard that she was home getting things delivered in the afternoon. But I did not see her and that wasn't until after the fact.

L: I know she was home Tuesday from one o'clock in the afternoon until about two-thirty or two-forty. Did you have any contact over there?

B: No.

L: None at all?

B: None. I had no contact with her other than the walk through. Personal talking to her and the message on the machine because there were three things that she stated, the garage door not operating properly, the paint and the demaster of the locks. It was those three things that she needed done. And I didn't verbally discuss anything with her. I attempted on the Wednesday to get ahold of her. I was told she wasn't going to be there most of Tuesday by the message on the machine. But these are the items that needed to be taken care of.

L: Is there any particular reason why you were working there on that Wednesday that you didn't check out the extra bedroom up on the second floor where Terri was ultimately found?

B: There was really no need to.

L: Well you checked the extra bathroom and you checked a few other spots for any paint . . .

B: Well it was just in the process of my travel pattern. It was basically the bathroom because of the enamel paint, the cleaner that they use to do the windows stains, puts a yellow stain.

L: I'm familiar with that.

B: So that's why . . .

L: You did, though, paint a scuff mark on the outside of that door.

B: Correct.

L: Now, I'm just asking a question, okay? I know that this has bothered you personally. You've taken time off work and it's an emotional situation to be

involved in and to be there when Terri was found. I'm just wondering is, in that time when you were working, did you by any chance open that door and see Terri in there sleeping and then close the door not to disturb her? And you don't want to say anything now because it's, it's not practical that a person in that small of a house is going to work there for three hours, paint the door to that bedroom and look for other items that need repair and not check that bedroom. And if you was to look in there and seen Terri and thought, well, she's sleeping, that doesn't mean that you've done anything wrong to Terri that you committed any crime.

B: No, I know that.

L: It might just clarify or make it more in tune with what a normal working process would have been. Did something like that happen that day, Dan?

B: Yeah, it did.

L: What time did you find her there?

B: It was, it was after the gas man left.

L: It would have been about nine-thirty?

B: It was after nine-thirty. It was when I was doing the paint touchup. 'Cause I did open the door and I was scared.

L: Could you tell at that time that Terri was dead?

B: No. I mean I just glanced in and I just closed the door real quickly and I was really surprised and I was going, man, she's a quiet sleeper 'cause we were up in the attic making a lot of noise.

L: At the time that you cracked the door and you know, you saw Terri laying there, did you get any odor from within the room?

B: No because it wasn't, I just basically cracked it and I saw this dark hair and sleeping, what I thought was sleeping. You know, I just closed the door real

quick. Not more than an inch or so was the door opened and I just, I was holding the paint in my hand so I did't get any odor until I went into the room and knelt down.

L: And was that after her . . .

B: That was after her mother had gone in and after Dan.

L: (Inaudible)

B: I was with him.

L: After you had opened the door and saw Terri laying there, you immediately closed the door or did you say anything to her or did you just say excuse me or . . .

B: I just closed the door real quickly, oops, you know like you walk in on somebody changing or something. I was really surprised and I just closed the door and I did the paint touchup on the door.

L: When you found Terri appeared sleeping in there, was this after or before that you checked the second bathroom?

B: It would have been after.

L: So you'd already seen her purse.

B: Um hmm, (affirmative).

L: And was there any suspicion that, wow, I mean if she's gone she would have taken her purse?

B: No, because a lot of times I leave my house without stuff. Especially if I'm going over to a friend's house, so, no, I didn't think anything of that. I mean if I'm not driving or if I'm not going anywhere, a lot of times I'll just take cash, you know. I don't carry any credit cards anyway. But I leave my personal stuff at home. So, no, I didn't think anything of it.

L: Is everything you're telling me here the absolute truth? You're not leaving anything out, Dan?

B: No, it's not, I mean I've told you the absolute truth, everything.

L: Is there anything else besides you just peeked in the room and you saw Terri laying there?

B: No.

L: Did you have a confrontation with Terri?

B: No. I had no dealing with Terri verbally after the walkthrough. And she was going to be out of town for a week on a golf tournament.

L: After you had found Terri there and then her mother came later, is that the reason you said she might be in the upstairs bedroom?

B: Um hmm, (Affirmative).

L: Okay. And can you explain to me in your own words now you've had time to think about it, about for what reason didn't you want to let it be known that you had peeked in the room and saw Terri lying there?

B: I was scared.

L: You were scared because of what?

B: I just was scared. I didn't know, you know, I've never run across anything like this.

L: Were you scared because you thought somebody might blame you for Terri's death?

B: No. I could have no reason, I just, I don't know how to answer that one. I was just scared.

L: After you had gone up with Terri's mother later and you went up and, well, after Terri's mother, but you went in and you said you felt Terri's pulse?

B: Um hmm. (Affirmative).

L: Okay. At that time you observed an odor in the room.

B: Yes.

L: Obviously and what did that odor indicate to you?

B: I'd never smelled anything like it before.

L: I mean from watching tv or reading books,

whatever, what would you think? What would that tell you?

B: That she'd been there for a while. Just the discoloration of her feet. I had never seen, I mean her body looked like it had been bruised but when it started to turn yellow, there's lack of circulation.

L: And looking back now, is there any doubt in your mind that when you peeked through the door that Terri was already deceased?

B: I didn't know. But at that point in time I would say there would be no doubt. You know, I mean, just that time span there wasn't, you know.

L: After you'd gone through the door and you saw Terri in there for a second and you closed the door, at that time you had already demastered the lock.

B: Correct.

L: You had already had the gas man there.

B: Correct.

L: And you had already painted the master bedroom?

B: Um hmm (Affirmative).

L: And you had painted...

B: Bathroom.

L: Bathroom, excuse me. And you had painted or checked the second bathroom?

B: Correct. And I painted, I don't know if I had painted the door before or after I opened it.

L: And this would have been somewhere around, between nine-thirty and ten roughly?

B: Correct.

L: For what reason did you remain in the house between nine-thirty or ten and whenever it was that Terri's mother came at eleven? If all those chores had been completed, your job should have been done.

B: The gas man, the, my job was done, but the

heater guy was going to be coming in to get into the attic to turn the furnace on to get it so it would operate and he had gone in and been up in the attic and then was done (S/B down) below working on the condenser in the garage.

L: The gas man came first.

B: Correct.

L: He left at nine-thirty, nine-fifteen. B: Nine-fifteen, nine-thirty, correct.

L: Now your talking about the heater man, that's Safeway.

B: Safeway, correct.

L: Did the Safeway man come up and go into the attic?

B: He went in the attic also, yes.

L: That's Mr. Brown.

B: There were two of them working together.

L: A big fellow.

B: Yeah, well there was him and then there was a smaller guy and he was working, I know he was in the garage and I don't know if he had gone upstairs into the attic or not as of yet. I know I turned the blower or the air conditioing unit off for him when he was working in the garage.

L: This is the big fellow?

B: Um hmm (Affirmative).

L: I think his name is . . . he works around there all the time, maybe you know him?

B: I'm not that familiar with him. I think he works the production end of it and I'm more in dealing with their customer service people. But it was the first time that I had met him.

L: So you let somebody there to go back upstairs. Did he bring the ladder back up or I thought the ladder had been returned?

B: We returned the ladder to him. They were going to come back in when they got done with the unit across the way and come over and work on this unit.

L: I'm just trying to get the time sequence down. Now, the last man's gone. You've discovered Terri's in there, apparently sleeping. You've completed your work. And where did you go then? Where did you remain, where did you situate yourself in this house for an hour?

B: Well I wasn't in the house for the total time. I had done other work in other units. I know that I had gone into the neighbor's unit to check out some painting that needed to be done over there. My car stayed there because I was going to be going back in with these guys when they went up to do whatever needed to be done with the heating unit, why it wasn't firing. So they could get the heating and the air conditioning unit working. It had to be charged and the whole shot. Normally it's called the startup procedure.

L: When the gas man, not the gas man I guess, the man from Safeway Heating and Plumbing, did you take him upstairs to do some work?

B: I believe I showed him where the attic access was.

L: This is between ten . . .

B: I would say about ten-thirty.

L: At that time did you tell him or warn him or caution him that somebody was sleeping in that room?

B: I didn't say a word to him.

L: And while he was up there working did you remain there with him?

B: Yeah, when he was upstairs, I remained upstairs with him.

L: Then he left.

B: He was down in the garage, working, when Terri's mother showed up.

L: Okay. I know that you're a religious individual, correct?

B: Yes.

L: Do you feel that the person responsible for this should not only pay to somebody higher than our authority but also do you think the person should be punished for this crime?

B: I do, yeah. I mean, I feel when somebody does anything in violence it should be, punishment should be rectified, yeah. There are times when, you know, in self-defense and things like that. I don't agree with some of . . .

L: Do you think Terri's death could have been self-defense?

B: I don't know. I don't know Terri. I don't know if she, I have no idea. I don't know if she gets angry and gets violent with somebody and you know, somebody turns around and hits her. I don't know.

L: Do you think this could have been the circumstances around Terri's death though?

B: I don't know, I have no idea. I don't know. I asked questions when, you know, I was asked to have some pubic hairs and things like that, if she was sexually abused. I was told you know, we're not at liberty to say. I dont know. I mean I've never been involved in a homicide. I mean I don't know what . . .

L: If I was to tell you that Terri was strangled, do you know or have you any idea or did you have any inclination as to what was used to strangle her? If there was an instrument or an item or hands or?

B: I'd be honest, I didn't even see her face. They said there was some dry blood around her mouth and nose. I never saw that.

L: Who's they?

B: I believe Brad. I think he was in the room when they turned her body over. I wasn't in the room. I didn't even really see her face when I put my hand on her neck 'cause her head was facing away from me. So I have no idea.

L: When you were in the house earlier, Dan, did something happen between you and Terri?

B: No.

L: Was there a confrontation?

B: No.

L: Were you working and she came out and was-startled and started to make a big fuss or something?

B: No.

L: There was no problems at all between you and her, you know, no confrontations?

B: No confront.., I had no communications with her other than the message she left on the machine. I did the walk through is the only time that I actually talked to her and when I attempted to try and call.

L: Okay, why don't we take a break just for a second. Let me get my train of thought. I'm going to turn off the tape recording for a minute.

TAPE STOPS

TAPE STARTS.

L: Okay, I've started the tape again. We took a short break. Going over a couple of questions which I've asked. Do you think any of the other workers could have looked in and seen Terri or anything?

B: No.

L: You were up there the time that you were up there?

B: Yeah.

L: Is there any particular reason why you didn't warn the other guy that Terri was in that room?

B: I just didn't think there, he wasn't going to go in there and there wasn't no need for that.

L: What if Terri would have awakened and walked out? Wouldn't she have been startled to find workers in the house?

B: I would have apologized and, you know. It's happened before. I've been in units where people have been sleeping and have come out or they've been in the shower and we didn't even hear the water and they've come down in their robe-type thing and make apologies but they're usually very happy that the work is being accomplished for them.

L: And there was no confrontation on that day between you and Terri?

B: None whatsoever.

L: When you got there in the morning and you started work, Terri didn't come out and was startled or pissed off because somebody was in her house?

B: No.

L: Terri's mother informed me that Terri was of the opinion that the locks had already been demastered prior to that Wednesday and I have a note left by Terri where she was requesting some of the work and indicating that it should be done on a day other than Wednesday because she thought she had to be there to undo the lock.

B: No. She told me that she would be there on Wednesday according to the message that was left on the machine and it had not been demastered prior to that because when she was out of town one of the other guys was going to be doing some work in the unit for her.

L: When she was out of town, that was going to be after the 31st or before?

B: Before. It was after the walk through.

L: She was out of town and Mateo did some tile work.

B: Did some tile work, sealing the grout.

L: Okay, that was accomplished. After Mateo had finished that though, Terri and her mother were of the opinion that the unit had already been demastered.

B: It had not been demastered because I hadn't gone over and demastered it.

L: Okay. Terri had a scheduled golf appointment where she met with her golf pro every Wednesday morning at eight o'clock. So, and then she would remain there for several hours so how was Terri going to be there, or how would, if she said she was going to be there on Wednesday, when it's even in her calendar book? And it's on a note she left before, that I can show you the note, if that'll help you.

B: No, no. I just, I don't know. The gas man was scheduled for Wednesday morning.

L: Through you or through Terri?

B: Not through me, it was through her or through somebody that was going to be there and the message that I was told, that she would be there on Wednesday. There's no way that I can get that message back on the machine because it's recorded over and over.

L: You see the couple little conflicts that I have. One, that Terri, according to Terri's mother and notes that I found by Terri, was of the opinion that the unit had already been demastered. Two, is that the work according to the message left on your phone was to be done on Wednesday, however, she knew previously and had told her mother and had indicated on appointments that she was going to be tied up on Wednesday. She would not be home.

B: Well, her mother came over looking for her on Wednesday, knowing, I mean asking where her daughter was. I mean, the message I had that she was going to be there, the gas man coming, so I mean, I don't know what, I'm just . . .

L: Okay. I was just trying to put the pieces . . .

B: Yeah, I know. You're asking me questions that, I mean, I don't know what her schedule was. I had, this was the first work that I had done with her or in her unit for her. Normally I get to know the homeowners when they're going to be home and when they usually work and things like that after they've been there a month or two. And depending on the unit and how much work is required in the unit. I'm just going by what I was asked to do. And I did what I was asked to do.

L: Let me cover another point. Because if there's anything else that we're leaving out, even minor, it should be brought out now. Okay? We don't need to pull teeth on this case as we go along and say, well, yeah I did this and I should have told you but I didn't because I was afraid.

B: Yeah. I understand.

L: Okay.

B: The only thing that I have not told you before is that I knew that she was in the room. Other than that, everything else has been . . .

L: If something had been taken out of Terri's purse, again, that does not mean that the person that would have taken that item would have been the person that committed a homicide, by any chance did you take anything out of Terri's purse when you were in the bathroom and you saw Terri's belongings? If you did, tell me now.

B: The only thing I remember seeing is credit

cards and her license. I don't even know, I can't even recall where her purse was.

L: Did you take any currency out of Terri's purse?

B: No.

L: And you can say that honestly?

B: Yes.

L: Did you kill Terri?

B: No.

L: You can say that honestly?

B: I can say that honestly.

L: Do you know who killed Terri?

B: No.

L: And you can say that honestly?

B: Yes sir.

L: And you have nothing in your conscience that would make you feel any guilt?

B: No.

L: Okay. As our investigation goes and you're kind of seeing how we work these things, we have to close out these things. That's the reason I was asking you in my own mind it helps me verify that first of all, Dan, you're telling me the absolute truth so I can look at another area because I have to continue to work these cases as long as there's any remote chance of solving them. It's fair to Terri, it's fair to her family.

B: What I went through, the mother, if demastering the lock the week earlier could have prevented this, I wish I could have done that. The look in the mother's face when she asked me about demastering the locks I'm sorry, I have not broken up since . . .

L: That's okay. You Take your time.

B: I have told you the honest truth about everything right now.

L: Okay. Let me ask you one thing, I know that

you said that you had some ill feelings about it but would you take a polygraph if only those questions were brought up? And that's mainly, did you take anything from Terri's purse. Did you kill Terri or do you know who killed Terri.

B: I told you before that I failed a lie detector test telling the truth.

L: Was that in a civil matter or something?

B: That was a civil deal when I was working for, there was a theft at a gas station.

L: Okay so they brought in some company polygrapher?

B: They brought in the police. My dealings with the police on situations, they kept me on the phone one time, said I was a witness to a robbery. They came to my house and picked me up on warrants because I had, I think, nineteen warrants out and most of them were parking tickets and there were two moving violations back fifteen, eighteen years ago, The polygraph test that I took, I failed. Dealing with the police I get scared to shitless, excuse me.

L: That's okay, I can understand 'cause that's a very serious investigation that we're conducting here.

B: And seeing different, I saw a deal on television, "20-20" or "Sixty Minutes" or something on people being totally
SIDE TWO OF TAPE ONE ENDS

SIDE ONE OF TAPE TWO BEGINS.

L: The tape ran out. I'm not sure where it did but . . . As far as the polygraph, you know, I can't make you take one. You don't have to take one. I can't order you to take one. It can't be used against you criminally. All it is, is a tool for me to try to go on with my investigation. I'll try to work around it. Maybe, just

give it a little bit more thought and see if, you know, if you change maybe, I believe you've spoken, you haven't retained but you've spoken to a friend that's an attorney. if you get a chance you might speak to him again.

B: I'm supposed to call him this afternoon.

L: Let him know what we talked about. Let him know what I'm telling you that, you know, basically I'm trying to put one chapter behind me and go on in my case and perhaps he knows a polygraph operator that is not connected with the police. As long as the man is a qualified expert at, you know, has been working in the field, then it's still a tool I can go by. I'm not saying you have to use our man, you know what I mean. Just something to try to help me go along.

B: He made mention of that and I said "I'll be perfectly honest with you, I'm scared of it." You know, it doesn't really, and he goes, well, tell you. Just be honest with you and tell you. I'm supposed to call him today and I'll talk to him and I'll let him know what was discussed and everything else.

L: Well, let me go over, you know. As far as our conversation here, we've basically covered everything that we need to cover. I'll go over my case again. If I have any other questions, I'll just call you on your work number, I'll just say give me a call or something like that.

B: Okay.

L: For Terri's sake, you know, there might be some little thing that you can't recall now or I might say something that might say what, you know, I did see this or I do remember somebody saying something. And you know, I'm down to that point in the case. It's going to take some little piece here or there if I have any chance of solving this homicide.

B: Well, you've made me question, I mean, you talk about shows and whatnot and cop shows and this and that. And you've got your good guy and your bad type situations and things. And you mentioned you have these things that her schedule says this, this and this and I mean, I had this, this and this for me to do and other things were scheduled and I don't know what to tell you on those things. I mean you're making me think and I know what I was told and what I was doing.

L: Well what you're told and what you're doing is all I want you to tell me, that's all. I'm not here to put words in your mouth. I'm not here to confuse you.

B: I understand that and the only thing that I did not tell you the first time around was that I knew she was in the room. My attorney knows that 'cause I told him and he says well, just go talk to the man. You don't need to tell him that. It doesn't need to come up. But those two weeks I was in (inaudible), it was bugging me 'cause I wasn't honest and I don't like being honest . . .

L: Okay.

B: . . . and I apologize and the reason I came in today is because I know that I'm innocent and I needed to tell you that other fact. Okay, it was going to be told one way or another.

L: Is there anything else, Dan, that's going to come up?

B: No, I have nothing.

L: That for whatever reason . . .

B: No.

L: . . . fear, embarrassment, anything that you have told me?

B: No.

L: Okay. I'm just asking you.

B: I know. I don't, I cannot think of anything that, you know, you ask me specifically three questions. I can say without a shadow of a doubt, I have nothing, I have no contact with her. I didn't do it. I don't know who did. I didn't steal anything out of her unit, out of her purse, out of her unit, out of anything.

L: Do you know what Terri was killed with?

B: No, I don't. When I was in the room I saw some scuff marks on the walls. I was told that you guys were doing your deal, and you were getting everything squared away. I don't know if she was killed with an instrument, whether she was killed by bare hands. I don't know if she was sexually abused, I don't know. Part of me is curious, but part of me doean't want to know. I mean, that would just, I don't understand things like that. I don't understand, you know, there are people out there that do weird bizarre things but . . .

L: Okay. Let me go over my case. I don't want to hang you up anymore. You can go ahead and get back over to work. I'm going terminate the interview now. The time is 1300 hours. Is there anything else you want to say while I still have the tape on.

B: I have nothing, no. I've said everything.

L: Can you think of anything that you recall now that I haven't asked you about?

B: No.

L: Okay. I'm going to turn off the tape then.
TAPE STOPS.

Chapter XIII

COUNTY OF LOS ANGELES, STATE OF CALIFORNIA
PROBABLE CAUSE COMPLAINT IN SUPPORT OF FELONY ARREST WARRANT

On 31 May 89, your Affiant and fellow officers were detailed to 3200 Alder Street, Unit #66, in the City of Urban, County of Los Angeles regarding a possible homicide investigation. Upon arrival at the location, your Affiant observed the deceased, identified as Terri Horgan, a female, 26 years of age, to be lying in the northwest, upstairs bedroom of a two-story condominium. Upon viewing the victim's body, it appeared to your Affiant that the cause of death was possibly ligature strangulation. It further appeared that the victim, Horgan, had been battered in the head area prior to or during the time of her death.

Your Affiant learned that the victim had been found at approximately 11:30 hours on 31 May 89 by her mother, Mary Gandy. Your Affiant also learned that Mr. Dan Black (employed by the condominium builder) had arrived at the Unit #66 at 0800 hours on 31 May 89, where he utilized a master key to gain entry to complete work previously requested by the victim to be completed. Your Affiant spoke with Mr.

Dan Black who stated when he made entry into Unit #66 he observed a bent screen to be inside the front door. He noted that this screen belonged on the den window, east side, first floor of the unit. At this point in the investigation, point of entry into Unit #66 was unclear, due to the fact that Mr. Black and other workmen had been in the unit between the hours of 0800 and 1130, utilizing various doors as points of entry and exit. However, it was pointed out to your Affiant by Dan Black who supervised the work on 31 May 89, that the screen, as previously mentioned, was bent and at that location when he entered into the unit. Further, Dan Black could not explain how the screen got bent and recalled that the previous time he had been in Unit #66 the screen was intact, placed in the first floor, east window.

Your Affiant spoke with Mrs. Gandy (mother of victim Horgan) who stated she was in her daughter's condominium, Unit #66, on Tuesday, 30 May 89 and at that time, the screen previously mentioned was in the window frame on the first floor, east window and was not bent.

On 01 June 89, your Affiant attended the autopsy of victim Terri Horgan. The autopsy was performed by Dr. Smiley, Deputy Medical Examiner. Dr. Smiley determined that the cause of death was ligature strangulation.

On 02 June 89, your Affiant's fellow officer, Detective Conley, interviewed a subject who identified himself as Jody Williams, a negro male adult with a date of birth 27 June 65. Mr. Williams stated he resided in Los Angeles. Mr. Williams stated he was employed by All State Security Systems in Urban as a security guard for the condominium complex. Mr. Williams stated he was on duty during the night of 30

May 89 through the morning of 31 May 89 and indicated his work hours were 2300 to 0600 hours. Security Guard Williams stated his duty post was approximately 40 yards from Unit #66 and he further
stated that during the hours while he was on duty, he
observed no unusual activity within the complex.
Williams further stated he had only met the victim,
Terri Horgan on one occasion; that being on a Sunday morning previous to 31 May 89. Williams stated
he observed the victim to be going through a trash
container and consequently, he had a short conversation with her. Williams indicated to Det. Conley that
he had not personally ever been in Unit #66 (the
victim's) and further stated that during his shift, he
does not have keys to the condominium unit.

On 05 June 89, the victim's clothing and other
possible physical evidence, including vacuumed
debris from the northwest bedroom were transported
to the Los Angeles County Crime Lab, where it was
assigned to Senior Criminalist Turk.

On 29 June 89, your Affiant and fellow-officer,
Det. Conley, contacted Jody Williams at his security
post, located at 3200 Alder Street, City of Urban.
Subject Williams was asked if he would voluntarily
submit hair samples for comparison in the homicide
investigation regarding Terri Horgan. Williams subsequently consented and was provided with a form:
"Consent for Hair Sample," which he read and subsequently signed. Your Affiant and fellow officers, at
this time, did receive both hair and pubic samples
from Jody Williams and on the same date, these
samples were transported to the Los Angeles County
Crime Lab for comparison by Senior Criminalist Turk.

On 25 July 89, your affiant received a report from
the Sheriff's Crime Lab, dated 25 July 89. Included in

the supplemental report Criminalist Turk wrote the following results and conclusions:

"The two hairs found on the victim's shirt (GB-6A), were found to be dissimilar to the pubic hair standards from Jody Williams. Two of the four hairs found in the vacuum debris from the victim's bedroom (GB-BC), were found to be similar to the pubic hair standards from Mr. Williams. These two hairs could have originated from this person."

On 31 October 89, your Affiant was advised by Urban Police Department Identification Analyst Todd Philcox, that he had made a Cal I.D. "hit" on the Terri Horgan homicide. Your Affiant was advised by Philcox that a fingerprint from the window screen frame, found inside the victim's front door, was identified through Cal I.D. to a Jody Williams, SID number W1212121.

On 31 October 89, your Affiant and fellow-Officer Conley contacted Parole Agent Gina Prater at Los Angeles. Agent Prater advised your Affiant that she was the Parole Officer for Jody Williams and further, provided your Affiant with a photograph of subject Williams. Your Affiant, upon viewing the photograph, verified that her parolee, Jody Williams, was the same Jody Williams that your Affiant and fellow-officers had previously contacted at the condominium site. Your Affiant was advised by Agent Prater that Williams was currently residing in Los Angeles with his father. She also advised that Jody Williams' mother, Vonni Williams, resided in Los Angeles also. Your Affiant, in reviewing the parole package on subject Jody Williams, noted that he had several gang affiliations, the last one being with the Rolling Sixties Crips. Your Affiant and fellow-Officer Conley further noted that Jody Williams had a serious arrest record, including arrest for crimes in which he had inflicted great bodily injury on his victims.

31 October 89, your Affiant received a copy of
fingerprints from the Beverly Hills Police Department
on a previous booking of Jody Williams. These prints
were subsequently transported back to the Urban
Police Dept. where they were again analyzed by Identification Analyst Philcox and confirmed as being the
same person who had left the fingerprints on the
screen inside the victim's apartment. It appears to
your Affiant that suspect Jody Williams had gained
entry during the late evening or early morning hours
on 30 May through 31 May 89 into victim Terri
Horgan's condominium by unknown means. Once
inside, the suspect had confronted Terri Horgan,
where a brutal struggle ensued, resulting in her death
by ligature stangulation. Victim Horgan's purse had
been ransacked and it appears at this time, through
verification by the victim's mother, Mrs. Gandy, that
the only item taken was currency. It is further appar-
ent to your Affiant that the screen, as mentioned in
this Affidavit, was in place on 30 May 89 and found
on the morning by witness Dan Black to be bent and
removed from the window and had been placed next
to the front door. Suspect Williams stated to Detective Conley that he had met the victim on one occasion outside her residence and at no time had he
ever entered into Unit #66 prior to or after the time of
death of the victim.

That based on the foregoing, your Affiant believes that there exists probable cause to arrest Jody
Williams for the crime of 187 PC, Homicide.

WHEREFORE, your Affiant prays that a Warrant
of Arrest be issued for the arrest and seizure of the
person of Jody Williams.

DATE: 11-2-89.

RICK LANDER
Signature of Affiant
Police Officer
(Position of Affiant)

Sworn to before me and subscribed
in the presence at 1:45 PM,
on: 02 November 89

xxxxxxxxxxxxxx xxxxxxxx

(Signature)
Judge of the Municipal Court
of the Urban Judicial District

Chapter XIV

FELONY WARRANT OF ARREST UPON PROBABLE CAUSE

(SEE PEOPLE V. RAMEY, 16 Cal.3rd 263 and PEOPLE V. SESSLIN, 68 Cal. 2d 418, 425-427,n.6)

County of Los Angeles
State of California

THE PEOPLE OF THE STATE OF CALIFORNIA, TO ANY PEACE OFFICER IN THE COUNTY OF LOS ANGELES.

Complaint, on oath, having been made this date before me by Det. R. LANDER, of the Urban Police Department, I find that there is probable cause to believe that the crime of 187 PC, Homicide , was committed on or about 31 May 89 by JODY WILLIAMS (that is the person named or described below and in the attached complaint)

WHEREFORE, you are commanded forthwith to arrest JODY WILLIAMS and bring said person before any magistrate in the County of Los Angeles pursuant to Penal Code Sections 821, 825, 826, and 848. In lieu of bringing said person before a magistrate, you may release, prior to the time limitations of Penal

Code Section 825, said person from custody without bail or further appearance before a magistrate and then shall file with me no later than the next day on which the court is in session, a Declaration, under penalty of perjury, setting forth the fact that said person has been released without bail or further appearance before a magistrate.

Defendant is to be admitted to bail in the amount of $No Bail. This warrant may be executed at any time during the ten calendar days subsequent to its issuance (i.e.; until 12 Nov 89).

TIME ISSUED: 1:45 P.M.
XXXXXXXXXXXX XXXXXXXXXXX (Signature)
Judge of the Municipal Court

DATED: <u>02 Nov 89</u>   OF: <u>URBAN JUDICIAL DISTRICT</u>

AT: <u>URBAN, CALIFORNIA</u>

DESCRIPTION OF ARRESTEE

Sex: Male Race: Negro DOB: 27 June 65 Hgt: 5'7" Wt. 230

Hair: Blk Eyes: Brn DR #9807 VEH YR: --
RES ADDR: ----

INV. NAME(S): R. LANDER

Public Defender
INVESTIGATION REQUEST
by Trial Deputy Cory

CHARGE: PC 187, 459(res.), 664/261(2) Special Circumstances case (Murder in the commission of residential burglary, attempted rape.)

Testimony at the preliminary examination indicates as follows:

BACKGROUND:

This is a very complicated special circumstances case involving the strangulation murder of a white woman in her brand new condo in Urban. The homicide occurred in May, 1989. At the time of the homicide, the defendant, a rolling sixties crip on parole for ADW and robbery, was a security guard at a partially completed condo complex in the Urban area. He was on duty and stationed in the vicinity of the victim's condo where the victim was killed.

The defendant was arrested in October, 1989, when the Urban police got a California I.D. (i.e. print computer) "hit" on latent prints lifted from a bent screen found just inside the front door after the homicide. At first the police didn't believe the screen came from the point of entry because it was from a window 13 feet above the ground. The point of entry was initially believed to be a ,sliding glass door leading from the living room area to an outside patio. There was a slit in the sliding screen near the locking mechanism for the sliding glass door.

The victim was found dressed in casual clothes, strangled in an upstairs bedroom. The police

vacuumed the room for evidence. The criminalist testified at the preliminary hearing that three hairs found on the floor and two on her clothing were similar to the defendant's pubic hair. Before the criminalist, in a report, said that the two hairs on the victim's clothing was not similar to the defendant's pubic hair. "Similar" meant it could be the defendant's hair. In other words, the defendant could not be eliminated as the hair donor.

One of the most significant pieces of evidence was developed just before the preliminary: A partial distorted palm print was developed on the window sill where the bent screen probably came from. It was lifted using state-of-the-art techniques and photo-graphed under filtered laser light. The Urban print expert stated that it was a very hard print to read but that he was positive it was an inward pointing latent belonging to the defendant.

Defendant denied the homicide to Urban police in two long tape statements. He told them he didn't know how his prints got on the screen. He denied being in the victim's condo at any time.

The defendant has told me he probably had slept in the victim's condo before it was completed and that he had been in it on several occasions when workmen were there (one remembered occasion was when rugs were installed on a Saturday or Sunday). The defendant thinks he might have re-moved the screen on one occasion to see if he could see the nighttime supervision walking around the complex.

Urban police had three suspects they were in-vestigating during the first three months of the inves-tigation:

(1) Sammy Battles (security guard)

(2) Dan Black (first person in condo "after" death. Works for builder)

(3) Don Arnold (Builder employee)

When the print computer put out a "hit" on Williams in October, then he became the only suspect and the point of entry became the window thirteen feet above the grounds for obvious reasons.

The case is very complicated, possibly exceeding Maurice Hastings in complexity. It will require an exhaustive investigation. It will also require an investigator to sit down and read all the materials (police reports and PHT) to become familiar with the case.

The requests initially will not require any knowledge of the case. However, the investigation will have to quickly become familiar with the case because the defendant is desirous of getting a trial rapidly.

Realistically I will not be prepared to go to trial before Fall of 1990.

Chapter XV

Urban Police Department

SUPPLEMENTARY REPORT
02 April, 1990

Inv. Det. J. CONLEY

During an interview with defendant Jody Williams, defendant stated to me that he had been caught sleeping in a unit at Paradise West by his supervisor Billy Duncan.

I contacted Billy Duncan on 14 Nov 89 at approximately 0900 Hours at his home in Norwalk, California. His Date of birth is 26 Oct 26; business Statewide Security. I asked Mr. Duncan if he had ever caught defendant Williams sleeping on duty while he was employed by Statewide Security at the Paradise West complex. Duncan stated he never actually caught Williams sleeping on duty, but one time did accuse him of that. I asked Duncan if he could be specific on which unit he had seen the defendant in and he stated he would go to the complex in an attempt to identify the unit.

On 16 Nov 89 at approximately 0800 hours, Billy Duncan called me and stated the unit where he had

caught Williams inside was Unit #116 or Unit 69. He stated it was a second unit from the end. I asked Duncan the circumstances surrounding this incident; he stated he observed the lights on in the garage, with the garage door closed. He indicated he opened the garage door and observed the security cart inside. He indicated he went upstairs and observed defendant Williams's duffel bag lying on the floor. He then observed defendant Williams coming down from upstairs. Duncan stated he confronted Williams and stated: "Is this where you sleep?" Duncan stated Williams had no response for him. Duncan stated Williams was to call in every hour on the hour to Operations, which is located on Crenshaw Boulevard. Duncan further indicated he did not write up the defendant for this incident. FOR FURTHER DETAILS, SEE HAND-WRITTEN NOTES BY THIS INVESTIGATOR (Conley).

URBAN POLICE DEPARTMENT

SUPPLEMENTARY REPORT

LEGEND
L = DETECTIVE R. LANDER
J = DETECTIVE J. CONLEY
W = JODY WILLIAMS

SIDE ONE OF TAPE BEGINS IN MID-TAPE.
(The date is 06 NOV 89)

W: . . . you know, over there I talked to . . .
J: Who'd you talk to when the parents were over there, do you remember?

W: I don't know. I think he was either one of the neighbors or Fred. One of them I know I talked to.

J: You talked to the supervisors?

W: Yeah, the supervisors that was on dispatch during the time.

J: Did you ever find her watch?

W: Yeah. I jumped in the trash can, helping her out, you know, and reached in there and grabbed the bags out. And she said "it might be that bag right there," you know, so I grabbed the bag out and put it on the ground. She just got to folding paper towels and stuff and she reached in there and said "Oh, I found my watch." And I said that's good, you know. And she said "Oh, that's great." And I say so you just want to skip this calling in and she said "No, I want to let them know what's going on because I don't like things like that. That's not his job, his job is supposed to be security and if he's security he supposed to be doing his job." I said exactly, you know, and I will let them know. So that's the time that I left and went (inaudible) you know, the company.

J: You didn't see her anymore after that?

W: No. Oh, no, I seen her, or Sammy Battle came in, he came in about one o'clock, two hours before (inaudible) he came in. I got off on three on weekends, I work eight hours. During the week I work seven hours and I told him, I said the lady made a complaint on you, dude. I mean, I don't know why you been fucking up all the time and why you be doing that shit. I said because I told him before about some shit, you know, that people was coming to me and complaining to me about him, you know, doing some strange and weird shit around there , you know. I talked to Billy Whalen, you know, a couple of people who live around there and they was telling me that

you was doing some weird things and I would go to Billy's house, you know, and he's L.A.P.D., and I was talking to him and he was telling me that dude's kind of weird and strange and I don't know what's wrong with him. Even ladies come out of the house and told me that. And then recently when he was working on Glasgow and Arbor Vitae, the ladies was saying, you know, he was doing some weird stuff over there and they asked him not to do it and he was doing it anyway.

J: So that afternoon when Sammy came to work, he saw Terri again?

W: Yeah, she passed by and I told him, I said just don't say nothing to her. Leave her alone, man. You got a complaint on you. Just leave it alone, don't say nothing. So he was pissed off at that time. So I said man, don't even threaten - don't even act like you mad at her or nothing, just leave her alone. So he said, "Listen, man, I fucked up." He took off his hat and threw it in the back of the car and pulled his jacket off and pulled off his belt and put it on the car and he came in the car and sat right next to me and sat right there and he was talking to me, you know, for a little while and then, the next thing I know, she came walking by and she put her trash in there. And I said "How're you doing?" And she said "Oh, I'm doing just fine." I say, "Everything's alright now?" And she say, "It sure is." And I say, "Oh, that's great." And I say, "You going out?" And she said, "Yeah, I'm going out for a little while with my mom," and that's another thing, I met her mother, too. You know, talked to her mother, well, I didn't really hold a conversation with her. I just said, "Oh, how you doing this evening?" And she said "This is my mother, mother, this is the security guard, you know, work around

here and his name is Jody, you know. And I met her and we talked.

J: Do you know if Terri was living in her unit?

W: Huh?

J: Was Terri living in her unit at that time or not?

W: I don't know. All I know is she's moving in that day and the next day she came to me, I mean she was in the trash can and she just, you know, start pulling out the trash. And I asked her, I came up and asked her what she was doing because they told me, you know, when people's prowling on the premises like that, this is like private property. So don't let anybody see you coming back here or anybody you see messing with anything, call in and let us handle it. Or ask them what they're doing and if they give you a negative response, walk away and call us immediately.

J: So you may have had three contacts with Terri the whole time that you worked there?

W: Yeah, about three times I, well, not, about three times, yeah. The first time I talked to her with the moving guy. The second time was when she was in the trash. The third time was when she was passing by.

J: This was all on the grounds, never inside her apartment or anything?

W: No.

L: Have you ever been inside her apartment, Jody?

W: I sure haven't.

L: Do you know which one her unit is?

W: I think it was in the 80's, 82, something like that.

L: It was sixty-six.

W: Sixty-six, yeah.

L: But you know which one we're referring to when we talk about Terri Horgan?

W: Yeah.

L: You never had or possessed a pass key to any of the units?

W: No. Oh, yeah, one time I asked Cindy, the lady who works up in the main office, I asked her I wanted to go look for the guard cart because when I called it in and I told them, I said I don't know where the guard cart's at. The guard cart's not here. And they said the guard cart has to be here. I said Dick ain't came and got it? And they said no, the guard cart supposed to be there. And I said well, I left it in a stall yesterday and it's not there today. And they said well, just look around, you know, and you'll find it. So I went up to the office and got the key to the stall that I put it in and the Genie button and I pressed the Genie button and the garage came open and the cart was in there. It was plugged up and everything

L: And you returned that Genie button and the key back to Cindy?

W: Um hum (affirmative)

L: Okay, was that sometime prior to this?

W: That's the same time. I mean right after when I went in there and found the guard cart and everything. I left the door open, went back and just gave her the key.

L: When Cindy gave you the key and the Genie, that would have been prior to when you were employed there that Terri was in the trash bin or after?

W: That was a long time after. That was a long, long time after, that was about two or three weeks later.

L: So anytime up to while you were working there prior to the discovery of Terri's body, you didn't have the key to any of the units?

W: None, never. They don't even give you the keys to no apartment there or nothing. You know, just like I said, the apartments and the situation that goes on in the apartments is none of my business. Unless, like one time a man came by and hit the fire extinguisher and knocked it apart and the water was going everywhere and I called them in and he was gone before I came back. I was on the side like when you come through the back way on the A Street, Alder, right there in the Alder entrance, you know, I was in the first stall right there by the last one on this side. I was right there, right next door to the (inaudible) man I knew right there and I was in there and the dude hit it and I didn't pay no attention at the time, you know, cause I was doing my paperwork and soon as I heard the water going everywhere and the truck had gone, then that's when I came out. I looked and saw water going everywhere and I called it in and they told me they was coming out and stuff.

J: Jody, how long did you work for Interstate Security?

W: From May all the way to August.

J: So you got the job in May?

W: About the middle, yeah, about the middle of May.

J: How'd you get the job over there?

W: Huh?

L: How did you get the job, were you just going around . . .

W: No, my cousin, he was working there for them and he told me about it, you know. And I went down and filled out the application.

L: Who's your cousin?

W: Win Corcoran.

L: Is that a guy?

W: Yes. Black guy.

J : He was working there and he said that they needed some more guards so you just went down and filled out an application?

W: No, he said it was a nice job and they pay $5.00 an hour and he said, cause I didn't have no job at the time. I was working for temporary services, Porter Temporary Services and that wasn't getting me nowhere. So my father said go and see if they're hiring, even though you're on parole and everything, you know.

J: You're on parole?

W: Yeah, I'm still on parole.

L: Did you tell the people over there when you hired on you were still on parole?

W: No.

L: Didn't they take a fingerprint card from you?

W: Yeah. And that's when Department of . . .

L: Department of Justice?

W: No. Of civil services. Isn't that civil services? Federal Bureau, Federal Bureau wrote me up a paper back and said that I couldn't get my guard card due to the fact that I had a felony. You know, I had one felony on my record.

J: How about your brother? Did he work over there?

W: Yeah, my brother, Lumus Williams.

J: Uh huh (affirmative).

W: Yeah, he worked over there too.

L: He did?

W: He worked at Freeman though, Freeman Hospital.

L: For the same company?

W: For the same company, yeah.

J : So you hired on probably in the middle part of May until September?

W: No, until August.

J: Till August.

W: Right.

J: And you got the job through your cousin, Corcoran?

W: Right.

J: Anybody else work over there in the office or anything?

W: That I know?

J: That you're related to or anything?

W: Oh, no, no. Oh, yeah, well, he didn't work out of that office. He worked at Glendale office. Glendale office, out there. It's the same owner as here but the manager out there handles it out there and he deals with it out here because he's always at his main office and I had two cousins working out there and me and my brother was working out here.

J: What were you on parole for?

W: Assault.

J: Assault on who?

W: My family.

J: Your family?

W: My family.

J: What happened?

W: One day I had just got a job working for a custodian for this company and I came back home and I was happy about getting the job and everything so I had a few beers, you know. I say I told my daddy I be back, I going to go over to my auntie's house and he say sure. So he left and he went to work and I left and went over there. Well on the way back instead of going the way I had came, I went around to the store to get me another beer and I walked down the street and I bumped into this lady and during the time the beer was going in my hand

and the lady bumped into me. She didn't say excuse me or nothing. I said what's your fuckin' problem. And she looked at me and then her husband and son just start talking real crazy, you know, "Don't be talking to my mother like that, you fucking asshole. Get your ass out of here," and all this, you know, so at that time I socked the dude and I hit his mother and that's when his father tried and wrestle me and I started swinging and I hit him. Then the daughter got into it and then . . .

J: You just assaulted the whole family?

W: Yeah.

J: What made you snap on that?

W: The beer.

J: Just the beer?

W: Yeah.

J: How bad did you hurt anybody?

W: The baddest I hurt somebody was, I busted the lady's nose.

J: Yeah? How'd you do that?

W: When I hit her the first time. But, other than that, you know, (inaudible).

L: How much time did you do for that?

W: Three, three, I mean four years and three months. Wait a minute, I got locked up in July '84, July '84, 85, 86, '87, '88, July, August, September, October, November. I did four years and four months.

J: What facility?

W: Folsom.

J: Folsom.

W: Folsom, San Quentin, Soledad, Tracy.

J: You hit them all, huh?

W: All of . . .

L: Let me get back to this point a little bit. We've gone over this twice. You've never been into her house, right?

W: No I haven't.

L: Remember when we took some hair samples from you back on June, I think it was 26th or 28th?

W: Yes.

L: Okay and we submitted those hair samples along with numerous other people up to the laboratory and the conclusion when they wrote it back to me was the only person that the hair sample appeared to match was you. And that they matched four hairs which they believed came from you, the scientist at the laboratory did that. Is there any explanation why your hair samples would have been in the, inside the house?

W: I don't have no idea. I don't have no idea how the hair samples, hair got in her house or what happened where. I have never touched that lady. I have never did anything wrong to her. I have never cussed that lady. I have never did nothing wrong to nobody in that whole townhouse complex. I have only got into it with one person, a black dude. One day he was trying to get in the front gate and I talked to him and I told him he could not in behind another car. He had to submit either over the phone with somebody and have them buzz him in or he have to have a code number to come in the gate. Other than that, I could not let him come in that gate. That's the only thing that I run into with a person in here. Period. Everybody in there could tell you that I was not a negative person there. I have always done my job. I have never had a complaint. I have helped two or three people in there, you know, with complaints with other people, you know, and they made complaints on other people who was there all night long with the garage door open and a lot of noise and stuff . . .

J: And how about that hair?

W: I don't know.

J: Were you ever inside her apartment?

W: Never, never. I was never in her apartment, not one time. I don't know, I don't know how or when or where or what. I know that I have never touched the lady in no kind of (inaudible).

J: When you worked over there, you were basically out in the construction part?

W: That's right. That was my area. My construction area was the only construction area that I did in there all the time.

J: Did you have access to any ladders or anything?

W: I didn't have no access to nothing in there. The only thing that was in there that you can climb on is the, where they got wood where you can go up the stairs and you can climb back down, which I did a lot of times, you know, in the back part where, in my construction area and stuff like that, other than that, no ladders or nothing back there was, you know (inaudible) back there.

J: Well, the night of the murder you were stationed at an apartment or a garage less than maybe sixty-five, seventy yards from Terri's.

W: Exactly, exactly.

J: It was right down the alley, right?

W: Exactly, exactly.

J: You never wandered down that area that night?

W: No, no. I have never went down there. I have been down there, but I didn't go down there during that time or the time before that because I had just talked to my supervisor not too long ago, which is Bob Carney. And I had just talked to him and he told me, you know, he said, the construction area is the only area that we mainly involved in right now. I said

why did you tell me. He said during that time it was nothing over here, it was, you know, nothing. It was like nobody was living in that whole area back there or nothing. The only main problem was the construction area all the way around. And that's where I stayed, right there, in the back sitting in the cart. Or I stayed right there where the lady Cindy told me to sit, right there, you know, I can plug the cart up cause it ran off a big generator battery with the batteries up under the seat. And plug it in the wall and charge it and we'd go from there, down that way and go down there and come back, then go all the way around and check the front gate. And I'd go by and I'd check the time right there and the first thing and come back out and go all the way around and come back and stop. Other than that, I do not know how they say that my hairs got there. I don't know how it got there. I did not touch that lady. That lady to me was one of the sweetest persons I ever met in my life. She was sweet.

L: I've got one more problem here. Your fingerprints have been identified four places inside her apartment.

W: Mine?

L: Yours. Unit sixty-four. We've had it checked by three different experts.

W: Sixty-four?

L: Sixty-six, excuse me. Her unit, number sixty six.

W: Sixty-six I, I . . .

L: Sixty-six is her unit. You know which one is her unit?

W: Right.

L: The one you said you'd never been in. Your hair, prints . . .

W: I have never been in that lady's apartment. The furthest I have ever been to her house was when I told her about what was going on. I made the complaint and that's it. And then after that me and Billy, the L.A.P.D. guy walked over there and we was looking where they fingerprinted, you know, put the dust up there and everything. That's all. That's the farthest I've been to her townhouse complex, period. I have been in, I have been in every one back there, every last single one back there when nobody was living there when I was going back there. That's when I had to stick the tags in the doors all the way through the other side over there before they moved in. Other than that, I have never been in that lady's apartment. I don't know how my fingerprints got in there. I did not go in that lady's apartment. I did not mess with that lady in no kind of way. Nowhere, shape or form.

J: Did you snap that night or what?

W: Huh?

J: Did you snap that night?

W: Snap what night?

J: That night she got killed?

W: No. I didn't even know what happened. I didn't even know what happened until . . .

J: Why don't you tell us what happened?

W: . . . the next day. Huh?

J: Why don't you tell me what happened?

W: What happened when?

J: To Terri?

W: I don't know what happened to her.

J: You said you found out something the next day. Why don't you tell us about it?

W: Oh. The next day I came in and the officer that was working he left right before I did, an older guy, I forgot his name right now. He told me, he said

did you hear what happened? I say hear what happened to who? He said the lady got killed in sixty-six. I said the lady in sixty-six, the one that just moved in? He said yeah. I said man, I said, no, I know Sammy ain't did no shit like that to that lady.

J: You thought Sammy did it?

W: Huh?

J: You thought Sammy did it?

W: Yeah. Cause at the time the only person that was going through drama, you know, with her back and forth, was Sammy. That's the only person . . and then the lady there that lives over the other side she told me that Sammy threatened her and she heard it, you know, that Sammy . . .

J: So where'd you hear that happened?

W: That's what I heard. And then he told . . .

J: How'd she get killed?

W: Oh, they told me what happened.

J: What happened?

W: That she got beat up and strangled.

3: How'd she get strangled?

W: I don't know.

J: Beat up and strangled.

W: Yeah.

J: It's funny that your hair was up there in that room where she got beat up and strangled.

W: Man, I don't know, man. I ain't saying man, that . . .

J: Do you know what room it was?

W: Uhh huh (affirmative). I didn't even know she was there.

J: You didn't know she was there?

W: No, I didn't. I did not know she was there. I do not go around to people's doors at that time of night, at no eleven, twelve o'clock at night. I did not

do that. Nowhere, ain't nobody in there that can tell you that.

L: Did you see any lights on in her room, or her unit that night when you went to work?

W: I did not pay no attention to that.

L: You got to work

SIDE ONE OF TAPE ENDS.

SIDE TWO OF TAPE BEGINS.

W: . . . in there at all. I do not go around in people's houses at all at nighttime.

L: Okay. I agree with you, Jody.

J: How's the three ways for people to get in?

W: Just only from the front door or the side door, the sliding door.

J: Yeah.

W: Yeah.

J: Or?

W: Through the top. You got to go through a window or something.

J: With a ladder.

W: With a ladder. Or come off the roof, coming off the roof, they'll jump through a window.

L: Both Jim and I agree with you that that would be the three most practical was of getting in. Right?

W: Exactly.

L: What we're wondering is, how did your prints get on this bent-up screen that was found inside her unit that was taken off during the night when she was there, the night that she was killed? We can already verify that the screen was on there in good condition earlier in the day on the 30th and it was found when the apartment was unlocked on the morning of the 31st, bent up and inside the house and your fingerprints have positively been identified on four

separate places on that screen. Can you explain that at all?

W: I sure can't. I cannot . . .

J: The screen was removed from the window and down, and set by the front door.

W: The only way you can removed a screen from a window from out there is you got to have some kind of tool. And we do not have no kind of tools at all.

L: What if somebody went into the sliding glass doors, could they have done that?

W: The you have to . . . you can't go into the windows, the sliding glass door unless its unlocked.

L: I opened it. I opened Terri's within two seconds myself. Those are cheap doors.

W: I have never broken into nobody's house, not like that.

L: Let's get back to the point. Maybe you're forgetting something. How could your fingerprints get on that bent-up screen inside Terri's apartment?

W: I do not know. I did not go into that lady, I did not enter that lady's apartment.

L: You know what I think happened?

W: What?

L: I think you were always nice to Terri and I think Terri, did Terri invite you in for some reason that night Did you guys have some, you know, a cup of coffee or something and something went wrong?

W: No. Never.

L: You never went in there?

W: Never. I have never been in that lady's apartment. And if I would have been in that lady's apartment, me, by knowing exactly what I know and how to do what I know how to do, I would not bent-up no screen or nothing like that. Or I wouldn't leave my fingerprints in the apartment.

L: How would you do it?

W: I wouldn't have did it like that. I would have got her outside of the apartment. I would have stopped her down the street, around the block or I would have asked her for a ride somewhere on a busy street somewhere and stopped somewhere and I'd have hurted her. I wouldn't have did it in the townhouse complex, not where I'm working.

J: Hey, you were there all night? You know . . .

W: I was there all night.

J: . . . (inaudible).

W: But I was there all night. A lot of people come through there at nighttime, you know.

J: No. Not at two, three o'clock. I used to work security over there. Two, three o'clock in the morning it's dead over there.

W: No, it's not.

J: Yeah.

W: You got paper-throwers come through there.

J: That's five o'clock in the morning.

W: No, and you got people coming early, four o'clock.

L: Okay, okay.

W: And three o'clock. You got paper throwers. I don't know how my fingers, fingerprints got in that lady's house. I don't know how my hairs got in there.

L: Let's talk about something else, okay. Because we're going around in circles, Jody. Let's try to put all our heads together here and try to come out with a logical explanation. Fair enough?

W: Sure.

L: We know a couple of things. We know that there's hairs there that appear to be yours.

W: Appear to be mine, but know exactly they're mine.

L: Okay. I'm not an expert. All I know is what they wrote back in the report, okay?

W: Okay.

L: I'm telling you what I know.

W: Alright.

L: I know for a fact that your fingerprints are there, there's no doubt. It's not anybody else's fingerprints, no two people have the same prints. They're your fingerprints. They on a screen, bent-up inside. I know for a fact . . .

W: I don't think they're my fingerprints.

L: I know something was taken from inside.

W: And what was that?

L : Well, somebody might have been in there just to commit a simple theft, maybe see, maybe they were bored. Maybe they wanted to look around. Maybe they wanted to see if there was something small in value or whatever. And maybe someone was confronted by Terri.

W: Um hmm, (affirmative).

L: Maybe somebody was attacked by Terri and the whole thing just got out of hand, is that what happened that night?

W: No, not with me.

L: Maybe you went in there on your own and at the time you were just looking around and seeing if there was anything small, you now, a few boxes or something. Times are hard, you don't make very much money over there, five bucks an hour, right?

W: No, man.

L: Did Terri come out? You didn't expect her to be there that night, did you?

W: Huh?

L: You didn't expect Terri to be there that night, did you?

W: I didn't even know she was there that night. I didn't even go to thinking about her being there or not being there. I do not work in the townhouse complexes. I work in the construction area.

L: I understand.

W: My only detail that night in that area was right there in the last garage where I stay at due to the fact that the wind is blowing, it's cold out there. There's no guard house there at all. I have to be right there or be out there standing in the cold.

L: Okay.

W: So, therefore I do not ....

L: Then let's think of a way here to explain why your fingerprints are in there.

W: Man, I don't know.

J: Somebody (inaudible), come on.

W: I don't know, man.

L: Somebody put your fingerprints there?

W: No. Could nobody do that. Then again you know, I don't know, man. I mean . . .

J: Jody, why don't come on, just tell us what happened.

W: I'm telling you what happened.

J: No you're not. I can look at you, buddy...

W: You can look at me . . .

J: Yeah.

W: . . . straight in my eyes . . .

J: Straight in your eyes.

W: . . . and tell me I'm lying.

J: That's right.

W: No, I'm not.

J: Yeah, you are.

W: No, I'm not. I wouldn't lie about nothing like that. Shit, I never did nothing like that to nobody before in my life, ever.

J: How about the old lady you bumped into?

W: Yes.

J: Couldn't you say excuse me before you (inaudible) on her?

W: You got to think about it. I mean, that was a natural reaction of something that happened to me, you know what I'm saying?

J: Jody, maybe you're in Terri's unit going through and she opens the door.

W: No. What would I want to go in her unit for? And there's a whole bunch of other units to go in.

J: Well, why are your fucking fingerprints in her unit?

W: I do not know. I don't know. I mean, to you it sounds unlogical for a person not to know how their fingerprints got into that apartment.

J: And you are not giving me a logical explanation on how your fingerprints got inside her unit.

W: How can I? And I did not enter her apartment.

J: Well, then think back. You tell me how they got there . . .

W: I didn't, I'm telling you.

J: . . . unless you had to be inside of her unit for your fingerprints to get there.

W: No.

J: Yeah.

W: No. I did not go in that lady's apartment at all.

L: That night did you find a screen outside or anything, a bent up screen that you handled?

W: I do not look for screens. I do not look for nothing around there but somebody's come over there messing with the construction area, that's my main topic.

L: Okay, listen to me for a second. That night in that little garage area where you have your security

cart where it plugs in, do you remember if there was a bent-up screen you could have been handling there or something?

W: I do not know. I do not investigate the area that I'm in. The only thing I worry about is the guard cart and . . .

L: What I'm asking you is, do you remember handling any bent-up screen that was over there by the cart?

W: I don't know. I wasn't, you know, that night. I don't know what I was doing that night. All I know is I was sitting there. I probably went around the front, which I normally do, come back, go down the construction area, go inside the stalls, come out, go in, come out, go in, come out, go in and come out. As far as messing around over there in the townhouse complex area, I do not do that. Messing up screens and like that, I do not do that. I know my detail in the apartments, you know, before, you know, they went up after he told me that I wasn't supposed to be there no more because the people start moving in now, I did not go in there.

L: Do you know if they remove those screens to the windows to the inside or the outside?

W: Excuse me?

L: Do you know how the windows, the screens are removed from the windows? Do you know if they are removed from the inside or the outside of the building?

W: I can't tell you that. I mean I never did no detail in that building at all. And to be able to do detailing to know where the screens come off and come on at and how they put on and put off and all that, you would have to know exactly what's going on in unit (inaudible).

J: Haven't you told us earlier in this conversation that you needed a tool to get that screen off?

W: You have to have a tool.

J: What kind of tool do you need?

W: A screwdriver mostly. I mean, every screen that you look at everywhere is . . .

J: Most screens can be taken off very easily without a tool. I used to live in one of those units, I know to take a screen off.

W: I ain't never lived in those units, like that. I never had the money to live in a unit like that. The screens where I live at they always bolted in from the outside. They got screws on them in four places, at the top, the sides and at the bottom.

J: Okay.

W: Other than that I do not know how that lady's screen got off. I do not know how my fingerprints got in her apartment but I'm willing to go through a lie detector test and the whole shot that I did not mess with that apartment that night at all. I would never did nothing like that, that would be the first thing I knew. That would be the first thing that would pop into you guys mind, knowing that I'm on parole, first of all.

L: Well, it wasn't until the fingerprint things. That's something we can't explain away. Because somebody is on parole or something, well, that may make you take a second look. But that doesn't make any case, you understand? You know what I mean, Jody?

W: Yeah.

L: Okay, that don't make a case. I'm not an expert in hair fibers, I mean the laboratory says they appear to be your hairs, but again, I'm not an expert.

W: They appear to be my hairs. How could they say . . .

L: They say of all the people we submitted in there that . . .

W: Alright, tell me this. Alright, you listen to this.

L: Let's just cut it short. This is my question.

W: Don't cut it short. I just want to ask one question.

L: Your prints is what I can't under . . . we all know how they work. And they've been verified and rechecked and verified again. Those are your prints inside that unit. Now, if you weren't in that unit, how did your prints get in there? There must be some way or somebody would want to set you up. Did you have some enemy?

W: I could have. I could have. It could have been Sammy Battle. It could have been anybody, I mean, you know what I'm saying. I mean, I know for a fact that I did not touch no lady's screen in there. I did not go in that lady's house and I did not hurt that lady in no kind of way. I did not have no reason to enter that lady's house. I did not know that the lady was in there. All I knew was that her property was in there and that due to the fact that she . . .

J: What kind of property was in there?

W: I do not know.

J: you just said . . .

W: Her furniture. Her furniture that was moved from the truck to her house. That's all. Other than that, I do not know. I cannot come up with a logical explanation on how my fingerprints got on the screen in there because it did not.

L: Did you see any other employees there that night? Do you think any other employees could have been there? Could somebody have come around there that night?

W: Could have been. I didn't see nobody though. I mean, you know, I don't really pay no attention to

what's going on in the complexing part of the apartments. I just keep my mind and everything of what's
going on inside.

L: Jody, this is a capital punishment case, do
you understand?

W: I know that.

L: Okay.

W: That's twenty-five life off the top. Plus a career criminal; I can't get life without or death row. It
doesn't . . .

L: This appears to be . . .

W: . . . I mean, then again, it really don't make no
difference because I already been to the bus stop,
Folsom. You can't go no further than that.

L: I want to tell you this, by any chance did somebody you know from your neighborhood come up
that night and was going to rip off a t.v. or something and for whatever you felt obligated or threatened you, and did you say man, I just want you to
help me get into a unit and maybe he thought that
unit was empty.

W: My neighborhood?

L: Well, maybe somebody new from the neighborhood.

W: I don't know nobody from the neighborhood.
I just moved in that the neighborhood. I just got out
of jail November 13, 1998.

L: I know your whole background. And I also
know that you have numerous affiliations, the last one,
at least on your parole record, is that you associate
with the Rolling Sixties Crips.

W: Exactly.

L: Okay, did somebody that you knew from the
crips or used to run with come up there and threaten
you . . .

W: I do not even associate with the Rolling Sixties Crips no more. Just because it's here and it's there, doesn't mean that, you know, that it's me anymore. You see what I'm doing.

L: I'm trying to find out how your prints could have got there. If maybe somebody came up from you used to associate with heard that you were working there and they says, brother you going to have to turn your head because we need to rip off some t.v. or something. Well, then maybe they did it and you were forced to help them get in. Well, that could make sense. Maybe you put a ladder up there once the screen was gone, you said okay, that's the place, I'm done.

W: No, no.

L: What happened is your prints ended up there and somebody else did this.

W: No.

L: What happened?

W: I can't tell you what happened in there at all. All I can tell you is this. I do not associate with the Rolling Sixties Crips no more and if you was to go over there and you was to grab one of them, they will tell you they haven't seen me in so long that they wondered where am I.

L: Jody, I'm looking for possible explanations for your fingerprints. That's a fact that I can't remove from this case. It's there, okay?

W: I mean, all we can do, man, is just go to court and you officers give me time, man. But as far as the prints, you know what I'm saying, whatever, man, the hair, whatever, I cannot explain that to you because I do not know. I mean, I was not drunk. I do not drink. I do not drink on job. I do not drink no time coming to the job. I have drunk. I have smoked marijuana. I have

never smoked nothing else but marijuana and drunk only (inaudible). I was not drunk at the time. There was nothing wrong with me and I did my job, what I was supposed to do and I left there. As far as somebody coming there, they do not even know where my father lives at, but one person. And he's nowhere near Los Angeles right now, he's in Glendale.

L: Well, our situation is here, Jody. Me and Conley, we're here to find out to the best of our ability who killed Terri Horgan.

W: That's what I want to know.

L: If it's not you, then our job is not to send an innocent man to jail, do you understand that?

W: You going to do that anyway.

L: I ain't going to do anything. I don't send people to jail. I work the case and I submit it to the District Attorney who takes it to the court.

W: Exactly.

L: So that's why we're talking here.

W: Right.

L: We felt, let's just say you had nothing to do with Terri's murder, nothing.

W: Alright.

L: We're still stuck with the fact that we've got your fingerprints inside on an object inside of her house which was removed sometime during the night hours on the night that she was killed. Now, that we know.

J: That's a fact.

W: That's a fact.

L: I can't . . .

W: You sure that they my fingerprints?

L: Oh, I'm positive and I ain't shitting you.

J: Your fingerprints.

L: Your fingerprints are positive. Hair, I'm not a hair

expert, okay, but I have enough background in finger-prints to know that it's been checked, rechecked again and again, and there's no doubt, and, that is the basis on that information that the judge has signed the arrest warrant. Now, I've put my cards out on the table . . .

W: Then I can go to the court man, and deal with it there. And I mean, cause . . .

L: Well, listen . . .

W: . . . as far as you guys trying to tell me that I did something that I didn't do, you ain't never going to get me to say that I did and I didn't. I mean, it's going to go back and forth all night long or all night long or all week long or all month long.

L: Okay, I understand what you're saying and I just told you it's not our job to send you to jail if you're innocent.

W: Exactly.

L: I'm telling you, understand me what I'm say-ing. We have this piece that we have to explain how it got there.

W: Right.

L: If somebody put it there or something . . .

W: I don't know how it got there. I don't know if it was there or not. I'm going by what you telling me. I do not know. I was not there.

J: How about this, Jody.

W: Was you there, did you take the fingerprints out of there?

L: Yeah, I was there.

W: Did you get the screen?

L: How about if I get a picture and I come show it to you and show you the screen?

W: Alright.

J: And we'll show you the I.D. expert that ID'd you and we'll also show you your log from that night.

W: Alright.

J: Maybe that will refresh your memory.

L: The log you know, right?

W: Yeah, I know the log.

L: You filled out the log.

J: I'm going to turn this tape off for a minute, it's three-twenty, twenty of . . .

TAPE PAUSES

TAPE CONTINUES

L: The tape started again. The time right now is fifteen twenty-six, it will be three twenty-six p.m.

W: Um hmm (affirmative).

L: I didn't want to bring out a lot of the other picture. This is what you call a proof sheet. Okay, these will be blown up, it's a regular photograph, colored picture. You see that, that's the inside of the front door.

W: I can't see.

L: You see the screen right there? It's bent in half.

W: This one right here?

L: Yeah, I don't have a blowup that you can look at.

J: It's right inside her front door.

L: Now that's the screen we're talking about here. Okay, you can take that piece of paper and read it. That's from our identification section and that's been checked by several experts as far as the fingerprints.

J: Right here. Can you read it out loud?

L: Yeah, he can read it.

W: It says homicide, DR number 89-8970. Location 3200 Alder, number 66, victim Terri Horgan, suspect Jody Williams, as a result of fingerprints comparison between latent prints on (the screen) and the inked fingerprints of the above suspect, the follow-

ing identification was established. Latent fingerprints from window screen frame found bent just inside front door marked numbers ten through thirteen, were identified as having been made by Jody Williams, the latent prints and the inked fingerprints of Jody Williams will remain on the file in the identification system for possible future references. The writer of this report will be called as a witness to testify that he/she is a identification analyst employed by the City of Urban Police Department did the comparison did form the opinion stated above and states under penalty of perjury that the above statements are true. Reported by Detective Philcox; date of report November 2, 1989.

L: Okay. There's a picture of the print. That's what I'm trying to say. My job isn't to put you behind bars if you're not responsible. I have to figure out . . .

W: Put me behind bars if I'm not responsible.

L: my job is not to try and convict you of something, you know, if you're an innocent man. My job is to work with evidence that I seen, that I have.

W: Tell me this. You talking to me now, right?

L: Yeah, I'm talking to you.

W: Okay. If I'm guilty or I'm not guilty, you still got to put me in the holding cell and book me and all that, right?

L: Well, I still have to detain you here until the case is presented to the District Attorney. Like I said, I do the case and I present it to the District Attorney, you know how the system works. They file the case and then it's the judge and the jury. My job is to try to get as much of the truth presented to the court.

W: Yeah.

L: I've had cases before where I've filed on individuals and they've called me or somebody else has

come up to me before and gave me new evidence that it looked like that person which is already in the process of going through court is innocent and I go over and stop the trial.

W: Exactly.

L: Why would I want to send anybody to jail if they're innocent?

W: I'm innocent.

L: I just need to explain why your prints are on that bent screen inside of Terri Horgan's apartment.

W: I do not have the faintest idea. I do not know. Let's go to court.

L: Okay. There's no sense going over this now. I want to leave you with this thought. Okay?

W: Umm (affirmative).

L: Think about what I've said. Could anybody wanted to set you up for this?

W: I don't know.

L: Okay. This evening think about that.

W: I mean why am I a suspect and Sammy Battle ain't a suspect?

L: Because we don't have Sammy Battle's fingerprints in there. We don't have Sammy Battle's hairs that are even close to the hairs that were found. We had a number of hairs that were not the victim's.

W: What, head hair or pubic hairs?

L: We've got two pubic hairs and two head hairs?

W: How in the world can you tell a pubic hair from head hairs?

L: Again, I am not a criminalist, okay?

W: Oh, fuck, man that . . .

L: Remember what I told you about the fibers on your shirt?

W: Yeah. Man that's . . .

L: It's that good anymore.

W: Yeah, but I mean that's, that's, I mean a person can't even correspond like that.

L: Have you heard of a new process called DNA?

W: No, I haven't.

L: I thought maybe when you were in the joint you might have heard about it. It started over in England a while back. Certain items from the body, like your semen, or . . .

W: Yeah, yeah.

L: . . . or your hair, okay we're talking about a head hair, can go through a process that they now have available with the new technology that they have that they can say there's a lesser chance of a mistake on their comparison than there is in fingerprints. The odds are something like sixty billion to one.

W: Exactly.

L: That's how far they've gone in this technology. When I hired on here we didn't have any of that. So I don't claim to be an expert, Jody, all I know is that's what they've told me.

W: I know exactly what you guys is doing. I mean I'm not doubting you for doing your job and you know, you got to do what you've got to do, you know what I'm saying. But I'm just telling you I do not know how my fingerprints got on that screen and ain't nothing in this world that can make me tell you that I do and say that they're mine. Cause I do not know. I was not there when they ran the test. Who was there with him when he ran the test through the thing. Who can come to court and say that the fingerprint that he took from off the thing, run it through the thing is mine and nobody is there to watch him do this.

L: Well, obviously it will have to be the people from the crime scene that lifted the evidence, right?

W: Yeah, it have to be. And it have to be more

than one person, and then due to the fact that, you know, nobody ever seen me do, or you know seen me enter this woman's apartment or bent up the screen, then how can you say that I did? All you have is fingerprints. Fingerprints can convict a person, true, and I wouldn't doubt that and I understand it happened before. But I'm telling you that my fingerprints was not on that screen. It was not mine if it was inside her apartment. I haven't been in there. I haven't been in none of them, not when nobody, been occupied, no. And ain't nobody can tell you that I have. Only one person tell you I been in their apartment since I been out there and during that time and it was the L.A.P.D. officer Billy. And he lives in, I think, eighty eight.

L: Okay, Jody.

W: He's the only one and I don't know, man, I do not know. Is my fingerprints supposed to be on these too?

L: That's only a couple of pictures. I just wanted to show you a picture of the screen so you could see where it was at and kind of get an idea and maybe it will recall something.

J: Why don't we leave you tonight and have another talk tomorrow morning?

W: No, man, I don't want to talk no more. Just take me to the County Jail, man, and just book me and let me go through the whole process. I don't want to talk about it. I don't. I do not want to talk to nobody else about this case because I mean I haven't did nothing. I'm completely innocent on this. I mean, the fingerprints could have been from the fingerprints outside, you know, somewhere around there or something . I mean, I been working in that townhouse and complex ever since May.

J: She got killed in May.

W: In May.

J: Two weeks after you started, yes.

W: No.

J: In May.

W: No.

J: She was killed May 30th, 1989.

W: No.

J: Yeah.

W: Uh huh (negative).

J: Want to bet?

L: That's when she died.

W: No, she didn't get killed in May.

J: May 30th, 1989, two weeks after you started there, Jody.

W: No she didn't.

L: Yeah, that's the date. Maybe . . .

J: Just like your fingerprints aren't there

W: No, no.

J: That's a fact. She was killed May 30th, 1989.

W: No, she wasn't. No, she was not. She was not killed in May.

J: Yes, she was. It was my wife's birthday. I ought to remember that.

W: I swear on my momma that I never . . .

J: How do you know so sure when she was killed?

W: Cause I remember the day that she was . . .

J: Unless you have knowledge of it?

W: I don't have knowledge of it. The only thing that I know is I know that she did not get killed in May.

J: Just like your fingerprints aren't on that screen.

W: I ain't saying that they not on the screen. I don't know if they on the screen or not. I'm just going

by what you guys are saying. Them pictures, that's not telling me nothing. You could have just wrote that paper up and just said that my fingerprints is on there and took them pictures. You do not know if my fingerprints are . . .

J: You think we're bullshitting you, is that what you're thinking?

W: I'm not saying you're bullshitting. I'm just saying, how do you know?

J: How do I know?

W: Did you run the tests?

J: Yeah.

W: Did you run the tests, fingerprint and everything?

L: I'm not a fingerprint expert, Jody. I've read the evidence and the experts tell me.

W: How you all going to sit up here and tell me that I did and I didn't.

J: Cause we have to rely on what the paper says.

W: The paper could be lie.

J: That guy's an expert.

W: Experts lie. Experts make mistakes. Everybody, ain't nobody's perfect.

J: You're just being argumentative.

L : This is what we're going to do. I'm not going to come back and bother you anymore, okay?

W: Alright.

L: If, by any chance, this is strictly up to you, you want to talk to me at any time while you're still here at Urban, my name is Lander.

W: How long will I be here?

L: You'll be here till day after tomorrow.

W: Good. As long as I'm here until the day after tomorrow I don't want to talk to nobody.

L: Okay.

W: If I'm here longer than that, I still don't want to talk to nobody.

L: We're going to terminate the tape it's fifteen forty-two.

W: Wait a minute.

L: Oh. You want to talk more?

W: You all say that I was, I hurted this lady. I had never hurted this lady.

J: I'll be right back. I'm leaving the room.

L: I'm not sure we're talking about the same, Terri?

W: Yeah.

L: Okay, well, I told you . . .

W: Well, what I'm saying is, the only thing that I have ever said to this lady since I have been in there in that townhouse in complex is that she asked me a question. She asked me twice a question and I said, hi, how're you doing and that's it. You know, oh, you're leaving, okay, bye. You know, oh, bye mom, you know, told her mother bye mom, you know. I haven't even never got into a nothing with her. The only person who got into a nothing with her. The only person who got into something with her is another guard by the name of Sammy Battle.

L: I know Sammy.

W: You know what I'm saying.

L: I checked Sammy from one end to the other.

W: And therefore by him you know, you know doing that, it would more make him look like a suspect than me.

L: Oh, believe me, I looked at Sammy real hard.

W: Then due to the full point you say you got my fingerprints, my hairs, you know what I'm saying. Fingerprints and hair don't prove nothing.

L: All I'm telling you is the physical evidence.

SIDE TWO OF TAPE ENDS

SIDE ONE OF TAPE BEGINS AGAIN

L : Okay, then as far as the prints, the prints are positively yours. Nobody planted them there. Nobody . . .

W: How do I know that? And how do you know that?

L: The only thing I know is that I know these people. They do a lot of cases. What reason would they have to plant your prints? And where would they have gotten your prints from?

W: The guy next door, he said that the construction guys was in her apartment, too.

L: Who said that?

W: The guy next door.

L: Told you that the construction guys were in her apartment?

W: Um hmm (affirmative).

L: When?

W: Not the construction guys, the painters.

L: When were they in her apartment?

W: That same morning that she was found dead.

L: That's what the guy next door told you?

W: Yeah.

L: That's a fact, they were.

W: Yeah, so I mean, how could . . .

J: She's was already dead when they were in there.

W: How can you tell?

L: Time of death.

J: Time of death.

W: Oh, time of death? When was she supposed to have got killed?

J: You tell us.

W: Why would I tell you?

L : It was during the night, Jody. Late hours or

early morning hours, the night of the 30th, the morning of the 31st.

J: About the hours that you were working.

L: Well, obviously it happened during that time. I
mean, that's medical fact. It's a medical fact during
that time somebody killed her. It's a physical fact that
your fingerprints are on that screen.

W: That doesn't mean just cause my fingerprints
was on the screen that I killed her.

L: I don't know. Tell me.

W: No, well, I didn't and I don't know how my
fingerprints got in the screen.

L: And it's a physical fact that according to the
lab expert up there the hairs found on the victim and
on her clothing appear to be your hairs.

W: On her clothing?

L: Yeah.

W: And on her?

L: Right.

W: How did my hair get on her . . .

L: Now we're back to how did your fingerprints
get there. We don't know. That's the reason we wrote
the Ramey warrant.

W: Man, this is way out, man. This is way, way
out. First it was my hair was found on her and in the
apartment. Now, it's fingerprints, hair found on her in
the apartment and on her. What is it man, is it that
you know, that you think it was me and I'm the one
that did it . . .

L: I don't know. All I know is what I've told you.

W: Alright.

L: Everybody else we've talked about, I checked
their alibi's over and over. I checked their fingerprints.

J: We've checked their hair.

L: I checked their backgrounds. Okay, there's

been a few people over there we've looked at that are no cherry pickers. They have some backgrounds but okay nothing else come through, until the mistake was corrected on the prints we have up there that we thought were yours, were your brother Lumus's.

W: Yeah.

L: As soon as your prints come up, they made them like that. They notified me at seven-thirty in the morning. By nine o'clock they made them three more times on that screen. There are four makes on that screen.

W: Well why did it take you all that time all the way into now to come and get me?

L: From last Thursday?

W: From last Thursday.

L: That's when the print was made through California ID Section, that was last Thursday.

J: They kept putting the wrong finger in, they have to rotate the finger back and forth. They were putting a right one and it was a left one.

W: I don't know.

J: Your prints because you just got the job and probably weren't over Statewide when they sent them over.

L: They sent your brother's over.

W: How did my brother's get over there?

L: They sent them over on the last name of Williams. So they run over to a series upstairs and as far as we knew we said do you have Sammy's prints, yeah. Do you have Williams' prints, yeah. Well, they had Lumus Williams. They didn't have you. Cause they probably sent yours over to DOJ or whatever to have them compared to see if you could get a license.

W: Yeah.

L: But that's not even here or there. We're still stuck with the hair and the prints.

J: And where all this stuff was is what we're stuck with. You're stuck with it too because you haven't given us an explanation on how they got there.

W: I'm stuck with them. I don't know how they got there. I mean, I could sit up here all night long with you and it's not, . . . I'm doing the best I can. But I don't know how they got there, man. I did not touch that lady. I wouldn't even do nothing like that to nobody. I mean, that's like, I know, I won part of a Buddhist practice, man. I chant, man. And I go to church, too. And I know completely well that all Buddhist practice is placed on cause and effect and I know good and well, through by what I've seen from my Buddhist practice, you know what I'm saying. If I was to do something like that, I would cause and effect, and I'd be like it'd come right back on me. And I know I ain't did nothing like that to nobody.

L: Are you sure that night that maybe you didn't just let somebody get in or whatever because they weren't going to commit a theft and somebody else did this murder?

W: If somebody else did the murder, what would my fingerprints doing up there?

L: Maybe you just put a ladder on the window and you just pushed in the window and you said okay, man, that's it, I ain't doing anymore.

W: Did you find the ladder up there with my fingerprints on there?

J: We're just doing maybes here.

L: No. I'm just trying to say . . .

W: You can't live on maybes.

L: I know. But how can I try and find somebody else who's responsible if I can't explain anything.

W: Cause nobody even knew around nowhere, not even from the neighborhood even know that I was working security.

L: Okay, we're just throwing out ideas, okay.

J: The fact still remains that your prints are on that screen. We can't get away from that, can we?

W: I guess not. You got to do what you got to do, man. And I'll say that they wasn't. And you all say that they is and we going to go through the whole nine yards, man. And I ain't did nothing to nobody. I haven't did nothing to that lady. I haven't even talked back to that lady. I always gave everybody in there their proper respect at all times. Anytime they asked me to handle something, I did it. I did not do nothing wrong in there the whole time I was there. I did not harm that lady. I did not mess with that lady. I did nothing, man.

J: But you got the job there in mid-May, right?

W: I got the job to work with Interstate in May, yeah. About mid-May, yeah.

J: And she was killed at the end of May.

W: That don't mean just she was killed the end of May that I did it. I still work for them and I still worked during that time I was in (inaudible) after she got killed.

L: Jody, this going around in circles ain't going to get us anywhere. I'm going to tell you again, my name's Lander.

W: Right.

L: If you have any ideas tonight, anything that comes up that you think, any ideas, I don't care how wild they are, I'll investigate them for you, you understand? If you want to talk to me in the morning, just tell the jailer I want to say something to Lander. Otherwise, I'm not going to bother you.

W: Right.

L: If you've got an idea how they could have got there some way, and like I told you a little while ago, you'll find out I'm not lying to you about any of this. None of these prints were planted there by us whatever. I don't know your run-in before. I don't guys you done time with, what stories they've told you about, but it ain't going to happen here.

W: I ain't worrying with nobody and nobody told me nothing.

L: Okay, let me just let it go at that and I want you to know if you want to say something to me, just ask to see Lander, otherwise I'm not going to come back. I'm not going to interview you again. Understand?

W: Sure.

L: Okay, we're going to terminate this interview now, it's . . .

W: What is my court date scheduled?

L: It will be day after tomorrow.

W: Which is eighth or the ninth?

L: Well, today's the sixth, it will be the eighth.

W: That's just arraignment. Where I'm going through.

L: Arraignment?

W: No, from here?

L: You'll stay here until arraignment. After arraignment you'll go to County.

W: What . . .

L: L.A. County.

W: Oh, okay. That's (inaudible).

J: You got friends there?

W: A whole bunch of them.

L: We're going to terminate the interview. It's fifteen-fifty or three-fifty in the afternoon.

FIRST HALF OF SIDE ONE OF TAPE ENDS.

URBAN POLICE DEPARTMENT
SUPPLEMENTAL REPORT

LEGEND
L = DETECTIVE RICK LANDER
J = DETECTIVE J. CONLEY
W = JODY WILLIAMS

The date and time is November 7, 1989. It's ten-fifty in the a.m. This will be a second interview with Mr. Williams. It's taking place in the Urban Police Department. Present in the interview is myself, Detective Lander, my partner, Detective Conley and Mr. Jody Williams.

L: Mr. Williams, for the record, will you state your date of birth please?
W: 6-27-65.
L: Okay, Mr. Williams, do you remember us having a conversation yesterday?
W: Yes, I did.
L: Do you remember me advising you of your constitutional rights?
W: Yes, I did. I mean, yes, you did.
L: Do you remember stating you understood your rights, stating you waived them at that time?
W: Yes.
L: Okay, I'm going to re-advise you of your rights because it's a second interview. Mr. Williams, you have the right to remain silent, anything you say can and will be used against you in a court of law. You have the right to speak with an attorney and have an attorney present prior and during any questioning. If

you want an attorney and cannot afford one, one will be appointed, free of charge, to represent you prior to any questioning. Now, again, do you understand your rights?

W: Yes.

L: And at this time do you wish to give up your right to remain silent?

W: Yes.

L: And at this time do you wish to give up the right to have an attorney present during this interview?

W: Yes.

L: Okay. Go ahead and ask all the questions.

W: Now, I just wanted to know, man, know, you said that the screen was found in her apartment?

L: Yeah. I showed you the picture taken at the crime scene of the bent screen found in the apartment that your fingerprints were on.

W: You guys know for a fact that it was my fin-gerprints?

L: Yes, we do.

W: Did the D.A. pick up this case?

L: I take it to the D.A. this afternoon.

W: When will I know?

L: If it's filed or not?

W: Um hmm (affirmative).

L : This afternoon when I get done with the D.A.'s office. We talked yesterday about a couple of things. When you were working there that night, you were just in your uniform, right?

W: Yeah.

L: The uniform is, describe it to me.

W: Blue shirt, blue pants, black shoes and black, blue hat.

L: The black shoes, are they rubber soled shoes, tennis shoes, what?

W: Yeah, they're tennis shoes.

L: Black tennis shoes.

J: Do you know the brand name or anything?

W: Nike

J: They were Nikes.

L: And what size do you normally wear?

W: Eight and a half, nine.

L: An eight and a half or nine in your tennis shoes?

W: Yeah.

L: Okay and I think you said yesterday you're not sure where they're at now, those tennis shoes?

W: They should be at the house.

L: You mean your dad's house?

W: Yeah.

J: We talked to your mom and dad this morning.

W: What'd they say?

J: They were quite concerned.

L: They seemed like real nice people.

J: Your stepmom was really upset.

W: My mother's going to be really upset, too. The rest of my family.

L: We explained to your dad and your stepmother the same thing that we explained, you know. We're here just to get facts and try to clarify what happened when we present it to the District Attorney's office. We're not here to determine your guilt or innocence that's why when we left yesterday I said if you have any thought or explanation as to how your fingerprints or those hairs could have got in the apartment, I was hoping when you called us back you might have thought of something.

W: I was just, you know, I was working in that area and for awhile in that area right there. Every . . . as soon as they got finished with one, they had us where I was stationed at, right there on the end, . . .

L: Uh huh (affirmative).

W: . . . they had us stationed in one right in front of that one, right across in front of that one. And they moved us from there to down the alley, over . . .

J: But you were always stationed in the garages, right?

W: Yeah, so, you know, I mean, there's a couple of times I was caught sleeping in the little townhouses, you know, by my commander, Bill.

L: You mean inside the condominiums itself?

W: Yeah.

L: Is that the ones under construction or that have been completed?

W: The ones that was construction and being completed.

L: Do you remember ever going in and sleeping in Terri Horgan's unit?

W: I think I have. I think I was.

L: And do you have any idea when that would have been?

W: No. I just know that we was moved around there several times, you know, and it wasn't just one place that we was stationed. My fingerprints could be all over that alley and everyone of them was, you know, like I said, I slept in upstairs, downstairs, all away around that alley. And I was caught by Bill a few times, you know and he made a complaint to his boss, you know, the supervisor overall.

L: Well, let's explore that. Maybe we got something here. You said yesterday that at the time you couldn't remember being in Terri's apartment, correct?

W: I couldn't, no.

L: Okay.

W: I said all I know, man, is that I've been in a

few of them, up and down the alley cause we was moved up and down that alley the whole time. We was even moved in like the next alley over. Even in there, the alley over there. But I was doing like all three buildings, you know, this one over here, this one right here and the one on the end. You know, so we was moved all the way around. And when it was being construction and everything, they had a lot of stuff in the places all the way around. The stuff that they was fixing up the apartment with and everything, everything all around.

J: I thought yesterday you told us no way shape or form were you ever inside her unit.

W: I ain't saying that I was inside her unit. I'm saying that I could have been inside her unit. I'm not saying that I was in her unit. I'm just saying I was stationed, it's in my files that was presented on my daily activity report.

J: Who was your supervisor?

W: Doug Gunter.

J: No, that you said that caught you sleeping.

W: Bill . . .

J: Bill who?

W: Can't think of his last name - it's a funny one. Yeah, he's the commander. He's the next one in charge.

J: When you went into these various units while previously . . .

W: Before they was occupied?

L: Yeah, Had you ever gone into the units after the people had started to move in?

W: No. It was locked then. You couldn't get in, no way.

L: Well, Terri's unit had been locked or secured, what they called "demastered," you know, to where

the average workman and that wouldn't have been able to get in. You had to have a master key that was held by the supervisors in there.

W: Exactly.

L: At that time though, if you went to a unit, it was cold and you wanted to sleep, how would you get into the units?

W: How would you get into the units if they was locked?

L: Yeah.

W: You couldn't get into them.

L: You couldn't get in.

W: The only thing you could get into was the garage and it would be open and they would leave the garage door open due to the fact that the guard cart had to be plugged in to run. You know it runs off batteries and the charger we had to plug it in the wall cause the electricity was on, so we plugged the electricity into the wall, I mean the cord into the wall and it would charge the batteries up so we used the cart to run around.

J: At what point in construction would they put the lock on the doors and lock them where you could not get in? Was it when they put the (inaudible) in or . . .

W: It was right when they get all the property, you know the function in there. You know, the microwave, the sinks, the stove, after all that stuff's in there and they get ready to move somebody in, they say, well, you know, these people will be moving in, then they lock up the whole place and then secure the garage doors up.

L: This is before the carpet goes down.

W: Yeah. No, well, sometimes you know, they have some doors open after the carpet was put down. And it was the guy, I had went into you know,

some of the townhouses while they was doing the carpet.

L: Now, prior to Terri's death to our best estimate, you were employed there for approximately two weeks.

W: Yeah.

L: Okay. And you knew Terri, you talked to her.

W: Yeah, I talked to her.

L: On a couple of occasions I think you said.

W: Yeah.

L: And you knew which unit or which condominium Terri was moving into?

W: Yeah.

L: Okay. That's pretty clear in your mind.

W: Yeah. She asked me did I, was them, the mover guys supposed to move her stuff in and I asked her at that time, which one was hers. And then she told me, you know, it was sixty . . .

L: Sixty-six?

W: Yeah, sixty-six.

L: That's a corner unit?

W: Huh?

J: That's an end unit?

W: End unit, yeah.

L: During that two week time period then, do you remember ever going in and sleeping in Terri's apartment? I'm not talking about many nights?

W: No, not after, not after she moved in or moved her stuff in.

J: About the time you started working there . . .

W: It was locked then.

J: About the time you started working there her unit was pretty close to being finished, wasn't it?

W: Yeah, it was almost, but it wasn't finished because, like I say, they had us move you know, first

one was right there, right in front of the one that they had me in, right there. And then they moved us down the alley again and up and down.

J: But your main job there was to guard the units that are just under construction, not the completed phases. You were supposed to watch for theft of lumber and stuff like that.

W: Theft of lumber, excuse me. Theft of lumber, anybody coming on the premises that wasn't supposed to be there, you know, in the construction site.

J: The new construction area would have a fence around it, right?

W: Yeah. They had a fence around the whole complex, period.

J: Yeah.

W: And during that time there was a lot of them that was still open and I was, where they put me at in the job that they told me to do at the time, it made me go into the apartments, at will. It was like, you go by a door and you see a door open into an apartment and see what was going on and if you find somebody in there sleeping or anything, then call in and let us know. So, that was exactly my detail all the time.

J: Back up. The night that Terri was killed which was May 30th or 31st, you were working there, you got to work at approximately what time?

W: Eight or nine, at night. I would come in early, I've been coming in early for a while.

J: I think your log stated you came in about ten-forty that night.

W: No.

J: Maybe earlier?

W: I probably called on at about ten-forty but I was there earlier.

J: Can your supervisor . . .

W: Where did you get that from?

J: Oh, this is from your mom.

W: Oh, is that right?

J: Yeah, we put it into property after we got done. You're referring to this newsletter here?

W: Yeah. I was wondering what's he doing with that, (inaudible) on Buddhism.

J: Now, let's get back. You were visited by your supervisor that night. What's his name?

W: Uh, uh . . .

J: Bob something?

W: Yeah, Bob. I forgot his last name.

J: Ricks, or . . .

W: Ricks.

J: Ricks.

W: Ricks, yeah.

J: Where were you at when he visited the site, do you remember?

W: Right there in the garage.

J: In the garage?

W: Yeah. He pulled up, I came out of the garage, you know, and then he was talking to me for a little while and then he left. And then it be about two hours later, then that's when I left.

J: And you don't recall ever seeing Terri that night?

W: No, not at all.

J: Any lights on in her unit or anything?

W: I talked to the guy next door, next door to her.

J: Across?

W: Well, same end that I was on at first.

J: About how far away were you from Terri's unit that night?

W: She was in sixty-six, sixty-seven, sixty-eight . . . sixty nine, seventy, I was in seventy.

J: You were in seventy, at the end, right?

W: I was all the way at the end.

J: About five units down from her?

W: Yeah.

J: And you talked to who? The guy right across from her?

W: I think his name was Dick Wolf.

J: Wolf? '

W: Yeah. And I talked to him.

L: What time did you talk to Dick Wolf.

W: I talked to him about, I think about two day, the next day or the day after that, or something like that. And he was explaining to me he know, he said that I wasn't supposed to talk to nobody you know, and that nobody know what the police had said and everything. But he was telling me that somebody had went up there and killed her. And what happened to her and stuff. He said he had seen her lights on earlier but he said it was like the lights went out and he didn't even know what happened. He didn't even hear nothing or nothing and I was explaining to him the same thing. I said, man, I was down that way, you know I'm down here all the time. I said I didn't hear nothing going on. And he said that's kind of weird. He said my first instinct, you know, I was thinking, he said my assumptions could be wrong, you know, but anytime you assume something like that, you got to go with that sometimes because you never know. He said he assumed that it was one of the guards. Or . . . what's his name, Sammy.

J: Sammy?

W: Yeah, Sammy Battle. He said that's who he was thinking that it was because he heard, you know, what happened with him and her, you know, about the threatening and stuff. And from that day on, I had

told Billy, he works for the L.A.P.D. in ninety-nine, and I talked to him about it and everything and he left with me and we went over there to where the death line was up and everything and we had looked and he had said, yeah, that's where they're fingerprinting. That's the dust. And he took me around the back and showed me some more where they had dust, trying to find fingerprints and stuff, and to the front. And we were out looking at it and we left and then Dick came out, you know . . .

J: This was a couple of days after the . . .

W: Yeah about a couple or few days after, you know.

J: Let's get back to the night. You said there was nothing unusual on your shift of duty. You saw nobody. You were visited at one time by your supervisor.

W: Yeah. I was . . .

J: Did you fall asleep that night?

W: I probably did. I just . . .

J: Well, think back a bit, it may be important.

W: I can't even remember. I was asleep for, let me see, I slept in Mr. Quinn's car for, from about nine all the way into about quarter to eleven or about ten thirty-five, something like that.

J: Let's get back to the screen, the screen where your fingerprints were.

W: I was thinking about that last night. About the screen, you know. I was just thinking, I mean the screen could have been there from the time that I was working and I had to go into them and check them and put the tags up on the door and stuff. I could have had the screen, put the screen down, somebody (illigible) take the screen out or something, man.

L: Well, we know that the screen was intact in

the frame the day before she was found. The screen was in the window frame.

W: The frame, the screen has always been there. They haven't been there for a long time. The screens was there for even I got there. When I got there all the screens was on.

L: Now, the next morning when she was found, the screen is taken out of the window, it's bent in half and it's found at the front door and your fingerprints are on the edges of where it's in the window frame, it would have been inside the frame itself or touching against metal and wood. Understand what I mean? You know when you take a frame out of a window?

W: Yeah.

L: Well, the part of the frame, of the window screen itself that fits into the framing mechanism?

W: Yeah.

L: That's where your prints are at.

W: They're on the screen and the window?

L : The frame of the screen that would normally fit inside the window. So in other words, if you was to come up to that screen and just touch it with your hand, that's not where the prints were found. The prints were found as if somebody would have taken that screen out.

W: I mean how . . .

J: The screen sets inside of the window frame and the metal part is not exposed to the outside and you have to physically remove that screen to get your fingerprints on it. Follow our thought?

W: I understand what you all are saying but . . . I was . . . how could I remove the screen off a window. I have, you have to do something, you know, you have to have something to get, you know . . .
SIDE ONE OF TAPE ENDS.

SIDE TWO OF TAPE BEGINS.

W: I don't mean to smoke you out.

J: Go ahead. There's no ladders out there you're saying.

W: No, I didn't, you know . . .

J: Okay, let's assume then we got into the apartment some other way and say, well, we better make this look like a burglary so someone's going to have to remove the screen.

W: Make it look like a burglary?

J: Yeah.

W: How else would you get into an apartment unless . . .

J: You told us yesterday there was only three ways to get into those units.

W: Right.

J: Sliding door, front door or a window.

W: Right, that's the only way.

J: For the window you needed a ladder and there are, I'm sure there's ladders over there. I used to work there, security, and there's . . .

W: At Paradise West?

J: No, not at Paradise West, but I worked over at Porto Bello.

W: Porto Bello? When'd you work at Porto Bello?

J: Shit, I used to live right over there.

W: And you worked security at Porto Bello? I used to work security at Porto Bello.

J: Well, you guys replaced us.

W: Who was you working for?

J: It was all Urban Police over there before we were terminated and they hired Interstate.

W: Oh, is that right?

J: They said we were too expensive, I guess. I used to live in Lomita, that's when I bought my place

over there. So I know the ins and outs of all those places over there cause I worked there.

W: I don't know, man, how that screen got in there or how it got off the window, all I know is . . .

J: Your prints are on this screen, the screen was removed from the window, bent and set right at the front door, like I'm going to take this out of here when I leave, so to speak. That's where the frame is, that's where the screen is, right by the front door-like and it was in the window the day before. And your prints are on this screen. So you explain to me how . . .

W: I don't know. That's strange. How in the world can my prints be just on the screen and ain't on nothing else. Not even on her body. Or her room or nowhere. Throughout the whole entire house no other prints was found, just on the screen.

J: That's what so far they've made your prints. There's other prints. They're still looking at prints. The evidence is still being analyzed. We'll be finding prints other places in there, too.

W: How come you couldn't have . . . I mean, just like I said, I worked in that area there for about ever since the middle of May.

J: Yeah.

W: And I had been working there for awhile.

J: It's not your job to go touch all the screens.

W: I probably didn't touch that screen. I don't know how that screen got right there with my fingerprints on it. But like I said I worked in there for awhile, I probably could have touched the screen you know, I probably could have touched a doorknob or I could . . . my fingerprints might be all over that alley. It just due to the point that I have worked up and down that alley a while and I have worked . . .

L: We're not talking about any prints on door-

knobs, any prints in the alley, any prints outside of Terri Horgan's unit. We're talking about prints found on a screen which had been removed and bent during the night of the 30th and 31st and left at the front door. That's the only prints we're talking about.

W: How did you know that the screen was removed during the night of the 31st?

L: Because she had spoke with her mother on the day of the 30th. Her mom had been over, the family had been over. They're in the process of moving in and the screen was in the window. I mean, you walk into your house you know if there's a screen right there. You know if it's off the window and bent.

J: These screens have to be taken off from the inside. They can't be taken off from the inside unless you push in on at and bend it, which this screen . . .

W: Well, how do you know she didn't do that?

J: Who did that?

L: Her prints aren't on it.

W: Nowhere?

L: No.

W: Mine are.

J: Your's are. And your hair or a similar type of hair is found in the room where she was killed. So that's the two points you have to explain to us.

W: That's the two points that I can't explain, that's what I'm trying to say. That's the hard explanation, I mean . . .

L: Your mother when we talked to her earlier she was explaining what you mentioned yesterday. In your religion that you cause and effect.

L: And she expounded a little bit on what you were saying that if there was a cause that sometimes the effect can be greater than the cause.

W: Yeah

L: What I'm asking you is that is there something you're holding back because you don't want to get a friend in trouble or you don't want to do this.

W: No, it ain't even that at all. It's like I said, if, I know that I'm in the Buddhist practice and it's based on cause and effect and all the things that I done seen that people done did to me and what happened to them in the end, believe me, I do not want to go nowhere doing nothing wrong and have to deal with that. Even if somebody's accusing me wrongly and I in here like this and you're badgering me to death like that, something could happen to you guys.

L: We're not going to badger you. We're just trying to find out if you've thought, of anybody who had a vendetta against you.

W: I mean it could have been Sammy. He could have did it. You know what I'm saying, I mean . . .

L: It could have been who?

W: Sammy. It also could have been the old guy. It could have been anybody. It could have been anybody.

L: Sammy's prints aren't in there.

W: It could have been a boyfriend.

L: Nobody knew she was living there that night.

W: I didn't know that she was living there that night. The only one that knew she was there that night was Dick Wolf. The guy that lived right next door and he told me that he had seen her lights on.

J: And that was two days afterwards.

W: A couple days, the next day, something like that, when we had that little talk.

J: We checked all these people out.

W: I had went over and talked to Billy

J: Every one of those people you just named, we had checked out.

W: Hair samples, everything?

J: Yeah.

W: Even Billy and Sammy's hair?

J: A couple of the employees, Arnold's hair, we did Dan Black's hair.

W: You even did all of them?

J: All of them.

W: All the employees that worked there?

J: And guess what, what comes up? Yours.

W: I mean, why would I want to hurt somebody like that.

L: I don't think whoever did this wanted to hurt Terri. I think whoever did this went in there, looking to take something and that's the way it appears. It looks like they were looking for some loose money, something small.

J: Maybe he went in there to sleep?

W: What would I want to look for some loose money for or something like that for, when I got a job and I'm getting paid.

L: Whoever did this . . .

W: Plus overtime.

L: Okay. He didn't move any big items. There was a brand new television and stuff like that. It wasn't disconnected and moved to the door, so this isn't a standard burglary where somebody's going to come there and say I'm going to steal this 25" television. This is a time that somebody's looking for small items.

W: The only one that been in her apartment since she moved in was Sammy. And she made it plain about that. And I had never been . . .

L: we checked Sammy out very thoroughly. Sammy, we know where he was that night. We know who he was with. He was there well past the time

that this was committed. His fingerprints weren't there. His hair doesn't match. We basically eliminated Sammy. We have nothing.

W: So I'm the only one.

L: You're the only one we have hair matching and fingerprints.

J: And you said you've never been in her unit.

W: I don't think I ever been in her unit. I'm not saying that I ain't never been in there, but if I been in there, it probably be because, like I said I was putting a tag or something on the door and it was way before she . . .

J: What about this. Maybe you went in there to sleep that night.

W: No.

J: And she caught you. And you go, hey, you've already complained about Sammy. I'm going to lose my job over this. She starts something.

W: No.

L: She starts screaming at you and yelling and . . .

W: If she starts screaming and yelling at me, don't you think the guy next door would have heard.

J: Not the way he sleeps (inaudible).

L: I don't know. I'm trying to think, Terri seems like a pretty ballsy girl, from what I knew about her. And she would be more of a on the offensive that she would be more like a, you know, a little scaredy cat over in the corner. I think she would be more, confront somebody than she would be to hide or retreat or try to hide in a closet. So I think that somebody that was in there was obviously there to commit a theft. There was some items taken, property's missing and I think there was a confrontation by Terri and the person that was in there.

W: No, I would never. That's one thing, I could

tell you for a fact. I have never even argued with her. I wouldn't have nothing but a conversation with her.
L: We don't think whoever went in there knew Terri was there.
W: Probably didn't. I don't know.
L: I think it was a surprise to whoever went in there that Terri was even inside the unit. I don't think somebody went there with the intention of killing Terri. First of all, nobody knew that she was staying there that night. She has no enemies. I think it was she was in the wrong place at the wrong time.
W: Who?
L: Terri. And whoever ended up being in there and killing her went there for a different reason than to kill her. Went there to commit a theft or went there because he was bored and wanted to look around or went there to sleep. I don't know what, that's an unknown, okay?
W: I ain't never went into, especially when these people are moving in these places. I ain't never went into one of these places. The only person's house that I had been over was Billy.
J: Yeah, but you didn't know Terri was there that night.
W: I didn't know nobody was at home that night. All I knew was I came home and I was sitting and talking to another officer and then he said you know if you want to kick back until the time for your shift. Then I said yeah and he wanted me to just sleep it out so I just went in there and slept for a little while, then the next thing I know I woke up and one thing, Carney came too, he came too that same night.
L: Who did?
W: Carney.
L: Who's Carney?

W: Bob Carney.

J: The manager.

W: He's the next supervisor.

J: And he came just as you were coming on duty?

W: Yeah.

J: Let's go back to those prints though.

W: Man, I don't know how those prints got in there, man. I cannot tell you that. I know you all probably don't believe that and probably the judge won't believe it, the jury won't believe it, but I do not know, man. And that's the God's honest truth.

J: How about on Buddha?

W: On what Buddha?

J: Well, the statement you were telling us.

W: What about it?

J: Do you swear on Buddha that it's the truth?

W: Yeah. I swear.

J: Only one person can make one person's fingerprint. And that's the person (inaudible) with their hand.

W: I don't know how, man. You never know.

J: You'll feel better if you tell us about it.

W: What?

L: We know you didn't go there to kill her.

W: I didn't go there to kill her?

L: We know you didn't.

W: I didn't go to work at all to kill nobody.

L: We know that. Something happened that night.

W: I did not even see her at all that day.

L: And you didn't let anybody in there?

W: I don't know how, it's a lot of ways you can get in there.

L: Well, I know, but I mean by whichever way the person got in there originally, did you help anybody get in there?

W: No. I didn't help nobody in there.

L: Did somebody come up to you that night and hand you a screen and said would you bend this and give it and then he took it back from you?

W: No.

L: Well, I mean, we got a bent screen taken off a window that occurred that night.

J: Set at the front door like somebody forget the damn thing.

W: How did somebody . . .

J: Like the person wanted to take that screen out with them that night, but they didn't, they forgot. After killing somebody you're not thinking right.

W: Okay, then I don't know.

L: Especially when you go there and you didn't want to hurt anybody when you went there. You went there and something happened and it got out of control. The whole thing went to shit.

W: I don't know what happened.

J: If that screen had been carried out that night and discarded in the dumpster, you'd have been home free.

W: I wasn't even thinking about nothing like that. I wasn't thinking about nothing. I don't know how that screen got in there. I don't know how or what happened to her into the next day when I came home.

J: How about your hair? How'd your hair get up there in that room'?

W: As far as hair, man, you go by what somebody else told you.

J: He's an expert.

W: Experts make mistakes.

J: (inaudible) criminalist.

W: Then again, you all did not submit no evidence to me that, you know, or show me that . . .

J: Hey, we've been straight with you this whole investigation.

W: I haven't seen no hair . . .

J: You've read the fingerprint analysis.

W: Yeah, but you still didn't show me that you had the hair.

J: We showed you the picture of the screen.

W: But that still didn't have shown me no picture of my hair.

L: If I go get you a report written by the criminalist from the Crime Lab dated and signed, then will you believe us that we, that the hairs were found there and they appear to be your hairs?

W: No.

J: It said they could have originated from Jody . . .

W: I want to see my hair that was took.

L: Well your hair that was took was taken by Detective Conley and myself.

W: You were the guys that took the hair.

L: We were in the garage.

W: Yeah, I'm talking about my hair that you all took from me. But I'm talking about the hair that you took out of the apartment.

J: Well, that was collected the day of the crime.

L: The day that the body was found.

J: We took vacuum, vacuumed the whole room, vacuumed the whole body and took all the stuff up and we took it to the lab. And we took your's up there with several other people's.

W: You guys vacuumed?

L: Yeah.

W: And took it up there?

L: Yeah.

W: And my hair was in the vacuum?

L: That's what the expert at the crime lab says.

He looked at all the hairs. He looked at Sammy Battle's hair. He looked at Dan Black's hairs. He looked at everybody's hair.

W: He even looked at her hairs?

J: Yes. Her hairs.

W: Man.

L: At the autopsy we took hair samples from her. We have everybody's hairs. The only person he says it that it appears that some of the hairs collected . . .

J: Could have originated from Jody Williams.

W: Could have.

L: Well, that's how they word that. They appear to be the same.

W: We can't live on appear to be.

L: Well.

W: I mean, we got to live on facts. That's just like you guys trying to tell me . . .

J: Well, that's what he's going to come and testify.

W: That's just like me saying you all, you saying that I did it. You saying that I did it . . .

J: We're not saying you did. We're saying facts. We're saying we have hair that could have come from you.

W: Could have come.

J: We have the fact that your fingerprints are on the screen that was removed during the commission of this crime.

W: You might as well not even take that to the District Attorney, cause you got to have facts, man.

J: That is facts.

W: That's not fact.

J: Yes, it is.

W: No it's not.

J: Well, then you have a different interpretation of facts.

W: Well, put it like this, man. Due to the fact that I have been through the judicial system and the law that I have studied going through the judicial and what I know, murder is one of the easiest things to beat. First of all, cause first of all, you got to have facts. And if you don't have facts, you don't have no case. And it can go on to two more times. You can come and get me again and bring me back and we can go through it again.

L: If you're a learned student, as you say, on the law, then you should be fully aware that many people have been convicted and sentenced on less evidence than fingerprints.

W: No.

L: Did you ever hear of motive, did you ever hear of things like that? People have been sentenced by that.

W: Yeah, but I still, they going to look at a motive. They going to look at the facts, which there isn't any facts.

J: The facts of this case are, you were on duty that night. You are there at the scene.

W: Yeah, I was there. But it's a whole lot of people living there.

J: Not during the time she's killed.

W: Yeah, there's a whole lot of people there.

J: Yeah, that are living there.

W: Yeah.

L: But none of their fingerprints . . .

J: None of their fingerprints were there. None of their hairs were there.

W: Did you check the whole, everybody in there?

J: All, everything.

W: Well, I mean this morning just me.

J: You said that murder was the easiest rap to beat. How do you know that?

W: How do I know that?

J: Yeah.

W: Because, man, you got to have facts. And without facts you cannot win a case like that.

L: Well, how about evidence? How about evidence?

W: Evidence, you got to have factive evidence.

L: Factive evidence?

W: And you said it could be. You said it could be my hair.

J: That just all adds up.

W: No. You can't.

L: That's the hairs.

W: No.

J: The fingerprints is the best evidence.

W: Alright.

J: Fingerprints is the best evidence in any case.

W: No.

J: Yes.

W: Only on the screen?

J: A screen that was removed during the time of the murder.

W: But how you know that . . .

J: (inaudible)

W: But how you know it was removed when, when, the night she got killed? How you know it wasn't . . .

J: Because we have her mother . . .

W: . . . Three or four days before . . .

J: No.

W: . . . or six or seven day before . . .

J: It wasn't removed before then because the mother was in the apartment that day. She saw the screen in place.

W: They went around and checked?

J: That morning, that morning at eight o'clock.

W: Oh, man.

J: Listen to me, at eight o'clock at night (S/B in the morning) when Dan Black came into her apartment he noticed that screen by the front door. He said well, this is unusual. Why is the screen not in it's place.

W: He didn't touch it?

J: He didn't touch it. His prints aren't on it.

W: Dan Black, who is Dan Black?

J: Customer service representative for Dunn Homes.

W: Oh.

J: He was the person who opened up the apartment at seven-thirty in the morning or eight o'clock on the 31st. He worked there until eleven o'clock that morning. The mother came in that day and said, where's my daughter. He goes I don't know. And that's when they found Terri up in her room.

W: She was (inaudible)

J: Yeah. So you're saying that's an easy crime to beat and we're saying . . .

W: I'm saying that it's not easy to beat. No, I can't say that. But I can say this though, for a fact, though, I can say this. I don't know, man, how my fingerprints come up in that woman's on that woman's screen on in there, period, when in fact, I did not enter no houses at all that night.

J: You've been saying that ever since yesterday and you said yesterday I never was in there. And today you're saying I could have been.

W: I'm saying that because I have been up and down that alley the whole time.

L: We're not talking about the alley, Jody. We're talking about the bent screen found at the front door.

W: The bent screen found at the front door I do not know.

L: We're talking about hairs that were found inside the room that she was murdered in. Those are the big questions.

J: It's like a jigsaw puzzle. You put all the pieces together and . . .

W: And what you have?

L: We got a picture of you.

W: You got a picture of me. I can't see how you got a picture of me.

L: Well, we're going around in circles now. We've already explained to you.

W: Alright, take for instance, that you're 100 percent sure that they was my hairs. I'm talking about, don't say . . .

L: That's not for us to say. Jody, let me tell you this.

W: I just want to know . . .

J: Jody, let me tell you this.

W: . . . Is you for sure that they was my hairs.

L: We have the first report that says it appears, believe it, it's verbatim, (inaudible) hairs and that were compared to hairs found in this location and they matched the hairs received from subject Jody Williams. It appears it is the same person. That's the way he wrote it.

J: Now, if you know hair evidence, it's not conclusive. But taken with fingerprints and hair, it becomes pretty damn conclusive.

W: Yes.

L: Cause everybody else's hair that he submitted, he was able to say these hairs are definitely not from the person.

J: It's something you can rule out, it's not.

W: How could you tell that they were my hairs?

J: The criminalist can. He does a microscopic test on it. It's the same thickness, the same length, the same color, the same pigmentation, the same everything.

W: How he know it could have been butt hairs, man?

L: Well, he said they appeared to be pubic hairs?

W: How do you know that they was pubic hairs?

L: I'm not an expert.

W: Did he smell . . .

L: That's what he says, okay?

J: By the slides, by the texture, by the curling of it.

W: The curling of it?

L: Look, we're not hair experts, he is. He's the one that has to come to court to testify as an expert.

W: It's stupid though, how in the world, Jesus . . .

J: We know there was a struggle in her room that night. Hair could easily have been pulled or stretched or . . .

W: My hair ain't even long enough to be pulled and it haven't been.

L: Well, the hairs that are on your head couldn't have been your hairs cause I saw the hairs being examined. Your hair on your head right now, you've had a short haircut for sometime. They're not head hairs. He said they weren't your head hairs. He said they were your pubic hairs.

W: My pubic hair ain't that long either.

J: Your belly hair. Let's see your belly.

L: I saw the hairs that he examined, okay.

W: No. You all got the wrong person.

J: I think we got the right person, Jody. And you think, you're ready to tell us what happened.

W: I'm not ready to tell you nothing like that, man. Especially nothing like that, especially when I ain't had nothing to do with that.

L: You told us yesterday and you told us today you think you could beat this case. You said murder is one of of, how did you put that? Murder is the hardest case to prove.

W: Yeah.

J: Easiest case to beat.

L: And yesterday you said the easiest case to beat.

W: I said it was the one of the hardest cases to prove, man.

L: What makes any harder than anything else?

W: Because you got to have facts.

L: Well, I think we got facts. We're going to have to present the case.

W: I mean if you get up there in front of the courtroom and you tell them that there appeared to be in his hair, that's not . . .

J: We're not going to get up.

W: That's not substantial enough.

J: The experts have testified in probably a hundred cases like this and probably sent several people to jail just on hair, fiber.

L: He's the expert and they do convict on that evidence.

W: Well, I guess I won't ever see you guys no more. (inaudible).

L: Well, this is going to be the last time we have an opportunity to do a conversation, Jody.

W: When is we supposed to be going to court?

L: I'm going to take the case over this afternoon to the District Attorney. After he files the complaint, you'll be taken over tomorrow morning for arraignment.

W: He going to file a complaint tomorrow, you sure he's going to file the case? Are you sure?

L: I wouldn't tell you if . . .

W: Are you sure?

L: I've been doing this for twenty years. He's been doing it for over twenty years. If I didn't think . . .

W: I mean, you all don't have no witnesses, no nothing, man.

L: I'd rather have fingerprints in any case than an eyewitness.

J: There is no witness in a homicide case almost 90 percent of the time. The victim's dead.

W: I mean nobody didn't hear nothing. I mean, that just, that's stupid. I mean, even I, where I was sitting at I didn't hear nothing, man.

J: You heard. You were probably in her apartment.

W: Why you want to say something like that?

L: Because that's what the evidence points to.

J: That's what the evidence points to. You asked me a question, I'm telling you. That's a fact as I see it.

W: You (inaudible) sit tell me up and tell me that I was there. You can't tell me that I was there. You wasn't there. You didn't see me.

J: We got work to do Jody.

L: Okay, Jody, unless you want to tell us something enlightening, we're going to take the case over and file it as is. If you want to tell us how your prints got there, this is your opportunity, otherwise . . .

W: I already told you, man, that I don't know, man.

L: Okay.

W: I been working in that area for a while.

L: Okay.

W: And I been sleeping in places and I been doing a lot of stuff around there but I know man. . . .

J: You only worked there two weeks.

W: No, I've worked there longer than two weeks.

L: Okay, the time is now eleven-forty hours. We're going to terminate this interview.

TAPE STOPS

Chapter XVI

INVESTIGATION REQUEST
SUPPLEMENTAL
April 4, 1990
(Trial Date Not Yet Set)

Request by Trial Deputy PD Ron Cory

REQUEST

(Read testimony of Douglas Bonner at prelim. See me for transcript.)

1. Interview Douglas Bonner, Helen Bonner, 3200 Alder, #65, Urban, California. Please interview Mr. Bonner about the night of the homicide. Is there anything else he remembers that he didn't testify to at the prelim?

Interview Mrs. Bonner independently (i.e. maybe call her at home before interviewing Mr. Bonner) about the night of the homicide. Does she agree with the times (i.e. victim's light on, off, dog walk, got to bed, etc.). Does she remember anything that Mr. Bonner doesn't remember (i.e. screams, the presence of a ladder next day, seeing Sammy Battle that night, etc.)

Please interview Mr. Bonner concerning the following:

(1) Does he know when his carpeting and the victim's carpeting was installed? Locks installed?

(2) Please have Mr. and Mrs. Bonner describe all the facts he knew about Battle to make him (Bonner) call him a "5150" (walking crazy).

(3) Did Bonner ever see defendant Williams with the carpet installer at Terri's condo? See him inside the condo? See him talking to Terri?

(4) When Bonner left for work the day the body was found (5/31) did he see a bent screen by Terri's front door?

Ask Mrs. Bonner if she recalls the events of the day the body was found. Did she see Dan Black enter Terri's apartment? Did she see any bent screens? Did she see workmen enter and leave? Can she just narrate every thing she remembers up until the time the police finally <u>left</u> (6:30 p.m.).

4/23/90
Phone call — William (Billy) Duncan.

Duncan was "astounded" to hear Williams was arrested for murder.

Duncan may have caught him sleeping. Just can't remember. Had open heart surgery. Lost a lot of blood. Memory became faulty.

1st suspect would be Battle a "mental case." Always trying to hit on women at complex.

Time caught William's graveyard shift. Early morning hours. D hadn't called in on radio. Duncan driving around and saw garage door close. Pretty sure unit #17. Duncan entered. Saw Williams on stairs leading in from garage. Duncan went upstairs into top bedroom and saw D's bag with clothing in it. D obviously sleeping in that room.

Doors of units with locks but unoccupied were supposed to be locked at night but were frequently left unlocked. Harold Nolan instructed guards to enter and see if anything missing.

Doors were frequently "tagged." If somebody opens door tag falls. Guard then enters to see if that person inside or something taken.

Carts were charged from open garages.

Caught a big black guard sleeping at Paradise West sometime after murder of Tracy. Hired after Williams left to guard in Inglewood.

Sammy Battle and Williams became good friends at Arbor Vitae Complex.

Duncan caught them together at Donut Shop in Inglewood once when Williams supposed to be on duty. Wrote them up.

"Real strange" for Battle to go back to Paradise West in Sept. at 2:30 a.m. looking to see if Williams on duty.

Sam Battle most cooperative. Knows case evidence is not strong. Basically said "it could be anybody" [i.e., any guard could be charged because they sleep? or leave prints? He didn't elaborate].

Duncan seems to want to help Williams. Called me at his boss's [sic] insistence.

Ron Cory, Dep.PD

Public Defender
County of Los Angeles

INVESTIGATIVE REPORT

Investigator: Robert E. Gonzales

Date: April 8, 1990

Douglas Bonner
3200 Alder, Unit #65
Urban, California

On 4/8/90, 1 contacted the above.

He said that he started moving in about 5/22/89.
The carpet was installed in his condo, Terri's must
also have had the carpet. Neither condo had curtains/
drapes. The condo also had the lock's installed.

He re-keyed the locks after moving in, he does
not know about Terri's locks.

He does not remember seeing the defendant
(Williams) with the carpet installer at Terri's condo.

He never saw the defendant (Williams) speaking with the victim.

He did not notice a ladder and he did not notice
the bent screen by Terri's door.

He said that (Sammy) Battle is a nice, simple,
guy. To him he had the mental capacity of a 10-12
year old. Battle could not hold a conversation. He
could not maintain a thought. He rambled on and
on. Battle just wants to be liked. He would stop and
talk, he would knock on the door and just talk, talk
about nothing.

He would see him when he walked his dog. Battle
may even have been in his condo several times.

Chapter XVII

Gina DiBello
---- Torrance Blvd., #8
Urban, California

On April 11, 1990, I, Robert E. Gonzalez, Public Defender's Office Investigator, Los Angeles County, contacted the above.

She said she has known Sammy Battle for about six years.

She considers Sammy a good friend. She does not know Sammy's sister.

Her children are aged: 4 years, 3 years, and 2 years.

She has never seen Sammy angry. He is a private person. He is very easily embarrassed and is reluctant to discuss anything about himself.

Sammy is not a violent person. She would not let him baby sit if she thought that he was violent.

He never mentioned his job. She said that he wants to be liked and is always trying to do something for someone.

He never mentioned any lady, anything about any lady who was displeased with (him), he did not talk about his job.

She was gone for about two hours. She went shopping and to Michaels. She is not sure but Sammy baby sat between 8 p.m. and 10 P.M.

She had no reason to pay attention to the clock. The children were safe with Sammy.

She said that she cannot go over the evening hour by hour.

Sammy had no access to a car. He got around by walking and by depending on the bus.

The kids are to(o) young to be interviewed, besides, Gina said that she does not want me speaking to them. My contact with the kids was trying not to step on them and keeping them away.

She said that now she does not know exactly what time she left again but it was after 10:00 p.m. She must have come back about 2:00 a.m. however, she is not sure.

She got up about 8:00 a.m. and Sammy was there. He spent the night, he spent the night many times!

She does not know if Sammy and the defendant were or are good friends, she does not remember Sammy ever mentioning Jody Williams.

Public Defender
County of Los Angeles

INVESTIGATIVE REPORT

Date: April 12, 1990
Ekiko Yamada
3200 Alder
Urban, California

On 4/12/90 1 contacted the above. She said that she was living at the complex at the time of the mur-

der. She is surprised that she was not contacted by the police.

(Sammy) Battle talked to her just one time, she said that he was just strange. He made no sense in his conversation.

She was not surprised when Sammy was fired.

She talked to him several times while moving into her condo. At first he was very friendly, then she found him obnoxious

He would knock on her door and ask for coffee. Then he would ask her for something to eat. He just made her uncomfortable.

He would play the radio real loud in the early morning hours. He would be next to her condo. He would then talk over the walkie-talkie.

One day he asked her to go get him a hamburger.

She saw no ladder by the victim's condo.

Public Defender
County of Los Angeles

INVESTIGATIVE REPORT

Date: April 12, 1990
Patricia Channing
3200 Alder
Urban, California

On 4/12/90 I contacted the above. She moved in the weekend before Memorial Day, 1989. She does not know anything about (Sammy) Battle.

She does remember the defendant (Williams). She felt bothered and harassed by the defendant. He always seemed to want access to her condo. The defendant told her about the murder. He told her that

it was a family member. He told her that the victim had inherited her money.

She felt threatened by the defendant. He was constantly about her condo.

He would park under her window and she could hear him on the walkie-talkie.

He even asked if he could walk her over to the victim's condo.

He told her that he knew that she was by herself.

She would close her patio gate and in the mornings it would be open, she is certain, she is certain that the defendant was creeping by her windows. She was never contacted by the police

NOTE: It is noted that due to the passage of time between the murder event (5/30-31/89) and Ms. Channing's interview (4/12/90) it is likely Ms. Channing has reversed the identities of Sammy Battle and Jody Williams in her memory.

Chapter XVIII

On November 30, 1990, a confidential source of known reliability advised that DON ARNOLD was arrested on November 2, 1989, by the Los Angeles County Sheriff's Office for Burglary. He was convicted on January 19, 1990, for three counts of First Degree Burglary and was sentenced on February 7, 1990, to six years in the State Penitentiary. The source advised that ARNOLD is presently incarcerated at Deuel Vocational Institute, Tracy, California. His CII Number is A09317838 and his CDC Number is E044851.

URBAN POLICE DEPARTMENT
DR #9870   Supplementary Report

LEGEND
L: DETECTIVE RICK LANDER
C: DETECTIVE JIM CONLEY
X: WITNESS

L: The date and time is 4-12-90 is approximately 11:32 in the a.m. This will be an interview between myself Detective Rick Lander, my partner Jim Conley and X.

L: Okay. Part of this interview, did you write a letter to the Los Angeles District Attorney's Office?

X: Yes, I did.

L: And did you indicate in that letter that you have some possible information in regards to a homicide which occurred in Urban?

X: Yes, I did.

L: Showing you a letter that I have in front of me. Is this the letter that you wrote?

X: Yes sir.

L: Okay, and that's your handwriting?

X: That's my handwriting.

L: Okay. The person that I'm currently preparing for trial is a Jody Williams. Do you know Jody Williams?

X: Yes sir.

L: And where do you know Jody Williams from?

X: I met him in the Los Angeles County Jail.

L: I've previously shown you a what we call sixpack it has six pictures of male blacks and you circled one picture and you signed and dated it. Is this the person that you spoke with in . . .

X: Yes sir.

L: . . . the County jail?

X: Yes sir.

L: Prior to this meeting. Have I offered you any reduction in sentence or any leniency on any term that you are presently serving?

X: No sir.

L: Okay. Why don't you in your own words tell me why you wrote the letter or what information you have about Jody Williams?

X: Basically it's being eaten up inside you know ever since I heard of the gruesome crime and this is all I can get rid of, just bring it out like this.

L: And when did you first hear from Jody Williams whatever you heard concerning the crime he has being accused of?

X: We were together possibly three to four days before he came out with, you know details.

L: And what did he tell you?

X: He was just telling me about a murder he did that he is in jail for.

L: Okay. Can you go into the detail about what he told you?

X: Well, basically he's told me from how it started to how it ended and it started when he went to work. He worked midnight, swings, I mean graveyard and about 12:00 o'clock he said he smoked him a joint and so he then, well, you know, a little buzz and he was new at this apartment, I mean a townhouse or condominium; I have never been there and he used a ladder from the construction site which was across the street evidently or somewhere in that vicinity. He got the ladder and proceeded to put it by the garage, or the bedroom window, or somewhat of not. He entered the place just looking for something to steal. Okay, after he looked around, he went upstairs. I guess it's a upstairs apartment whatever. And he said, he went, he looked in the bedroom and saw a girl. So he ran downstairs and he realized, hey, this woman saw him and knew him. So then he proceeded to go back upstairs, then he grabbed ahold of the door knob, but she was on the other end. So he finally pushed her out of the way, and she was running to get the phone. That's when he gets to beating her up and after he beat her up for a while he shuts the bedroom window so no one can hear, whatever. So uh, she was wearing jogging, sweat pants. A halter top. That's what he described she was wearing, and okay he say he then proceeded to tell her to, she say she would do anything, just don't kill her or hurt her. So he told her to suck his dick. So which

she did, alright. Then after that, he says he wanted to have sex. So after she got all her clothes off, he said he didn't have sex in the vagina, he went in the ass. Okay, probably why investigators didn't say rape. And that's how the pubic hair got down on the floor. After that he realized he done fucked up. So he got to beating her real bad and started dragging her around on the floor. Then he just took her panties and put them around her neck, until she was out of it. Then he didn't know if she was dead or not, so he had on some construction boots, which are at his brother's house. If you can find his brother? Then he got to kicking her in the face and all over the body and then he put the clothes back on. I don't know if he set her back in the bed or what not. Then he proceeded, he went downstairs, he found her purse. He took 600.- out of her purse. And he went on about his business. And they found a fingerprint on the screen. That is supposed to, he said he had a glove on but he may have left his print there.

L: Okay, did he say if he took anything other than the $600.00 dollars?

X: Just cash is the only thing he mentioned.

C: He said that . . . he said that he went in there just to steal something did he say that he saw anything inside there?

X: Well he knew that the person that was moving in was very wealthy and he didn't expect her to be at home.

L: Going over it one more time. He said he put a ladder up on the window

X: Yes.

L: And he made entry into the unit from the window?

X: Right.

L: And then he looked around downstairs?

X: Right,

L: Then he went upstairs?

X: Right.

L: And then he saw her in the bedroom?

X: Right and then he proceeded to run down, then he change his mind and went back.

L: Okay.

X: And by the time she had got, put herself behind the door, he pushed her out and got to beating her up.

L: And he said that he used her panties to strangle her with?

X: Right, no, I take that back, quote, it was her bra. Her halter top or bra strap. One of the two, that he used.

C: You also said, he said that she was dressed in some type of jogging . . .

X: Sweat pants, jogging pants.

C: Did he mention a color or anything?

X: No . . . no color. He didn't mention the color. You know the way he says she's a very attractive young lady, very wealthy just inherited some money just moved in there two days prior that was her second day there or a first night there something I think that was a Tuesday if I'm correct.

L: But he indicated to you that when he went in there he went to do his burglary, he didn't know . . .

X: Correct.

L: that she was going to be in there?

X: Right . . . okay.

L: So after he had struggled with her in the bedroom then he wanted to have oral sex with her?

X: Right he did have.

L: Ok. Was, did he tell you if he was able to ejaculate or to come when he was having oral sex?

X: Not oral sex.

L: Anal sex?

X: Anal sex is when, but he didn't do it inside of her.

L: He ejaculated or come on the floor?

X: On the floor,

C: Or on himself?

X: On the floor and on himself and then he commenced to dragging her around on the floor to smear it up.

L: Okay.

C: You mention that when Jody told you the story he kind of broke down just cried.

X: Yes, he cried . . . cause it was eating him up and I know he's facing the death penalty on this case and it's a gruesome crime.

L: Did he tell you after how he left the unit?

X: Well, through a garage, garage, they got a double garage or something there I can't recall in there I just, by the time I didn't

L: He made mention to you that there was finger prints?

X: On the screen.

L: On the screen and then you said something about gloves?

X: Right. He said he wore gloves when he said he was gaining entry to the, you know, when he took the screen out and threw it in, going in.

L: Okay, did he say where he left the screen at by any chance?

X: Maybe, what was it down by the window . . . the window or either in the hallway or something like that. Is been months ago since I heard the story I am just bringing it back, that's what.

C: You said he smoked a joint before?

X: Yeah, well about twelve he knew he had to be back and check in with the supervisor every hour or every two hours or something like that.

L: Did he say what he did now after he left, what he did the rest of the night?

X: Yes. He hung around as normal then he told me he got rid of a bunch of clothes or something that he was in, he had a security guard uniform. But the shoes he said he had too much blood in stuff on it so he gave them to his brother.

L: Okay.

C: Did he mention his brother's name?

X: No but I know he has a father and his brother is somewhere around there in Los Angeles but I don't know where.

L: I have one last question that I have. Had you ever known Jody from the streets from Los Angeles or any other institution prior to meeting in L.A. county Jail in November of 1989?

X: No sir.

L: Were you ever associated of his or any gangs that he or you or . . . or either he or you had been associated with?

X: No sir.

L: Do you know if he was previously or is now a gang member?

X: I know he previously was I don't know if he's still a gang member.

L: Do you know which gang that was?

X: Rolling 60 or something one of those crip gangs.

L: Okay and are you currently a gang member?

X: No sir.

L: And have you previously been associated with other gang members?

X: No no sir . . . no sir.

L: So you have no running feuds between Bloods, Crips . . . ?

X: No sir.

L: or two conflicting crips?

X: No sir.

C: I have a couple things. You said that Jody mentioned to you that . . . that that was how the pubic hair got on the ground?

X: Right.

C: Or on the floor because she was orally copulated. Did he tell you how far he undressed or . . . ?

X: He just pulled his pants down to his knees.

C: And after oral copulation then he started to . . . ?

X: Yeah.

C: . . . and then after that, that's when he pulled out and ejaculated all over . . .

X: The carpet.

C: Himself and the carpet?

X: Right.

C: And then he drug her . . . ?

X: Around.

C: Around.?

X: And then after that he sit on the edge of the bed or sit her down on the bed or sometime later he put her in, put her clothes back supposedly.

L: What did he used to strangle her with again?

X: It's either the bra strap or the halter top.

C: Did he say where he found the money?

X: In a purse, in some purse he supposedly found. 600, 700 somewhere in there.

C: Did he say what he did with the money or anything?

X: No he didn't.

L: We are going to terminate this interview. It's

now, is 11:45. Is there any other thing you want to say while the tape's still running?

   X: No that's it.

   TAPE ENDS.

   It is noted that this tape transcription has not been edited.

Chapter XIX

On December 29, 1990, 1 left the Paradise West condominium complex at 3200 Alder, Urban, California, and drove non-stop to 7835 30th Street, Saugus, California. I started at 3:30 p.m. and arrived at 5:13 p.m. (travel time one hour, thirty three minutes), Distance 78 miles.

On the same date, I left the Acacia Apartments, 7835 Acacia Street, Saugus, and drove non-stop to the Paradise West condominium complex, 3200 Alder, Urban, California (using a slightly different route - see below). I started at 7:15 p.m. and arrived at 8:50 p.m. (travel time one hour, fifty minutes). Distance 87 miles.

The trip from Urban to Saugus was as follows:

Alder north to Torrance Boulevard - west to Hawthorne Boulevard - north to the 405 (San Diego) Freeway - north to the 5 (Golden State) Freeway - north to the Acacia Apartments in Saugus.

The trip from the Acacia Apartments to Urban was as follows:

Acacia Apartments to Palmdale Boulevard - west to Bouquet Canyon Road (11 miles) - west on Bouquet Canyon Road to Valencia, California, meeting the 5 (Golden State) Freeway - south on the Golden State Freeway to the 405 (San Diego) Freeway - south on the 405 Freeway to Hawthorne Boulevard - south

on Hawthorne Boulevard to Torrance Boulevard - east on Torrance Boulevard to Alder - south on Alder to 3200 Alder, Urban, California.

Chapter XX

Kathy Borders, Manager, Acacia Apartments, Saugus, California, was contacted on the evening of December 29, 1990, for the purpose of determining the present whereabouts of Connie Mae Arnold.

She furnished the following information:

Connie, her two children, both boys, ages now about 18 or 19 and 11 or 12, and her alleged husband Don Arnold, used to live in Apartment 415 there; however, they skipped out about 1.5 years ago, owing rent. Apparently they were having financial difficulties. She does not know where they can now be located but she has heard that Don is now in prison for grand theft or burglary. She does not know the names of Connie's two boys. She does not know where Connie lives now. Connie used to work for a Ralph's Market in Santa Clarita. She may still be working there. She was in some kind of trouble with the law before she moved out of the Acacia Apartments.

She is not sure Connie and Don were married or just living together inasmuch as Connie used more than one surname. The only one she can remember is Donaldson. That may have been her maiden name or the name of the father of her two boys.

Most of her knowledge of the Arnolds comes from what others have told her inasmuch as she was only the manager of the apartments when they lived

there. She said that Andrea Foreman, the former Assistant Manager of the apartments, is no long there. She said Andrea is now Assistant Manager of the Green Mountain Apartments in Lancaster, California. She doubts that Andrea would know the present whereabouts of Connie as they did not like each other.

Shortly after the Arnolds moved out of the Acacia Apartments, some detectives came from the Los Angeles County Sheriff's Department, Santa Clarita Station, looking for Don Arnold. They took all the records regarding the Arnolds and have not returned them. She heard they later arrested Don but she does not know where.

The Arnolds moved into the Acacia Apartments in early 1989. They had previously lived at the Pepper Tree Apartments in Saugus.

During the time the Arnolds lived at the Acacia Apartments, Don said he had several hundred dollars worth of tools stolen from his truck. She urged him to report the theft to the Antelope Valley Station of the Los Angeles County Sheriff's Department but he refused to do so. She does not know why he would not report the theft. Don even tried to make it look like she was responsible for the loss because the tools were stolen while his truck was parked at the apartment house.

Ms. Borders suggested that Connie and her two boys may still be living in or around Saugus. She thinks this because the older boy was seen within the past six months at the Park Place Apartments there. (Later observation of the directory at that apartment complex did not reflect any name identifiable with Connie's name).

She further advised that she heard only sketchy information about the murder that occurred in Urban,

California, on May 30-31, 1989 (Horgan) and she knows no details. She said that during that time, Don Arnold was employed by Dunn Management in Urban, Don had a friend, Josh Boxer (wife Maria), who lived at Joshua Tree Apartments in Saugus at the time the Horgan murder occurred. Josh got Don Arnold a job at Dunn Management in Urban, California. Later, she heard, Connie's older son worked there too. Josh Boxer was a Supervisor at Dunn Management. The Boxers now reside at an apartment complex called Meadowlands Apartments in Orange, California, where Maria is an Assistant Manager.

Kathy Borders can be reached at (805) ---------

Marriage records for Los Angeles County, California, reflect that Greg L. Donaldson and Connie Mae Grayson were married at Yosemite National Park, California, on December 9, 1980, by Rev. John Brown, United Methodist Church, Box 546, Yosemite, California.

At the time of this marriage, Greg L. Donaldson was described as a male, born August 9, 1948 in California. This was his second marriage, the first having ended in divorce on January 10, 1976. He was 32 years of age. He resided in Saugus, California. His occupation was Market Manager, Bob's Food Market. His education level was 15 years. His father was Chester E. Donaldson, born in Ohio, and his mother was Jennie Patterson, born in Iowa.

At the time of this marriage, Connie Mae Grayson was described as a female, born November 9, 1945 in Utah. Her maiden name was MonteLeon. She was age 35 and this was her third marriage, the second having ended in divorce on May 20, 1979. She resided in Saugus, California. Her occupation was Vet's Assistant, Vet. Hospital. Her education level was

twelve years. Her father was Mario Vigil, born in Mexico and her mother was Clementina Monteleon, born in Utah.

Records of the Department of Motor Vehicles, Division of Drivers Licenses reflect that Connie Mae Donaldson was issued License #A0218858 on October 10, 1989. It is a Class 3 license and is valid. It expires on November 9, 1993. She is described as a female, born November 9, 1945, 5'8" tall, 140 pounds, brown hair, brown eyes. There is one violation-conviction on her driving record. She was cited on June 13, 1988 and convicted on May 16, 1989, for violation of Section 25658A, Vehicle Code. The Docket Number is 8T01540 in Court Number 19413. There is no plate number for the vehicle she was driving.

On December 31, 1990, the following investigation was conducted in efforts to locate the present whereabouts of Connie May Arnold so that she could be contacted for interview:

A search of the Los Angeles County Registered Voters Index was negative regarding Connie Mae Arnold or Donaldson. These records were also mute regarding Greg L. Donaldson.

On December 31, 1990, Andrea Foreman. Assistant Manager, Green Mountain Apartments, Lancaster, California, was contacted telephonically to determine if she could furnish the present whereabouts of Connie Mae Arnold. She advised she has no information as to where or how Connie can be located. She suggested that Kathy Borders, Manager of the Acacia Apartments in Saugus, California, be interviewed, as she might be helpful. She was not apprised of the fact that Kathy had, already been contacted.

The Manager of the Meadowlands Apartments, Orange, California, (Name withheld), advised that Josh and Maria Boxer live there but that Maria is not Assistant Manager there. She said she does not know either Don or Connie Mae Arnold. Josh and Maria Boxer were contacted telephonically for the purpose of asking for an appointment for interview regarding Don and Connie Arnold. They said they do not know where Connie can now be located but that they have heard that Don is in jail somewhere. Josh advised that he was not working for Dunn Management at the time the Horgan woman was murdered. He said he had worked for that company previously. He advised he would have to consult his attorney before he would grant this investigator an interview. He would make contact during the first week in January, 1991.

The following page reflects results of a search of the Los Angeles County Superior Court civil index regarding the divorce of Greg and Connie Mae Donaldson.

NOTE: Some names, addresses and telephone numbers are changed or omitted to save innocent parties embarrassment.
•

Case Number NVD ------- filed September 17, 1987, was reviewed at the Los Angeles County Court Clerk's Office, San Fernando, California. It is styled Connie Mae Donaldson, Petitioner, and Greg Lee Donaldson, - Respondent. It is an action for dissolution of marriage.

The following pertinent facts were obtained from the file:

1. The parties were married on December 9, 1980. The date separated was marked, "Undetermined at this time."

2. One minor child, born to this couple, was JAMIE Donaldson, a male, age 7, born March 15, 1980. JAMIE's address was -------------------- Saugus, CA 91350.

3. Petitioner's address at time of filing was ----------------------, Saugus, CA 91350.

4. Petitioner had another son by a former marriage by the name of TOMMY or THOMAS Garner, age 16 at the time of this petition.

5. Petitioner drives a 1984 Oldsmobile Cutlass.

6. Petitioner's attorney was --------------------------- ---------------------- Saugus, CA 913501

7. Petitioner's employment was Ralphs Market.

8. Petitioner's Social Security Number is ------------

9. Petitioner's education level was 12th Grade.

10. Respondent's residence was ---------------------- Saugus, CA 91350.

11. Respondent's employment was Ralphs Stores ---------------------- Tujunga, CA.

12. Respondent's Social security Number is ------------

13. Respondent's education level was 16 years.

14. Respondent's attorney was----------------------- --------------------------------

15. Petitioners former name, Monteleon, was restored to her. Her last known address in May, 1988, was ----------------------Saugus, CA 91350.

16. The minor child was to get $300.00 a month child support from the Respondent.

17. The Respondent was to get unlimited visitation, with legal custody to both Petitioner and Respondent, with physical custody to Petitioner and Respon-

dent was to be apprised of the address of the minor child at all times.

18. Final dissolution of the marriage was entered on May 13, 1988.

Chapter XXI

On January 3, 1991, a confidential source of known reliability advised that Greg L. Donaldson now resides at ---------------- Newhall, CA 91321, telephone (805) --- ----- He is employed at Ralph's Market, Lancaster, California, telephone (805) --- ------
Efforts to contact Donaldson at work on the afternoon of January 3,1991, were unsuccessful; however, it was verified that he is employed as stated above.

The confidential source also advised that Connie Arnold, also known at Donaldson, currently resides at ----- ------- Street, Panorma City, California, telephone (818) --- -----. This number is subscribed to by someone unrelated to Connie.

The source said he could find no employment for Connie Arnold. A call to the number failed to find anyone at home. Observation of the address revealed a one story three-bedroom house located on a corner lot. There were no cars parked there and no people were seen. No one responded to the doorbell or knocks on the front door.

At 5:15 p.m., January 3, 1991, an attempt to reach Greg L. Donaldson at his residence was unsuccessful. The telephone was answered by Henry Donaldson, age 10, the son of Greg and Connie Donaldson (Arnold). Henry advised that his dad is

married again and he does not know where his dad works now. He said his dad would be home soon. Henry said his mother, Connie, now lives with George Eastley on Catalina Street in Pasadena, California and can be reached at telephone (818) --- ----- Tommy is in the Army. A call was made to (818) --- ----- A man, identifying himself as George Eastley, answered the telephone. He advised that Connie is out job hunting but will probably be home at around 7:00 p.m. He suggested the caller, this investigator, call at about that time. He furnished his address as ---- South Catalina, Pasadena.

I finally made contact and interviewed Connie Arnold at a fast food restaurant in Pasadena on the evening of January 3, 1991.

The interview elicited the following information:

She married Don Arnold at Las Vegas, Nevada On July 16, 1988. They have been separated since October or November, 1989, when Don was arrested for burglary in Los Angeles County. He was convicted and is now serving his sentence in a state prison at Tracy, California.

During almost all of the time Don worked at Dunn Management in Urban, He and Chuck Weller would alternate days driving to work. Chuck drove a gray Nissan car. Don would leave home in the morning at about 4:00 or 4:15 a.m., for the three hour drive to Urban. Chuck was a trainee as customer relations representative. She believes they left that time of morning in order to get to work by 7:00 a.m. The company was very strict and wanted them there by 7:00 a.m. and no later than 7:30 a.m. She believes they went by way of the Antelope Valley Freeway as it was not so crowded during the early morning hours. She doubts that they ever went by way of Bouquet Can-

yon Road, as Don never mentioned having used that route to go to work or to come home after work.

Connie gave the following account of her recollection of the events on and after May 31, 1989:

Don came home from work on the evening of May 31, 1989 and told her he had seen a dead woman that morning in one of the condos at work. He told her that he and another worker, Dan Black, had been working downstairs in the condo. They went upstairs and into one of the bedrooms where they saw the body of a young woman. It was lying face down and they thought she was injured. They turned the body over to see if they could help the young woman, inasmuch as some time before he, Don, had helped resuscitate a young girl who had overdosed on drugs. They discovered the young woman was dead, however, and they turned the body over to its original position. They both vomited, because it was a very gruesome sight. There was blood everywhere. It affected Don grossly for several days after that. He was nervous and irritable.

Two or three days after the discovery, Dan Black called on the telephone and Connie answered. Dan said, "Connie, can I talk to Don?" She called Don to the phone and he talked with Dan for a few minutes. After he got off the phone, Don told her that Dan said he was worried; that he had been having an affair with the victim (Horgan) and they had broken it off only a day or two before they discovered the body. Dan was worried that if the police found out about his affair with the victim and that they had broken off in their relationship, the police would make him Dan, a prime suspect in her murder.

Later, Don told her that he, Don, had taken a Polygraph test at the Police Department. He also told

her that Dan Black had taken three polygraph examinations and that he had "flunked" the first one. No comment was made about the second or third tests.

Don left his job at Dunn in August or September, 1989. He may have gone to work with Josh Boxer at Ripon Homes. She is not sure.

Chapter XXII

On January 17, 1991, Los Angeles County marriage records reflected that Dan W. Black and Lorna G. Wood were married on May 22, 1982, at Fullerton, California, by Charles R. Dwindell, Evangelical Church of America. Witnesses were Jeffrey Ault and Catherine Johnson.

At the time of this wedding, Dan W. Black was described as a male, age 30, born February 13, 1952, in California. This was his first marriage. His occupation was Tech. - Communications. His education level was 14 years. His father was Frank H. Black, born in Pennsylvania, and his mother was JOY EWING, born in Pennsylvania.

At the time of this wedding, Lorna G. Wood was described as female, age 22, born November 14, 1959, in Scotland. This was her first marriage. Her occupation was Pricing Analyst Aerospace. Her education level was 16 years. Her father was John N. Wood, born in Scotland, and her mother was Eileen Graham, born in Scotland.

Lorna G. Black filed for dissolution of the marriage in Orange County, California, on November 29, 1983, stating that they had been separated since June 1, 1983, after one year and one day of marriage. There were no children born of this marriage.

The Petitioner's maiden name, Wood, was restored to her.

On February 11, 1991, at 8:45 p.m., a light colored Toyota pickup with a camper shell was observed parked in the driveway in front of the residence of Dan Black in Fullerton, California.

Records of the California Department of Motor Vehicles, Division of Registration, reflect that California License is for a 1984 Toyota pickup, registered on June 29, 1990 (expires June 30, 1991) to Dan Black. He is the sole owner.

Dan Black was interviewed at home from about 8:50 p.m., until about 9:30 p.m., on February 11, 1991. He said he is not presently employed, except for doing free-lance work wherever he can find it.

He said that with regard to his knowledge and activities surrounding the murder of Terri Horgan on May 30-31, 1989, at the Paradise West Townhomes, Urban, California, he does not want to discuss the subject except possibly in general terms. He said this is not only due the passage of time but also because his recollections regarding the event are very uncomfortable.

He advised he is the one who originally discovered the body in the upstairs bedroom of Unit #66 but when he first saw it he thought Horgan was sleeping and, it was not until later, when Horgan's mother was there that he went to the bedroom with her and determined that Horgan was dead.

He advised that he has described in detail those events to the Urban Police Department and also testified in a court hearing. He knows of no details that he was not asked about or that he did not testify about in court. He said that although he may have seen him at one time or other, he is not acquainted with

Jody Williams. He is not sure he would recognize him if he should see him at this late date. He said that rumors flew around so fast and furious about the Horgan murder that he does not believe anyone except possibly the police knows anything of any certainty except that Horgan was slain. He heard one rumor, originated by Don Arnold, that Horgan's hands and feet were cut off and there were other mutilations of her body. He said Arnold was not present when he discovered Horgan's presence in the bedroom or when Horgan's mother came to the townhouse and they viewed Horgan's body in the bedroom.

When asked about possible telephone calls by him to the home of Don Arnold shortly after the date of the Horgan murder, or the allegation that he told Arnold that he had had an affair with Horgan, and therefore did not want the police to find out about it because they would make him a prime suspect in her murder, Black denied the allegation. He stated that he had never had any affair or other kind of romantic interest in Horgan, never told anyone he did and certainly never told Don Arnold such a thing, either by telephone or in person. He advised that he believes Arnold, at that time, lived in or around Lancaster, California. He never knew his address or telephone number. He said that of course Arnold's telephone number was on record in the company office but he never had reason to look it up or inquire about it. He said he had no personal social contact with Arnold and never met Arnold's wife. He does not know her name. He never met her at a company picnic or other social function. He did not attend the company picnic on July 4, 1988 or 1989.

Black advised that he has never been able to

handle death like most other people do. It is emotionally very upsetting to him. He recalls that he was off work for several days after the Horgan murder and he received professional counselling. He said also that he never took a polygraph test requested by the Urban Police Department. He said this was due to the fact that he had previously failed a polygraph examination given to him in connection with a theft. He was never charged or prosecuted in that case. He said he has no criminal record.

Black advised that he did not kill Terri Horgan and does not know who did. He said that if he ever gained such information, he would immediately notify the proper authorities.

An Urban Police Department crime report of Detective E.P Hall (#9127), dated May 31, 1989 reflects on Page 5, 9th Paragraph, as follows:

"Mrs. Gandy informed me that her daughter had no boyfriend and that she did not work or go to school. She was active with a group called Women's Track Gym, located at an unknown location in West Los Angeles. Her daughter was also known as Terri Gandy. The mother stated her daughter had changed her name approximately one year ago, but the reason she did so, was not clear to the mother."

Chapter XXIII

The pelicans had started to come back in pretty good numbers after being poisoned and shot almost to extinction by determined commercial fishermen five or six years ago. Lately I had noticed some brown pelicans and cormorants cruising around this little cove and perching on the support poles of the rickety two-board-wide pier and the boats tied up alongside. If they keep depositing their droppings on these little boats, the week-end owners, I thought, are going to take up where the commercial fishermen had left off.

As I stepped out onto the pier to get some good shot angles and tried to get a view through my camera lens swinging it to and fro, I couldn't help but notice a male figure climb out of one of the boats and come walking towards me. Busy with my shot-angle search, I paid no attention to his approach.

Reaching a point about two steps from me, his right hand came up bearing one of those leather BB-filled slappers and connected along the left side of my head, knocking me into the water. Fortunately, the water was only hip deep at that point and I was able to recover as I heard his steps pounding on the boards as he ran from the pier. I'm sure the blow would have knocked me unconscious or killed me if his aim had not been less than perfect and the blow

had not glanced off my left shoulder. Thank providence, the camera strap was about my neck so I didn't lose five hundred dollars worth of Leica. Involuntary reaction is a wonderful accident. If I ever see that bastard again he'll have a nice surprise when I recognize him from the photo the Leica took that day.

Chapter XXIV

Charles (Chuck) Weller and Penny Weller, nee Dobbs, were interviewed at home in Palmdale, California on January 14, 1993.

They furnished the following information regarding their knowledge of and association with Don and Connie Arnold: (Later, I fervently wished I had interviewed them separately - for obvious reasons). I'm sure separate interviews would have produced quite different responses to my questions.

They first met the Arnolds in Palmdale, California, in about 1987 before either couple was married; just living together. In July, 1988, they and the Arnolds went to Las Vegas, Nevada, and got married. They do not believe Don had been married before but Connie had previously been married twice. In the fall of 1988, they all moved into the Monte Verde Apartments in Palmdale. Don was working at that time as a Customer Service Rep for Dunn Management Company in Urban, California and Chuck was unemployed. He had been unemployed for about three months, having previously been employed by the San Fernando Valley Electric Company in Sylmar, California. In about October, 1988, Don got Chuck a job as a Customer Service Trainee at the Domani Serra Project for Dunn Management Company in Urban, California. He worked for and with Don there and on

Dunn's two other projects, both adjacent to Domani Serra on Acacia Avenue in Urban. Chuck left his employment there in April, 1989. He therefore was not working there at the time Terri Horgan was murdered, (5/30-31/89).

During the time he and Don worked together at Dunn, they would ride to work and back home together. On Monday morning, they would both drive their vehicles to work. At the end of the work day on Monday, Chuck would leave his car and tools on the street in front of the work site in Urban and ride home with Don. On Tuesday, Wednesday and Thursday, he would ride back and forth to work with Don and on Friday, he would ride to work with Don and at the end of the workday he would drive his own car home and Don would drive his own car home. They continued this system all the time Chuck was employed at Dunn. They would usually leave home at 4:30 or 5:00 a.m., and usually get to the job site at 7:00 or 7:30 a.m. He had to get up at 3:30 or 4:00 a.m., in order to make it to work on time. They started to work at 7:30 a.m. It usually took them about 1.5 hours to get to work in the morning. They almost always took the Antelope Valley Freeway to the Golden State Freeway, the San Diego Freeway, then to the Crenshaw Boulevard off ramp and Crenshaw Boulevard to a street going west to the job site. They would sometimes go the first leg of the trip on Sierra Highway as it had less traffic than the Antelope Valley but they did not do that often. They never, in his memory, went by Bouquet Canyon Road. Once in a while they would get to the work site at 6:30 a.m. When they did, they would take a nap until 7:00 or 7:30.

They usually left the work site between 3:30 and 4:00 p.m. and, it would usually take them two to two

and a half hours to get home, because of the traffic.

Chuck did not know any of the security guards at any of the three work sites and only rarely saw any of them.

Don and Chuck talked about many things during the time they rode together. Don told him that he had been raised in an orphanage in Texas from the age of eight until eighteen, along with two brothers. He does not know where the orphanage was located but Don told him he lived in Amarillo, Texas, before going to the orphanage. Connie told him that Don had told her that his father had shot his mother and that is why he and his brothers had been taken by the authorities and placed in the orphanage. Don told him that he has served three years in Texas for Burglary. He does not know whether that was before or after he got out of the orphanage.

Don has never told him about the killing that occurred in Urban because he had left that area in April, 1989, before the killing happened and he was no longer riding with Don. Connie had told them that Don said that he and Dan Black, another employee of Dunn, had found the body and that Dan Black (whom everyone on the job called Sierra), had fainted. Several weeks or months later, Don may have told them that a "guard" may have done the killing.

Don left Dunn Management Company some time in the late summer or early fall of 1989, and went to work for Ripon Homes in Canyon Country, California. At that time, they had all moved out of the Monte Vista Apartments and were all living at Weller's present address, the Monte Vista Mobile Home Park.

During the first part of the time Chuck worked for Dunn, a man by the name of Josh Boxer was his and Don's boss. Shortly after Chuck went to work for

Dunn, Boxer quit his job as Supervisor and went to work for Ripon Homes. Boxer had obtained Don's job for him at Dunn. When Don left his job at Dunn, he went to work with Boxer at Ripon. Don was working for Ripon when, in late 1989 or early 1990, he was arrested for Burglary. He is now serving time in the State Penitentiary for that crime.

Chuck and Penny have had no contact with Don since he went to prison. Neither do they know the current address or telephone number for Connie.

Something about Chuck's body language, tone and responses to my questions didn't strike me right. I didn't get the same feeling about Penny's contributions to the dialogue between us. It is strange how sometimes we learn something during a conversation or while listening to a speaker on the radio or whatever, that we pay no conscious attention to, that our sub-audio sense receives below the threshold of conscious awareness. That happened to me several times during my 25 FBI years. I don't know if it is a freebie bonus to training or even if it is trainable but I get the idea that I am more susceptible to the phenomenon than most other people. The most graphic example was when I was interviewing a male transvestite about her alleged friend whom I was seeking as a military draft dodger between the Korean and Vietnam Wars. I did not receive and realize the subliminal message I was receiving until a few minutes later, after I had left the interviewee, while I was driving down the street returning to my office, when it hit me like a ton of bricks: that it had not been a woman but a man I had been interviewing. (We later arrested her/him, our fugitive subject).

During my interview with Chuck and Penny Weller, it kept bothering me that I had seen Chuck

somewhere before, but, wracking my brain while still trying to keep the interview on course, I could not properly concentrate. A few blocks down the street, after leaving the Wellers and mulling over the interview, it snapped like a bolt out of the blue what the subliminal message was trying to tell me. I played hell with the DMV's speed limit getting back to my office. There, rummaging through the papers in my case folder, I found what I was looking for – the photo my Leica had accidentally taken of the guy who had blackjacked me off the pier and into the water. Staring back at me was my good buddy Chuck Weller.

VOILA! What a break! Things were starting to come together.

I started thinking back, as I had many times since the "Pelican Cove" incident, as to who or what could have caused me to be the target of someone who would do me serious physical harm – and why? Was it someone I had busted while in the FBI or one of his/her relatives? I could think of no one. Anyone who is or has been in law enforcement knows that it is rare as hen's teeth for an arrestee to stalk or harm an officer who has arrested him. But in my ruminations I did come to the definite conclusion that I had been surveilled and stalked before being blackjacked, otherwise, how had my assailant known where and when I'd be on that rickety trap of a pier. It was obvious that Chuck had been tasked and now I'm pretty sure who tasked him and why. Thank God I didn't let the cat out of the bag any more than I had while talking to Chuck and Penny.

Friends are friends and Chuck and his friend are no exceptions.

I can ideate one side of an exchange between Chuck and his friend who has asked him for a favor

and Chuck doesn't even have to ask him why: "Sure,
Buddy, you scratch my back an' I'll scratch yours.
You be my friend, best man at my wedding, get me a
good job when I've been out of work for three months,
haul me back an' forth to work, loan me money 'til I
get a payday – I appreciate it, man. Any time you
need me – anything – I'm your man mean it. – I don't
need to ask a lot of questions – that's what friends
are for."

Chapter XXV

It is not at all uncommon, especially in large departments, where the Robbery-Homicide Divisions are so undermanned and overworked that very limited amounts of time are devoted to the investigation of homicide cases. Whenever fingerprints at a crime scene connect or seem to connect with a prime suspect, the lead detective team will, due to pressures of other cases, of time and other important correlating factors, drop the ball at the point of finding and identifying the owner of the fingerprints and stop investigating all other suspects and possibilities. They'll believe they now have a "dead-bang" case and present it to the DA for prosecutive opinion. That's what happened in the Horgan murder case. The detectives then went on to other matters, congratulating themselves and each other on "breaking the Horgan murder case."

Preparatory to submitting my written investigative report, I had a sit-down with Lola and Marjie, to give them my theory resulting from my study of the material they had given me and from my independent investigation. I started by suggesting that they drop three of the four original suspects of the Urban Police Department, i.e., Battle, Black and Williams;

Battle and Black because there was no inculpatory evidence against them and Williams because he was no longer a suspect but the charged defendant.

Since my investigative endeavors had developed no new suspect(s) and I was in agreement with what the Urban Police Department had picked as the right suspects, I simply, by the use of common sense and investigative results, picked Don Arnold as the killer.

As we sat there, I was watching Lola's and Marjie's body language: eyes meeting, heads nodding or moving side-to-side, legs crossing and uncrossing, positions changing, etc. Seated side-by-side, it was almost like a choreographed mirror-image dance. Noticing my grin and being totally unaware of their own body language, Lola asked me what was so funny. Not mentioning body language, I told them:

"Looks to me like you two are agreeing with what I'm telling you."

They, with quizzical expressions, looked at each other, then at me, then back at each other and back at me. The second time they looked back at me, I was pointing a forefinger at each of them, turning my head back and forth, nodding my head, crossing and uncrossing my legs as if to imitate them. They both caught on and broke into gales of laughter – while I said, "Gotcha!"

Regaining her composure, Marjie said:

"Hey, wait a minute, we're working a Special Circumstances Murder case here. Get serious."

Hot to trot as I was for Don Arnold, I momentarily forgot what we were trying to do but Lola brought me up short:

"Steve, she said, I think we are all in agreement who the killer of Terri Horgan is and we can hope that

one day he'll meet his Waterloo but our job, believe it or not, is to prove a negative – that Jody Williams didn't do the dirty deed. The best thing we have is the knowledge of how the fingerprints got on the screen frame but at the same time, we can't put Jody on the stand. They'd eat that gangbanger alive, no matter where the truth lay."

"The next best thing we have is the 'point of entry' issue. The DA wants to hang his hat on the window thirteen feet off the ground when there was no fifteen or sixteen foot ladder found within a block of the victim's building during the crime scene search. Even if such a ladder had been found, a 250 pound man would have to be a real acrobat to maneuver himself from the ladder through half of a small casement-type window. If he had entered through that window, he would have muddied the snow-white settee sitting against the wall directly below that window. There was not a mark on it."

"Besides, there were two other possible points of entry and, I think you will agree, as any jury will, that one of those is one the killer used. One is the sliding door screen between the patio and the living room and the front door to which five builders had a master key, one of which was Don Arnold."

"The slit in the screen on the patio door could have been a red herring created by the killer on his way out but that is unlikely because the killer would have been in a hurry, not wanting to awaken Jody, who was asleep on the floor. Also, it is possible the killer could have left by way of the front door without making enough noise to awaken Jody."

"Then, there is Arnold's friend, Chuck Weller, willing to do great bodily harm to Steve, out of 'friendship' for Don Arnold."

"Again, we are not trying to build a case to convict someone but are trying to win an acquittal for Jody Williams. It is hard to figure the almost idiotic approach to this case that the Assistant DA is taking. Of course we never know what a jury will do in a Special Circumstances Murder case where the defendant is a South Central gangbanger but we do know that the prosecutor is no mental giant. Maybe he is being so careless because this is the last case he will handle before retirement and he is tired and just doesn't give a damn."

———————————

I sat through the trial at the counsel table alongside Jody. I don't believe I have ever seen a more lackadaisical prosecution or on the other hand a more spirited and professional defense than I saw there at the hands of Lola and Marjie. But the ultimate surprise came, at least for me, on the last day of the trial (I believe Lola and Marjie were holding out on me). Connie Arnold and Don Arnold appeared as rebuttal witnesses.

Connie testified that on the night of may 30, 1989, when she crawled into bed, Don had already been there for a couple of hours and she thought he was asleep. Apparently, he had been asleep but when she got in bed he was very much awake. Don tried to have sex with her but she pushed him away because she was tired and her period was about to begin. Don became very angry, got out of bed, got dressed and left the apartment. He was gone for several hours. He returned about 4:00 or 5:00 a.m. He just about had time enough to shower and change clothes before it was time to leave again for work. There were blood spots on his shirt. At that point in Connie's tes-

timony an objection was raised regarding the word blood and the objection was sustained, with judge instructing the jury to disregard Connie's answer and for the question to be restated without the reference to the word blood. Connie then referred the color of the spots on the shirt to be rust colored or something similar. Another objection was raised but the judge overruled it. She testified that when she got up in the morning the shirt was gone.

Don Arnold then got on the witness stand and was sworn. The judge then gave Don the standard "Miranda Warnings." Don said he understood them and waived his rights to remain silent and to an attorney. He then testified that on the night of May 30, 1989, his wife, Connie, "wouldn't give him any." This angered him because he was "real horny," so he got dressed, got in his truck and drove (the round trip of about 160 miles) to Urban, (California) to "visit some friends." By the time he got back home, it was almost time to leave for work again. There were no more questions and the trial ended. I was flabbergasted (happily so) at Arnold's final testimony.

Jody Williams was acquitted.

"Geez, Keisha, you're the coolest trim a guy ever had. The way you use your head to get me up an' then take me to heaven with your tight li'l snapper makes me forget about the three-an'-a-half years in the Biscailuz Hotel waitin' to stand trial for somp'n I never done. That was real hard time - hard in more ways than one."

"Yeah, I guess so, Baby, but I tol' you each time I visited, an' I meant every word, that I'd give you sex like you never dreamed of when you got out. Now

that I got you, I'm gonna do it. Like that radio talk show guy says, 'Well, that takes care of hour one. In the second and third hours we'll talk about sex an' more sex,' but you an' I, Baby, we won't jes talk about it, we're gonna do it."

"That's why I came out clean, Sugar, I never did cotton to the way those guys used to butt-fuck the queer inmates an' I jus' satisfied myself with ol' Lady Thumb an' her four daughters. An' I wanted to be ready for you an' I used to dream 'bout you. I saw a big sex poster one time that had couples doin' it in about thirty diff'rent positions - jus' 'bout ever' way you could imagine. If you're game, I'd like to try as many as I can remember with you. I got a lotta catchin' up to do. How 'bout it?"

"Sure, my offer still goes, Big Daddy. Lead me to it. But tell me, during that prior sentence - the four years you did up at Folsom for burglary - didn't you have a girlfriend or weren't you a girlfriend for someone else?"

"Not on your life, Keisha, I did my time at five feet eight, an' two hundred fifty pounds, pumpin' iron - no fat on me. I could bench press three hundred pounds, so nobody fucked with me. Sure, there was some other guys bigger an' stronger an' meaner'n me, but they was all "brothas" too. I didn't kowtow to no one. After 'bout a year inside - an' no hole time - they made me a trust-y. Did the same at Biscailuz, only it took jus' six months to make trust-y there."

"So stop yodelin' an' give me that ten pound sausage you big black studs call a love muscle. We'll see how much that thing can bench press."

"You might be s'prised but hey, I gotta be careful. My trial starts next Tuesday an' I'll have to be in good shape. That lawyer of mine is bossy as hell an'

she's tougher'n a steel-toed boot. When I hollered po'mouth an' the judge assigned her to my case, he couldn'ta done better. Ever'body tells me she's right on the top when it comes to crimnal defense lawyers. She gets big bucks when she sides with them Beverly Hills millionaires an' their fuckup brats. If I'da been as lucky with bail as I was gettin' a good lawyer, I'da been with you three an' a half years ago."

"Think you'll beat it, Honeybun? Gawd, murder's about as heavy as they can load you up with."

"Yeah, an' my record's the only reason I'm loaded up with it. My prints was found in the wrong place at the wrong time."

Chapter XXVI

In today's world, DNA comparison between a victim's DNA and that of a suspect is becoming quite common. When they meet eventually in a courtroom, civil or criminal, bells ring and whistles blow and someone ends up in prison or at the bank drawing out the cash to pay a heavy judgment. In its infancy then, DNA was not used in Horgan's case. I hope the time will come when the bloodstained brassiere used to strangle Terri Horgan can be compared with Don Arnold's DNA, then a long awaited closure can come for the Gandy family. I'm going to see if I can bring that DNA closure about.

EPILOGUE

A few days after the Jody Williams verdict I stopped for lunch at a fast food place in Urban. As I approached the "Order Here" counter, I heard a voice behind me say in a kind of crappy way, "Well, look who's here – the big FBI man." I turned and sitting there were Lander and Conley. I remember I had seen them sitting in the courtroom almost every day of the trial.

I wanted to ask them how they came up with the ridiculous "point of entry" theory of a ladder to a window thirteen feet off the ground. I didn't get to ask the question though, because their hurried statement to me was that they had the right guy, all right, and the lawyer, meaning Lola Lucia, was a damn liar. I wanted to ask them if the "Window" theory was their idea or that of the numbnuts prosecutor. It was just too hard for me to believe that two experienced homicide detectives, who had probably investigated dozens of homicides and crime scenes, could embrace that idiotic theory. I didn't get the chance for the questions I had or the discussion I wanted because, I perceived in the ever-tightening atmosphere that their hostile attitude was not conducive to conversation. Well, maybe later, when things have cooled down a little.

I wanted to ask them about a couple of things:

1. If they know what happened to the other white tennis shoe and, 2. If the blood stained garrote (brassiere) and other evidentiary material found at the crime scene search had been destroyed and their case closed.

I wanted to know if, due to the press of other work and the acquittal of Jody Williams, they considered the case closed or if they "shelved" the case, permitting it to become a so-called "cold case," with the possibly that at some later time it could be resurrected for the use of the relatively new science of DNA.